'In a world where inno... valued, understanding ... for all leaders. *Disrupt!* compile... ge – the question is: ...

... Cheshire

'If you know anybody that needs a deep breath of the cleanest air of the imagination, give them this book, because in these pages one will come across and savour the distilled genius of a generation of entrepreneurial thinkers and doers. Breathe deep, hold on to who you are, set your moral compass and fly. This book is a gift to everyone with a desire to enter a world where extraordinary things happen, and a roadmap by which to navigate it.'

Sir Tim Smit, Co-Founder, The Eden Project

'As a CEO, three things should keep you awake at night. Do I have the right people in my team? Is my business cost competitive? And, most importantly, are we still relevant for the consumer?

Disruption is about finding new ways to stay relevant, and every human enterprise aspires to it. However, I have learned one thing about disruption: you cannot plan for it – but you need to organize for it.

Disrupt! is a great way to get organized. You will access in this book ideas and concepts that you may be able to apply directly or by association to your own enterprise. Disruption may be everywhere but it is actually quite hard to locate. I believe you can find it here.'

Pierre Laubies, CEO, Coty

'Remembering the foundation of my own business, a thought remains strongly anchored: that of feeling isolated; of being misunderstood and clinging at night to dreams so as not to lose sight of them in the morning. I subscribe to the Springwise platform because it builds my desire to share in the innovation of emerging entrepreneurs' ideas. I often think that if it had existed much earlier I would have felt much less alone.'

Olivier Baussan, Founder, L'Occitane en Provence

'In an ever-changing world where decisions are being made which can't be predicted, we need more innovators to think about the world and business in different ways. *Disrupt!* is a fantastic resource of inspiration to stimulate new thoughts by highlighting amazing innovations and innovators from across the world who possess the creativity, resilience, entrepreneurial and interdisciplinary thinking that our 21st century society and economy is crying out for.'

Dr Kirsten Cater, Academic Director of the Centre for Innovation and Entrepreneurship, University of Bristol

'If you are even remotely curious about the future, mildly interested in how we sustain a healthy planet, pleasantly bemused by unexpected fixes to problems you haven't yet realized, or slightly piqued by new approaches to the ordinary, Disrupt! is a book that will intrigue and delight. Featuring a hand-picked compendium of the top innovations in categories ranging from sustainability, to retail, to the sharing economy, the book not only highlights these selections on their own fascinating merits, but also advances the critical viewpoint that it is the web of these innovations that will shape our future. Bidwell's thoughtful introduction situates today's innovations in the context of historical change, and provides a balanced framework for considering both the gains and potential losses as we innovate our future.'

Kate Williams, CEO, 1% for the Planetdfd

'Springwise has long been my go-to source for learning about the latest and greatest business ideas. Now James Bidwell has put those insights into book form with a collection of 100 amazing innovations. This inspired and inspiring book can be a crystal ball to help you see into your own creative future.'

Dan Pink, author of Drive and To Sell Is Human

'A fascinating testament to the power of human inventiveness and a clear indication that disruption is here to stay. The lesson for larger companies wanting to thrive in this new 'all comers' environment is to be every bit as creative, nimble and close to consumers as your smaller - often more entrepreneurial - competitors. For many large companies, that will mean finding the courage to disrupt themselves.'

Paul Polman, Chair of the International Chamber of Commerce

Disrupt!

100 lessons in business innovation

JAMES BIDWELL

First published in Great Britain in 2017 by Nicholas Brealey Publishing.
An imprint of John Murray Press.
First published in the USA in 2017 by Nicholas Brealey Publishing.
An Hachette company.

1

Copyright © Springwise Intelligence LTD

British Library Cataloguing in Publication Data: a catalogue record for this title is available from the British Library.

ISBN: 978 1473 69575 7
eBook (UK) ISBN: 978 1473 65476 1
eBook (US) ISBN: 978 1473 67409 7

Printed and bound in Great Britain by Clays Ltd, Elcograf S.p.A.

John Murray Press policy is to use papers that are natural, renewable and recyclable products and made from wood grown in sustainable forests. The logging and manufacturing processes are expected to conform to the environmental regulations of the country of origin.

Nicholas Brealey Publishing
John Murray Press
Carmelite House
50 Victoria Embankment
London, EC4Y 0DZ, UK
Tel: 020 3122 6000
Nicholas Brealey Publishing
Hachette Book Group
Market Place Center,
53 State Street,
Boston, MA 02109, USA
Tel: (617) 263 1834
www.nicholasbrealey.com

Also available as an ebook

DEDICATION

To Lili, Willow and Sage, inspiration for all my endeavours in life.

To Sophie, my muse and constant source of encouragement and love.

To the Springwise community, without whom this book would not be possible.

To the Springspotters, our unique network of amazingly creative, resourceful and inspiring people from all walks of life and from all over the planet.

To our readers who check us out every day and who share our commitment to the Springwise mission, to drive positive change through innovation, purpose and creativity.

To former Springwise Editor and principal collaborator in the writing of Disrupt!, Chris Kreinczes.

To our writers and collaborators: lead writer George Hammond, Editorial Coordinator Emily Uwemedimo and Managing Editor Linda Ligios.

And to Rebecca Trenner, Keely Khouri, Nick Atkins, Katy Young, Tom Hughes, Grace Wang, Isabel Farchy and Reinier Evers.

To Kirsty Ludbrook, who created the Springwise brand identity.

To our talented illustrator, Grace Holliday.

To Toby Mundy, our elegant and resourceful agent.

To the brilliant team at John Murray, Jonathan Shipley, Iain Campbell, Hannah Corbett and Jess Kim.

To 1% for the Planet for showing the way and allowing us to donate 1% of our royalties to Mother Nature.

And finally to my family and friends for their love and support in calm and disrupted times alike.

CONTENTS

INTRODUCTION

Two years have passed since we first published Disrupt! and two dominant themes emerge as this paperback edition allows us greater and more global distribution and accessibility. First, the disruption and innovation paradigm continues to shift, at an ever accelerating velocity as the pace of change continues to dominate all areas of our lives. Secondly, the Springwise concept of publishing the most exciting and inspiring innovations that really matter, every day, is more relevant than ever. In Disrupt!, as at Springwise, you will find a genuinely different collection of ideas and inventions from innovators across the globe. It will serve you not only as an educational resource for innovation, but also a beacon of hope in a disrupted world.

Since the 1960s the words of Nobel prize-winning songwriter Bob Dylan – 'The times they are a-changing' – have consistently rung true as society, politics, business and culture experience rapid development and transformation. If anything, as we survey the first two decades of the twenty-first century, the times are changing at a faster pace than ever before, as the third and fourth industrial revolutions, fuelled by technological advances and globalization, are changing our way of life and our planet in ways that are arguably more fundamental than at any time in history.

In this book you will find 100 innovations that are changing how we work, how we interact with others, how we learn new skills, travel the planet, save the planet, do business, and teach the next generation to innovate further. Some of these innovations are already well under way, while others hint at the future to come. All the ideas and projects described here are real and designed to inspire. They will give you a glimpse of the future and aim to provoke questioning, ignite fresh thinking and catalyse progress. Drawn from more than 30 countries, the innovations have come from a range of sources, from big corporations that are thinking differently to please their shareholders, to social entrepreneurs whose calling is to disrupt for the good of all.

Our mission

Our mission is to be the place of record for innovations that matter. At Springwise, the world's largest idea-spotting network (springwise.com), we have been spotting and publishing the most interesting innovations since 2002. We do this via our unique and trusted community of thousands of global 'Springspotters' in around 190 countries, who power our network. These Springspotters supply us with around 100 innovative ideas for review every single day. We research, commentate and present the best of these for publication on our website and newsletter, where they are tagged and sorted by industry, demography and business model. We are privileged to have an early view of the most important and impactful changes as they emerge: almost in real time.

Our *raison d'etre* is to spot the innovators, the entrepreneurs, the original thinkers, the disrupters and the outliers from across the developed and developing world and to bring these new ideas to a wide readership. You may already be aware of some of them. We survey the most innovative thinking to help you navigate the future. We also care deeply about positive change. In a world that is so often a maelstrom of conflict and confusion, great innovation and invention have never had a greater role to play in ensuring our wellbeing and survival. Applying this belief internally, we are proud members of 1% for the Planet (onepercentfortheplanet.org) and will donate 1 per cent of our share of the sales from this book to environmental causes.

Deciding which innovations to include here has been no easy task. We have tried to cover a broad range of ideas, while promoting a global perspective and citing many businesses from outside the mainstream Western media. We have also striven to strike a balance between technology-driven innovation and more 'lo-fi' creative thinking. Many of our favourite ideas are those that seem to mock more hi-tech examples with delightfully simple solutions created on a shoestring. One other aspect of the Springwise lens is to ensure that we provide robust coverage of the increasing number of social innovations we see. It is often easy to be obsessed with tech and Silicon Valley, but at the heart of the Springwise purpose – and, indeed, fundamental to a balanced world – are innovations that improve people's lives, innovations that matter.

We also consider whether the innovation has been published widely, since part of our mission is to bring our ideas to our readers before they are seen elsewhere. This is more of a challenge in a book, of course – although there is an element of timeless learning across the spectrum of innovations we have chosen for *Disrupt!*. Our website is dynamic and updated daily, but you will see that many of the ideas in this book are carried through the website, with the latest, evolved innovation iterations relating to each of our chapter themes.

As for what defines an innovation itself, we're very clear:

An innovation is a new solution to a problem. A Springwise Innovation can be digital or analogue, capitalist or social, start-up or corporate, academic or institutional, developed from an old model or creating a new one. Above all, it will be different, an outlier, part of the Zeitgeist.

A network of ideas

As on our website, the innovations featured here have all been arranged according to their industry or niche into chapters, to help you dive straight into specific areas of interest for a quick dose of inspiration. Within each chapter are ten innovations each representing the major themes and evolutions discussed in the chapter introduction, while the takeaways will encourage you to think about how these developments may affect your own practice or business.

Of course, separating these innovations out into discrete chapters in this way is also problematic. If each idea featured were written on a strip of paper and thrown on the floor and we were tasked with sorting the pieces into a logical order, it's likely that most of us would set about creating something more closely resembling a spider's web. To understand the innovations fully, it is best to see them as existing in an interconnected network of ideas, informing and signposting both the history and the future for ideas in other chapters. All the ideas here are in a discourse with one another, and we'd encourage you to read the book with this thought at the back of your mind. Not only will it, we hope, make the book more enjoyable, but it will also reflect the fact that the innovators we write about do not think in narrow terms. On the contrary, the greatest breakthroughs come from thinking outside the metaphorical box and allowing your mind to open up to all possibilities, to wander towards the most unpredictable, brave and lateral solutions.

As you read through the book, either from start to finish or by dipping in and out, the way the innovations knit together will become clear and you will start to see themes emerging. We'd encourage you to make links not only between innovations within the book but to your own business as well. And while some of the innovations – particularly those using the latest technologies – may seem prohibitively expensive, remember that it is usually still possible to adapt the idea, if not the delivery. For example, you will read about Mexico City's online **Plataforma Constitución CDMX**, which invited citizens to help shape the city's new constitution. This use of technology has implications for how we think about city management, citizenship and even democracy; the theory is fascinating, yet the delivery has its shortcomings, a lesson in itself.

We have seen the same idea adapted and reborn in retail, with online surveys asking customers to vote on a company's products and thereby help shape that company's decisions. The fashion retailer C&A found a way to bring customers' Facebook approval into full view in its real-world stores in Brazil. The company posted photos of clothing items it was selling on a dedicated Facebook page, where it invited customers to 'like' the ones that appealed to them. Meanwhile, the brick-and-mortar stores displayed the votes on screens in real time, giving in-store shoppers a clear indication of each item's online popularity.

A year later, fashion retailer Nordstrom made dedicated areas of their bricks-and-mortar stores designated Pinterest sections, which included some of the most pinned products from the Nordstrom

Pinterest page that week. The programme took into account the top items on a regional basis, meaning that products promoted in one store might not be the same as in another store, reflecting local preferences – and in the most analogue of formats. At the time of the scheme, the Nordstrom Pinterest page had nearly 4.5 million followers, making the pinned items a fair bellwether for trends — and at a fraction of the cost of C&A's initiative.

Another great example comes from S-Oil. The South Korean petroleum provider's 'Here' campaign chose a simple solution to one of the biggest problems faced in modern cities: finding a parking space. Hi-tech solutions to the issue include Germany's ParkTag app, which uses smartphone-enabled crowdsourcing to create a map of free parking spots to be shared among friends. But S-Oil sought a solution not reliant on smartphones or sensor systems, and joined with Korea-based advertising agency Cheil to tackle the issue – with balloons. Bright yellow arrow-shaped balloons were placed in the middle of parking bays, tethered to the ground by a piece of string. The arrows were boldly emblazoned with the word 'HERE', to indicate a free space. When a car drove into the spot, the string was pulled under the vehicle, drawing the balloon down. When it left, the balloon floated back up again, instantly alerting those nearby that the space was being vacated.

Both the Nordstrom and S-Oil campaigns show that innovation need not be expensive or lean on the latest technologies for delivery. By embracing this mindset, every innovation in this book can be seen not as an end point but as an inspiration.

Predicting the future

Because the innovation landscape is an interconnected ecosystem, predicting where it will go next is fraught with difficulty. With so many variable components, and with technological advancements often relying on success in other fields to progress, 'future-gazing' is a far from straightforward task. When we first wrote about Facebook back in 2006, it wasn't the first social network we had covered, and few could have predicted the exact magnitude of its success today. That was also the year we first began discussing virtual-reality innovations, but it was not until devices such as the Oculus Rift or even Google Cardboard entered development that VR innovations started gaining significant traction. Many of the innovations we covered back then would arguably have fared far better if released now, largely because of external developments. Political, social and cultural changes all have an impact, and are impossible to reliably predict. But, in uncertain economic and political times, future-gazing is also a necessary undertaking, regardless of how many caveats must be placed.

The effects of automation on the workforce are discussed in more detail in the Workplace chapter, and there can be little doubt that historical advancements in automation have led to fewer 'top-end' factory jobs. In the USA, for example, it's notable that employment in jobs that consist of routine operations, which are easily automated, has been largely stagnant since the 1980s, while employment in non-routine jobs has grown. The result is that there are fewer 'top-end' factory jobs compared to the total job base. As artificial intelligence (AI) evolves further and is capable of more human-like levels of complexity, it is likely to start encroaching upon these non-routine employment figures as well.

But this is hardly the first time that workers have been adversely affected by advances in technology. In *The Economic Singularity* (2016) by Calum Chace, the author begins by discussing workers' historical reactions to mechanization. In the fifteenth century, Dutch workers attacked textile looms by hurling wooden shoes — called sabots — into the machinery, giving us the origin of the word 'saboteur'. Later, during the Industrial Revolution in Britain, Luddism was a (relatively) small but noisy movement that destroyed the new machines that were displacing workers. From 1811 to 1813, death threats signed 'King Ludd' were sent to machine owners, and the government reacted in kind by making 'machine breaking' a capital offence.

But the Luddites were not reacting against mechanization or machines per se. However painful the circumstances, few people believe that technological advancements that remove repetition from the workplace should be stemmed, and even fewer believe that it can be. Rather, the Luddites were reacting not so much against the machines themselves as the workers' inability to share in the prosperity that those machines brought.

To look again at the present day, most estimates put the arrival of artificial general intelligence (AGI) at around 2045. At this point, AI would be as capable as a human in all areas of cognition, which, debatably, would leave humans nowhere else to move up the employment value chain. Over the coming years, the impact of automation on the workforce is only going to grow and we see examples of this ongoing revolution every day at Springwise and all around us, as companies learn to work in the new way.

The answer to the dilemma is to innovate more, and to disrupt further – to seek out models that accommodate these changes and mitigate the negative side effects. Technological advancements cannot and should not be slowed, but the systems around them can be disrupted to ensure that they bring shared prosperity. There is already plenty of inspiration to be drawn from many of the sharing economy and open-source models featured in this book.

We live in remarkable times, and in *Disrupt!* you will find 100 extraordinary and inspiring innovations to help you and your collaborators, friends and family innovate for a positive future.

James Bidwell

THE SHARING ECONOMY

In the early 2000s the original concept of the sharing economy emerged from the open-source community, a group of coders contributing to programs free of charge. Theirs was at least in part a normative concept: deploying the intelligence, endeavour and assets of individuals to solve collective problems.

Collaboration for the common good

A recent example of this open-source approach is the WikiHouse Foundation, a non-profit open-technology foundation that brings together companies, organizations and governments to develop new open technologies, standards and common infrastructures for housing and sustainable development. Director Alastair Parvin describes it as 'an entity that exists only to host core assets, infrastructure and standards for the common good, and allow the work of any one company to be interoperable with that of any another'. He insists, however, that it is not a charity: 'it's a common armature that needs to work for every business and individual that uses it, not just a few shareholders. Effectively it exists to take the issue of ownership, as far as possible, off the table.' Parvin likens the ethos behind open-source projects to the Norwegian word *dugnad*, used to describe the collaborative production or repair of a community asset built by everyone, to serve everyone.

Today, it is not uncommon for Norwegian communities to organize a Dugnad day, where people will join together to clean, repair and paint joint assets. It's a day of sharing and of human connections, working towards a common goal. Crucially, money is not exchanged at any point.

From the open-source concept grew some of the purest real-world articulations of the sharing economy seen to date, such as Freecycle – which diverts reusable goods from landfill – and Couchsurfing – which connects travellers with free beds in hosts' homes. Rather than pay the homeowner for the stay, a couchsurfer would typically be encouraged to give thanks through a gift exchange, such as offering to cook a meal. They are also encouraged to list their own free bed on the site if they have one. But, increasingly, the meaning of the term 'sharing economy' is becoming distorted and pulled away from these open-source roots.

In 2009 Travis Kalanick tweeted possibly the most valuable 140 characters in Twitter's history: 'Looking 4 entrepreneurial product mgr/ biz-dev killer 4 a location-based service … pre-launch, BIG equity, big peeps involved—ANY TIPS??' A year later, that location-based service was launched as UberCab in San Francisco. By 2012 the company's domestic success was fuelling a rapid international expansion. Interestingly, Springwise had been writing about car-sharing innovations for six years by the time Travis posted his tweet.

Airbnb — an online marketplace for residential properties — and TaskRabbit — an online marketplace for freelance labour — were launched in 2008, a year earlier than Uber, and by 2013 Google was seeing a marked increase in searches for 'the sharing economy'. These companies and their business models have now become synonymous with the expression and, by doing so, have largely redefined it.

The sharing vs the access economy

But while these innovations helped to popularize the concept of the sharing economy, they did so without incorporating many of its key tenets: meaningful social exchange, absence of a market intermediary and payments in kind rather than cash. For that reason, they are now better understood as constituents of the access economy.

Sharing is a peer-to-peer act, motivated in part by altruism and typically not involving financial payment. In the access economy, by contrast, consumers pay for temporary use of a good – a car, a home or a tool – which is owned by another individual or organization.

Simply put, the access economy model sees large, centralized online platforms enabling asset owners to rent their wares for a fee, with the platform provider taking a cut.

Away from the mainstream, however, a number of fascinating innovations are emerging that continue the original sharing economy legacy. **Pumpipumpe**, for example, aims to bring communities offline and into relationships by encouraging the lending of items between neighbours. Meal-sharing company **Josephine**, which connects home cooks to hungry people in their area, aspires to make technology platforms less extractive and more community oriented. In France, **TalkTalkbnb** is a peer-to-peer language and accommodation exchange, which enables hosts to trade food and lodging for conversation in their guest's mother tongue.

These businesses capture something of the essence of the sharing economy, tapping into social exchange, efficient use of resources and altruism. There is an emphasis on gift exchange and human connection, which, while perhaps an add-on in an access economy model, is very much at the core of the sharing economy. As societies become increasingly fragmented, echo chambers restrict our breadth of view and levels of loneliness rise, the sharing economy is a model that offers genuine hope and excitement. It is hard to read about Pumpipumpe without smiling at its simplicity, its charm and what it represents.

The future success of the sharing economy requires staying true to these ideals, and as we begin to explore the full capabilities of technologies such as **blockchain**, which naturally lend themselves to the creation of a decentralized structure, there is plenty of innovation still to come from these original tenets. But success also requires learning from the runaway success of the access economy, streamlining services, shedding unnecessary intermediaries, increasing convenience and, ultimately, lowering prices.

The innovations described in this chapter sit on a spectrum across both the access and the sharing economy. They include some of the more novel businesses riding the prevailing current of facilitated peer-to-peer rental, and others that point to a future economy based on shared goods.

1

NEIGHBOURHOOD MAILBOX STICKERS THAT DISPLAY ITEMS TO SHARE

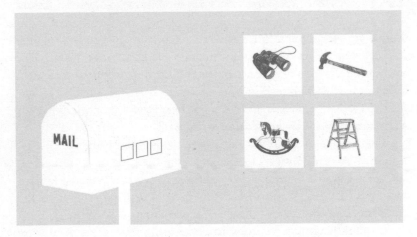

Pumpipumpe is encouraging people to place stickers on their mailbox listing the goods they're willing to lend to their neighbours.

If those nostalgic for the pre-digital age are to be believed, there was a time when people would simply knock on a neighbour's door to ask to borrow something, but this sharing and friendliness has been somewhat lost today. To solve this problem and renew a sharing community spirit, a Switzerland-based project called Pumpipumpe is encouraging residents to place stickers on their mailbox listing the goods they are willing to lend to their neighbours.

The idea was initially formed to enable those with bike pumps to indicate to fellow cyclists that they could knock and use theirs in the case of a flat tyre — hence the name Pumpipumpe. The scheme has since expanded to allow people to advertise any object they have available for others to borrow. Those who want to take part can simply order a pack of stickers from the project's website. Each sticker is a small blue square that features illustrations including a bike pump, lawn mower, kitchen scale, children's toys, and even Internet access and fancy-dress costumes. The idea is that homeowners place the stickers for the items they have on their mailbox so that passers-by can know that they can knock on their door and ask to borrow them. The stickers are free to anyone in Switzerland or Germany, with a 4-euro fee for shipping internationally.

Exactly how users wish to share their items is left largely up to them. In the case of higher-value items such as power tools, Pumpipumpe suggests that lenders may wish to take a small deposit to ensure that their items are returned. While actual monetary payment is actively discouraged – the point is to share items, not to rent them – it is suggested that there could be non-monetary ways to show appreciation for a borrowed item, such as offering a slice of cake to the person who lent you a cake tin. Users are also encouraged to explore other money-saving solutions such as sharing the cost of a common newspaper or magazine subscription.

Pumpipumpe aims to promote a reasonable and sustainable way for neighbourhoods to use consumer goods, as well as letting users build a local network, get to know their neighbours and buy less altogether. While the idea aims to recreate the offline networks of old, the team is working on an interactive map of all the neighborhoods participating in the Pumpipumpe scheme.

Perhaps Switzerland is just a naturally friendly place. Another innovation pioneered there is the Boîtes d'échange entre voisins scheme, which creates community boxes designed especially for leaving unwanted goods for others to pick up. The scheme aims to create a simple and open exchange, also providing the possibility for spontaneous encounters between locals and passers-by, or colleagues sharing a building. They can put any object into the box or take anything they want from it, books, CDs, DVDs, toys and other small, unwanted items.

There is potential to apply sharing networks like Pumpipumpe across the globe, provided that communities are receptive to neighbourhood interaction and respectful of each other's belongings. The unfortunate reality, of course, is that this is often not the case, which will inevitably limit expansion.

TAKEAWAYS

1 Could this idea work in your part of the world? Are the local people culturally receptive to this sort of interaction?
2 How else could your company restore nostalgic models lost in the smartphone age?
3 In what other ways could neighbourhood networks and a sense of community be fostered using the sharing economy?
4 Could this idea be expanded to offer goods and services not previously considered?

INNOVATION DATA

Website: www.pumpipumpe.ch
Contact: press@pumpipumpe.ch
Innovation name: Pumpepumpi
Country: Switzerland
Industries: Home & garden / Non-profit & social cause

2

CUSTOM ELECTRIC CARPOOLING OFFERING AFFORDABLE TRANSPORT

Denmark-based Spiri is looking to make car ownership redundant by expanding the concept of carpooling.

High transport costs, an overabundance of cars and a lack of convenient parking can make moving around cities stressful, costly and damaging to the environment. Carpooling has emerged as a solution to these challenges. In Denmark, Spiri is looking to expand the concept of carpooling further by using its own vehicles.

The carpooling element works on an app-based system where users locate and drive Spiri's electric vehicles to their destination and give rides to other users who also need to get from A to B. Firstly, users select either the Drive or Ride option. A user who has selected Drive picks up one of the cars and inputs their destination. A user who has selected the Ride option is then picked up by a user who is driving to the destination they require.

This is similar to the way UberPOOL works; the hailing app tracks vehicle locations and indicates pick-up points and times. As long as they pick up riders along the way, the driver's journey is free. Riders pay prices comparable to public transport costs. Payment happens automatically with a credit card registered in the Spiri app. Once riders have been dropped at their destinations, drivers are guided by the navigation system to the nearest Spiri parking hub to drop off the vehicle.

The electric vehicles are an innovation in and of themselves. The simple design of the vehicle comprises just 700 parts as opposed to the 3,000-plus of a conventional car and the car's weight has been kept down to 750 kilograms (1,653 lb) by using super-lightweight carbon fibre to build the bodywork. The vehicle's 36.5-kilowatt-hour battery has a 320-kilometre (200-mile) range – almost twice the efficiency of a Tesla model S – and charges in 40 minutes.

The car is designed to be both safe and comfortable, offering enough room that riders don't have to share their 'personal space' and can stow all their belongings. In order to avoid drivers losing keys, getting lost themselves or running into technical difficulties, each vehicle is fitted with navigation capability, is completely keyless – the car is unlocked and started using a smartphone – and uses remote vehicle monitoring. Spiri also offers live support to drivers.

Spiri is aiming to launch the scheme as a gateway towards encouraging the use of driverless cars and making car ownership redundant. They are also looking at the possibilities of launching a fleet of driverless 'micro-buses' to fully automate public transport in the future.

Other examples of vehicle sharing in cities include an Italian scooter-sharing scheme called Scooterino. The Rome-based 'Uber for scooters' connects those in need of a ride with scooter drivers heading in the right direction.

The overall aim is to reduce the number of vehicles on the road and to make those on the road more efficient. Vehicle sharing reduces unused car seats and the associated wasted costs and environmental impact. The more people sharing the fewer vehicles are required, and if those being used are electric, then emissions and costs are inevitably reduced.

TAKEAWAYS

1 Could driverless car concepts include office-style features that enable commuters to work while they travel?
2 What other vehicles could be shared in cities? Bicycles? Boats? Helicopters?
3 In what other ways could the issues of urban congestion and pollution be addressed by sharing schemes?

INNOVATION DATA

Website: www.spiri.io
Contact: hello@spiri.io
Innovation name: Spiri
Country: Denmark
Industries: Design / Smart cities / Transport & automotive

3

A PEER-TO-PEER HOME-COOKING START-UP THAT TREATS WORKERS FAIRLY

The Uber of home-cooked meal delivery, Josephine, wants to give employees stock options.

The gig economy is an environment in which temporary positions are common. It's not an industry well known for the good treatment of its workers. Josephine, a meal-sharing company that distributes home cooking, is hoping to change this. Josephine first set up its offices in Oakland, California and is now expanding into Seattle, Denver and Portland.

The app-based service connects home cooks with those looking for meals locally. The emphasis is on community connection rather than simple convenience. When would-be Josephine cooks apply to join the organization, one of the company's masters of public health inspects their kitchen to ensure that it meets standards of cleanliness. Once a Josephine cook is on the platform, users of their service can leave reviews, contact a cook or the central team directly, ensuring that accountability is built in. The company takes a 10 per cent surcharge on all the food sold, and supports its cooks by enabling them to start their own micro-enterprise, providing them with tools and resources — the payment processing, customer management, ongoing education and more.

'We've been thinking for a long time about how tech platforms can be less extractive and provide more value to communities,' explains Josephine CEO Charley Wang. The company is named after a friend's mother who took care of Charley and his co-founder Tal when they first moved to LA. This was their inspiration to build a compassionate, generous model for communities.

This is an ethically admirable and potentially globally applicable enterprise, but it is not without its problems. While there is built-in accountability to a degree, one of the key challenges of this model will be ensuring quality control and food safety across the board. While there is an initial food safety inspection of cooks' kitchens, it is more than likely that they won't be held to such a high standard of food safety as a professional business, and as people pay for this service, they must be expecting a certain level of professionalism and quality.

Josephine will give 20 per cent of its company to the cooks via stock options, which will be distributed according to how long the cooks have been with the start-up and how many meals they serve. Josephine is also launching a 'Cook Council', which will be a rotating group of cooks able to meet with the company's leadership team and function as a conduit for feedback from the chef community. The Cook Council will have at least one seat on Josephine's board of directors.

TAKEAWAYS

1 Would this model work where you live? Are people ready to get involved?
2 What other innovations could be built on initial generous investment and trust in people?
3 How could your company bring together a community while providing a platform from which all could benefit?
4 Are there other opportunities in the sharing economy to create fairer structures?

INNOVATION DATA

Website: www.josephine.com
Contact: hello@josephine.com
Innovation name: Josephine
Country: United States
Industries: Food / Food & beverage / Home & garden / Transport & automotive

4

A KID-TO-KID TOY APP INTRODUCING CHILDREN TO THE SHARING ECONOMY

Kidstrade lets children exchange toys and games
safely using mobile phones or tablets.

As every child knows, the playground is good for two things: running around and high-stakes trading. As football cards and various stickers change hands during lunch breaks, children naturally pick up valuable lessons for later life, gaining an appreciation of market forces and negotiating techniques – albeit through their childhood lens. Now, a new app is introducing these natural traders to the sharing economy by helping them and their parents exchange unloved or unused toys. Kidstrade is a Princeton-based start-up run by parents, aiming to create an entertaining and educational experience for children and adults alike.

The company's tagline says that users can make another child 'the happiest kid in the world', and the app taps into children's urge to swap toys and gadgets.

> With this app, children can set up their own trades and swaps, and
> reach agreement on the value of the items involved in the deal.
> For example, they could choose to trade two common
> collectors' cards in exchange for one rarer card.

To advertise items they would be willing to part with, the child simply takes a photo of an item, writes a quick description, and posts it within the app. The child's contacts can then browse these listed items, and express interest if something catches their eye. In response, the owner can then browse that contact's listed items and propose a trade. If it is accepted, they can arrange a time and a place to meet to exchange the goods.

Parents can control who can be added to their child's contact list. As a default setting, children will automatically be connected with other children from their school in their age group and with children in the age group one year above and below. It's then possible to add specific contacts using a unique ID number assigned to each user.

If activated by the parents, there is also the option to enable financial exchanges, giving children the opportunity to earn money using the app by selling off unwanted goods. Crucially, all listings, and eventual trades, must be first be approved by a parent — they can also veto trades if they need to. This keeps the experience safe and avoids horror stories like a child accidentally overspending in the App Store. There is a list of 'red-flagged' words, which prevent kids from posting anything containing offensive language, and parents are able to both report and block any activity or item they find inappropriate. Parents can even block entire categories to prevent their kids from browsing for certain kinds of toys, such as computer games.

As an extra feature, Kidstrade also offers features for easy fundraising. Rather than running a charity sale from their front garden, parents and children can start one-month fundraisers that are showcased through the app, to raise money and donations for their local school.

The platform is designed to teach kids three important lessons:

1 Toys aren't cheap.
2 It's important to take care of their items.
3 Sending something to landfill is not only environmentally unfriendly but also a wasted opportunity.

TAKEAWAYS

1 How could sharing economy apps not specifically designed for kids incorporate safety features to better accommodate a younger demographic?
2 How could apps such as Kidstrade evolve as their initial audience grows up, incorporating more advanced features for older children?
3 How else can peer-to-peer platforms be adapted to kid-to-kid?

INNOVATION DATA

Website: www.kidstrade.com
Contact: hello@kidstrade.com
Innovation name: Kidstrade
Country: United States
Industries: Education / Telecoms & mobile

5

AN APP BROADCASTING TO LOCAL USERS TO ASK FOR HELP

Getmii is a sharing economy app that lets users post any request – from ping-pong balls to a study partner – and barter with their local community.

Sustainable living is getting easier as more and more platforms are helping people make the most of their possessions; we previously saw Peerby helping local communities share large, expensive and infrequently used items. Getmii is an app that enables users to broadcast requests to the 1,000 nearest people. With a phone number and location information, the app connects users with their local community, helping them to share goods and services and cater to real-time, short-term needs.

Users first register with their Facebook profile. Then they post requests to the Need Feed, and can see what others around them are looking for. The app's chat enables users to arrange payment, pick-up or barter – a particularly important feature in building the Getmii community. Three of the most common requests on Getmii are for ping-pong balls, a study partner and first-date restaurant recommendations. The two main guidelines for using the Getmii app are to be positive and helpful.

Wanting to go against the grain of high-end premium service apps like Uber X, Getmii is designed to be available and useful to good Samaritans anywhere in the world, no matter what their socio-economic background. It focuses on the key sharing economy concept of taking advantage of the untapped resources in a local area, whether they be people, skills, knowledge or physical items.

The app was conceived at Harvard's famous Launch Lab by students Max Meyer, Darryl Lau and Matthias Juergens. They were first inspired to create Getmii when they embarked on a trip to Thailand together. Unable to speak the local language and in need of several goods and services, they realized how useful it would be to have an app where you could request and barter for goods and services from people nearby.

The team says that part of the trust base for sharing economies is using real identities online, which is why they decided to ask users to link their profile with Facebook. Future iterations of the app are likely to feature in-app points or incentive features. This is a key common theme within the sharing economy. Trust in our neighbours and those in the wider community is essential for these platforms to be successful. This is partly because the models themselves are based on community interaction and helping those around us, which cannot happen without trust and mutual respect; and partly because the systems are so open to abuse, whether this be the theft or damage of personal belongings or more serious issues of personal safety and security. Holding users accountable through using real social media-linked accounts is one way of reducing abuse of the system. We have seen ratings systems used previously, but trust remains the single largest obstacle in the sharing economy world.

The challenge varies hugely depending on geographical location and local cultures. For example, are those in an anonymous apartment block in a major city like London as likely to warm to the idea of community sharing as those in a close-knit town in rural Australia? That, however, is the most admirable aspect of the sharing economy: it does not wish to be altered or restricted by people's social inhibitions or distance, but to reduce these inhibitions and bring people closer together.

TAKEAWAYS

1 Are there ways in which a sharing economy could be scaled up?
2 How else could a bartering system be used to get users a great deal on local goods and services?
3 How could your company create a sharing economy model that could be deployed worldwide and accessible to millions of people?

INNOVATION DATA

Website: www.getmii.com
Contact: hey@getmii.com
Innovation name: Getmii app
Country: United States
Industries: Access exclusive / Home & garden / Nature & sustainability / Smart cities

6

THE AIRBNB OF FILM LOCATIONS

GETset is an online platform that allows those scouting film locations on a budget to source and rent them from members of the public.

If you're making a film on a budget, finding the right location can be difficult. Existing location services are often expensive. Now, new start-up GETset encourages anyone and everyone to upload their office, home or studio on to their platform, offering a wide variety of locations to filmmakers at reasonable prices.

GETset aims to be the Airbnb for film locations. Users can rent out their home, shop, treehouse or shed to music video directors, independent filmmakers, TV companies and even Hollywood, and earn money.

Those renting out their space can set their own price, taking into account the size of the location, parking, and whether it's rare or sought after. The idea was born when founder Jonny Wright was looking for a location for a short film he was making, but found what was on offer beyond his budget and 'too shiny and new'. Sign-up is free, and hundreds of locations are already on the site.

In the company's blog, they outline the main benefits of renting out your home as a film location. The first and most obvious is to make extra income. They explain that the amount likely to be earned by renting a property for filming varies depending on several factors, including the production size, whether the filming will happen inside or outside the home, and the number of people who will be working each day. But most users can expect to earn between £700 and £4,000 per day. If the person renting out the property is the owner and rents it for only two weeks each year, then the enterprise is tax-free.

Another benefit of renting out a property is the prospect of free home improvements. Filmmakers will often need to adapt some parts of a home to make it more suitable for their film. This can include landscaping, a fresh coat of paint and in some cases a new kitchen or bathroom. While filming work is under way it is normal for the production company to also cover accommodation costs while the occupants are out of the property.

GETset also provides a useful guide on how much to charge for the rental of your property for filming, which includes considering factors such as whether the production company will be using electricity, whether they will be using your furniture and whether they have an insurance waiver.

This raises an important challenge of the Airbnb model. It is important with these seemingly casual arrangements to consider insurance and liability. This is one of the benefits of using large corporate owned services like hotel chains and big studios – they have their own tried and true methods and processes and are covered in case of injury or damage to property. Users must be careful, when using Airbnb style set-ups like GETset, that they are covered in the event of such occurrences. The last thing a user needs is for a crew member to be injured while filming at their property and suddenly, having thought they were earning a few thousand dollars, be faced with a massive lawsuit. This is an example of where the trust element in a sharing economy needs to be backed up with some solid paperwork.

As the number of sharing economy platforms explodes, Springwise has seen numerous innovations designed to be the Airbnb of something, for billboards and for deliveries.

TAKEAWAYS

1 Is there anything that is yet to have the sharing economy model applied to it?
2 What other aspects of show business could use this model? Recording studios? Theatres?
3 How could your company benefit from renting locations, office space or equipment in this way?

INNOVATION DATA

Website: www.getset.media
Contact: info@getfilmtools.com
Innovation name: GETset
Country: United Kingdom
Industries: Entertainment & culture / Retail & e-commerce

7

THE SHARING ECONOMY FOR CURRENCY EXCHANGE

WorldKoins lets travellers exchange their unwanted foreign currency with 'collectors' through a web app.

Most people have experienced arriving at the airport on their way home from holiday, their pockets full of small change, having to buy something they don't really need in an effort to avoid transporting so many coins home with them. WorldKoins offers a web-based, highly scalable service to deal with this problem. Founded by Ali Zekeria, WorldKoins is a marketplace for leftover currency. Users can identify and locate 'collectors' through the WorldKoins app, transferring their spare change to them using the accompanying app, Dropkoins.

Collectors can be anyone from an Uber driver to a coffee shop barista. They validate the transaction using a verification code and credit the traveller immediately, via the app, with currency that is redeemable for a wide range of eGift cards including those for iTunes, Skype, PayPal and Google Play credit, or a charitable donation. A small commission is charged, split between the start-up and the collector. All currencies are accepted and exchange rates follow those offered by banks, updated in real time.

Collectors using the Dropkoins app benefit as much as users depositing their leftover change. For collectors already on the move in a city, such as Uber drivers, taxi drivers and couriers, it is a good way to make a little extra income for little extra inconvenience. Dropkoins advertises itself as an extra service that collectors can offer to their existing taxi or Uber customers. They can make collections in any currency from users visiting their country.

One of the key challenges in convincing users to get on board with such a model is the suspicion that they may not be getting a good deal for their money or a fair exchange rate. The developers insist that all transactions made through WorldKoins are completely secure. Each exchange is encrypted and validated through a one-time password. After collectors input the details of the transaction, a text message is sent to the traveller, breaking down the financial data and giving a password required to complete the transaction. Only when the traveller is satisfied with the deal they are getting do they relay the password back to the collector, who will type it into the app. This approach minimizes the chance of discrepancies and keeps both parties satisfied.

The exchange rate that the service uses is the prevailing one offered by global banks and is constantly refreshed in real time. At present, there is no option available where users can transfer their money directly to a personal bank account, but the developers are constantly looking to expand the marketplace and add new features to make the app more appealing, user friendly and profitable for all.

Of the idea, Ali Zekeria says, 'There are more than one billion international travellers per year and every single one of them is facing this problem: what to do with their leftover travel money once back home. The challenge is to come up with a simple yet effective solution that is scalable enough for worldwide reach and simple, with a user-friendly interface.'

If travellers and collectors both feel that they are getting a good deal and that the system is convenient, with the monetary and time benefits of using the app outweighing current systems of cashing in coins (such as physical coin deposit machines at banks), then the potential popularity and scalability of this simple model are limitless.

TAKEAWAYS

1 Where else will we see the sharing economy take hold?
2 How else could Uber drivers and other local workers be efficiently deployed to provide another service?
3 What other problems do all travellers face that could be solved with a sharing economy model?

INNOVATION DATA

Website: www.worldkoins.com
Contact: support@worldkoins.com
Innovation name: WorldKoins
Country: Malaysia
Industries: Access exclusive / Financial services & fin tech /
    Tourism & travel

8

FREE LODGING FOR TRAVELLERS CHATTING IN THEIR MOTHER TONGUE

TalkTalkbnb is a free peer-to-peer language and accommodation exchange.

The best way to learn a foreign language is to immerse oneself in it, and conversation is a resource that almost anyone can offer. TalkTalkbnb is a peer-to-peer language and accommodation exchange, which enables hosts to trade food and lodging for conversation in their guest's mother tongue.

To begin, hosts and travellers create a profile on TalkTalkbnb, detailing their first language and where they would like to travel to, or their home and what language they want to practise. Then, other users can browse the site and find a user who suits their needs. Once a match has been made, the host offers lodging and food in exchange for their guest spending time with them during their stay, speaking in their native language.

The service is completely free to use, and no money changes hands between subscribers. The host takes care of the guest free of charge – all they ask in return is for the guest to help them improve their language skills. For those travelling, it means free accommodation, good homemade meals, contact with local people, advice on where to go and what to do in the area. For those hosting, it's a unique opportunity to practise a language with a native speaker, at home, in an informal but very effective way.

TalkTalkBnb encourages hosts to welcome guests like a member of the family and create a warm and convivial atmosphere, and in this friendly environment language skills can grow. In contrast to other forms of free accommodation in private houses, which can sometimes feel like an awkward intrusion, with TalkTalkBnb guests don't feel that they are disturbing their host because they give as much as they receive.

This is a more cost-effective alternative to conversational language learning courses or immersion weeks, which can be extremely expensive. It is also a rejection of mass tourism, designed for those seeking a 'real' travel experience, and those who want to meet local people and experience authentic local customs, foods and lifestyles.

TalkTalkBnb is a French website, set up by an entrepreneur from Brittany, Hubert Laurent, with a group of students from higher-education establishments within the region, of a wide rage of nationalities. It fits into the space between free-but-basic accommodation, like Couchsurfing, and pay-for-comfort Airbnb. More than 3,000 pre-registrations in the two months preceding the official launch confirmed that there is strong demand for this service.

On an ideological level, TalktalkBnb believes that welcoming foreign tourists into your home, sharing a meal and learning to speak their language are all key goals that can help to 'bring people together in peace'. They believe that, if everyone across the world could talk and communicate well with one another, it would go some way towards easing tensions and helping everyone to understand others on a deeper level.

We have already seen similar models where people offer services in exchange for accommodation or workspace: at Berlin's **Blogfabrik** freelancers can work rent free in exchange for monthly content contributions, and GigRove enables hosts to offer short-term accommodation to skilled guests, who can help with their choice of tasks around the house.

TAKEAWAYS

1 What other skills could be traded for working or living space?
2 What free services could your company offer with a view to creating a warmer, friendlier global environment?
3 How could this model be adapted to incorporate the use of another commodity, like the use of a vehicle or even food and drink?
4 Could the system be made financially profitable by charging a subscription or small commissioned per-use payment?

INNOVATION DATA

Website: www.talktalkbnb.com
Contact: www.talktalkbnb.com/contact-us
Innovation name: TalkTalkbnb
Country: France
Industries: Education / Tourism & travel

9

A SOCIAL SITE FOR DATA SCIENTISTS TO BOOST COLLABORATION

Launching as invitation only, data.world's key tenets are open, secure, sociable and linked – the first social networking platform where data is the focus.

At least 18 million open datasets exist today. They hold great potential for the widespread sharing of data and knowledge across the globe. Data.world, a new public-benefit corporation based in Texas, has opened its social networking platform to invited researchers. As they describe it, it is a platform where the world's problem solvers can find and use a vast array of high-quality open data. Seeded with nearly 1,000 datasets, data.world hopes to transform research. Publicly available datasets are made machine-readable, discoverable and available for collaborative work.

Previously, researchers had no real-time way of connecting with others working on the same information. Members first create a profile and attach a photo, and then they can upload data and follow projects. Through semantic web technology, the platform provides data recommendations to members. Using this system, it should be easier to find, understand and use data, and make the data available more meaningful. This improves data discovery and interoperability so that people and machines can unlock its value faster. The idea is that new datasets energize and enhance everything they connect to, rather than just existing in isolation.

Membership is free, as is access to publicly available sets of data. Anyone wanting to work on private datasets must pay a fee. Data. world explains that some datasets will always be sensitive, some should only be shared with trusted collaborators, and others are simply not ready to publish yet. A key part of their mission is to build an environment where users' private datasets are safe and access is entirely under their control. As more people join the network, the data.world team believes that big data will finally begin to fulfil its revolutionizing promises.

Most corporations are required to prioritize shareholder returns above all else, but as data.world is structured as a public benefit corporation it can pursue its mission of easily shareable data and shareholder value simultaneously and equally. Data.world's aim is to:

- build the most meaningful, collaborative and abundant data resource in the world in order to maximize data's societal problem-solving utility
- advocate improving the adoption, usability and proliferation of open data and linked data
- serve as an accessible historical repository of the world's data.

The company sees datasets as social objects and believe that open data platforms should reflect this. They also believe that social networking can accelerate and enhance data science by improving decision-making, knowledge transfer, problem solving and more.

Data.world aims to be a community where conversation adds context to data and deep collaboration is the norm.

A key challenge for this corporation is the verification and quality control of the data being uploaded and shared. Due to the high volume of data that could potentially be shared, it is hard to conceive of a way in which it can be effectively reviewed and verified to as high a standard as traditional datasets. The responsibility for verification may fall more upon those gathering and applying the data from the platform.

We have seen a niche version of this idea with DataSpace, an international online collaboration platform for HIV vaccine research. And in the coming chapters we will explore the potential of open data in **mapping, traffic** and **location-based services**.

TAKEAWAYS

1 Where else could the power of connectivity help to improve research methods?
2 How else can open-source data be applied both in scientific research and other industries?
3 How else could scientists and researchers across the globe pool their resources and ideas?

INNOVATION DATA

Website: data.world
Contact: help@data.world
Innovation name: data.world
Country: United States
Industries: Education / Smart cities

10

TURNING ONLINE RATINGS INTO ONE REPUTATION SCORE

Deemly gives users one reliable, shareable 'trustworthiness' rating based on all their online P2P accounts.

The anonymity of the online world can provoke a lack of trust in both vendors and buyers. Positive ratings and reviews can make all the difference, but until now these have been confined to individual e-commerce platforms, meaning that newcomers have to start from scratch on each new site. Deemly aims to fix this by enabling users to consolidate all their scores into one reliable, shareable 'trustworthiness' rating.

To begin, users create a profile and connect it to their existing accounts – including peer-to-peer (P2P) marketplaces such as Airbnb. Then Deemly calculates an overall score between 1 and 100 using a unique algorithm, developed in collaboration with a statistician. Deemly takes into account factors such as how recently a score was given and assigns weighting accordingly. The Deemly score is the core of the Deemly profile, but you can enhance your profiles with additional images and a video to increase your trustworthiness. Then, newcomers can use their Deemly score to vouch for their reputation when using new services. Users can show their score on sites across the web. Deemly works with platforms to make it easy to display a profile when using a range of services.

From a business's point of view, it is beneficial to integrate the Deemly score API on their platform. It builds trust, which increases user activity. One of the main concerns for online users is that they will be scammed or taken advantage of by people who are less scrupulous. False Airbnb accounts have already been used to steal money from unsuspecting users. This system helps to verify users and therefore to minimize fraud. All the ratings and reviews collected are stored securely on Deemly's servers. The data from a business's site can be accessed by that business at any time through Deemly's admin panel. The integrated rating and review system is user friendly and quick for businesses to install, includes a customizable design and features, and offers a complete overview of data and analytics.

Deemly has proved to be a popular add-on and in some cases an essential feature of many online businesses. Laury Zwart, co-founder of HeelNederlandDeelt, says, 'Safety and trust are at the heart of everything we do. That's why we offer all kinds of additional services to enhance online safety and trust as well. With Deemly's review system, we can offer our users exactly that.'

The issue of trust has already been raised in previous discussions about innovations that use a sharing economy model. How can we be sure that the person we are trusting with our belongings, meals, transport or personal safety has good intentions? Various platforms have attempted to build in accountability through ratings systems and personal reviews. This is the first innovation to look at collating all that data in order to create a more comprehensive and reliable picture of an individual as a user or provider of these services. The system will never be infallible but this goes some way to improving it and making our online lives safer and more full of trust.

We have already seen Israeli social network PersonalHeroes reward good deeds online with kindness points. In the future, Deemly scores could be used in other fields such as in job applications, banking, crowdfunding and dating.

TAKEAWAYS

1. Are there any other positive characteristics that could be leveraged online?
2. What other common concerns of users should be addressed in this way?
3. Would your business or website benefit from a more comprehensive review and verification procedure?

INNOVATION DATA

Website: www.deemly.co
Contact: hello@deemly.co
Innovation name: Deemly
Country: Denmark
Industries: Retail & e-commerce / Tourism & travel /
Transport & automotive

SUMMARY

The innovations in this chapter are the latest shoots of an emergent sharing economy. While the access economy continues to thrive in its present format, these sharing innovations are likely to operate at a relatively small scale, focusing on communities rather than on market saturation.

However, two important factors indicate that the dominance enjoyed by access economy incumbents may not be as unassailable as it appears. Firstly, there are serious legislative questions that technology platforms operating in the access economy will need to get to grips with. In the UK alone, an employment tribunal found against Uber in 2016 – which prevented the company from classifying its drivers as self-employed – and this was closely followed by Airbnb's regulatory shift to comply with UK home rental law. Where these companies have flourished in legal grey areas and enjoyed tax advantages from doing so, they are now finding that the law is gradually catching up with them.

The second factor is the rapid advancement of automation and artificial intelligence. Although a great deal of debate still surrounds the impact of AI in the future, what seems certain is that it will result in swathes of job losses, and even the disappearance of a human workforce from entire industries. (For more on this, see the Workplace chapter.) That in turn could mean that people have less disposable income from their employment – a fact that has led to discussions in many countries about introducing a universal basic Income – and will ultimately require new ways of approaching the economy. In such a world, payment in kind may gain a new popularity, and innovations such as Pumpipumpe would be seen as foreshadowing a huge opportunity.

THE SHARING ECONOMY TAKEAWAYS

1 **Don't get sucked into the app trap.** Sharing economy services naturally lend themselves to mobile, with all the benefits of geolocation, real-time data and rating systems. However, including physical and tangible elements can inspire a sense of nostalgia and simplicity, which resonate well with the values of sharing and neighbourliness.

2 **Use peer-to-peer advertising.** Word of mouth is the best form of marketing: Pumpipumpe's stickers invite intrigue, meaning that as well as functioning as the basic mechanism through which the service operates, they are also brilliant marketing. The peer-to-peer nature of sharing economy services means that every user is a potential brand advocate. Consider how users of a sharing economy service can be made brand advocates simply by using the service.

3 **Take a step back.** Sharing economy services work best when users feel as if they are genuinely connecting with one another. For this to happen, it's often necessary for the creator of the service not to be too present in any exchanges that take place.

4 **Share to show caring.** A genuine constituent of the sharing economy must do more than simply generate profit. Instead, companies in the sharing economy should aspire to create additional value, whether raising levels of community, boosting efficiency or promoting sustainability.

5 **Understand that the access economy still predominates.** Uber has not become a verb because customers love its emphasis on meeting drivers and sharing rides. Its success is down to its more conventional indicators, such as convenience and price. Unless there is a dramatic shift in the law or public perception, our prediction is that Uber and its peers in the access economy will be with us for many years to come.

SMART CITIES

In 2014 the urban population accounted for 54 per cent of the total global population, up from 34 per cent in 1960. This is a significant shift that shows no signs of abating, largely because of the lure of service jobs within cities (more on this in the Workplace chapter).

Inevitably, as cities grow in size, so too do the number of challenges they are presented with. There are obvious logistical issues, from the need to provide enough housing for a growing populace, to ensuring that transport, health, education and emergency services can cope with demand. We also have an environmental responsibility to ensure that cities do not become pollution hotspots.

For example, try running a Google Image search for 'Beijing smog'. Insufficient pre-emptive consideration for environmental impact in China's capital has led to its residents becoming accustomed to emergency situations where cars are banned from the roads, schools are closed, and the air is deemed so toxic that going out of doors is considered dangerous. It's a frightening warning to the rest of the world.

Meeting the challenges of city life

By way of response, in January 2017 the famous fog mask maker, Kobayashi Pharmaceutical, teamed up with advertising agency Dentsu to 'gameify' the process of tracking air pollution levels in China – in an effort to make the situation feel a little less depressing. The higher the air pollution on the PM 2.5 Air Quality Index, the greater was the discount on the masks. Users could check the levels on their smartphone using the Kobayashi app, which reacts to real-time data, detecting each user's location to offer the relevant price reduction. It then dispensed a coupon, for use at some of China's biggest e-commerce portals.

The campaign claimed to 'Brighten up the days of everyone in China', but the campaign is problematic in many ways. Despite claiming to 'gameify' pollution checking, there is little to suggest this is a game other than the app's colourful interface. What's more, by describing it as a game, the implication is that the user is 'winning' when pollution levels are higher – which hardly promotes sustainable behaviour. Conversely, **TreeWiFi's** smart birdhouses, featured in this chapter, reverse this model by offering a reward (free Wi-Fi) when pollution levels drop. And even the birds get something out of it.

More generally, in response to these new demands, we are now seeing the evolution of the smart city. 'Smart city' is a broad term used to describe any metropolis using technology to deliver more efficient and effective public services – from transport to waste management to schools. Like so many innovations in this book, their development is underpinned by large-scale, detailed data collection, from both the built environment and from residents. This data, from peak travel times to seasonal shopping preferences, when analysed and interpreted in context, yields insights capable of solving any number of urban problems. In the Philippines, for example, congestion is being reduced thanks to **OpenTraffic**, which aggregates data from a ride-sharing service to improve traffic flow. And as the Internet of Things* gains momentum – adding an enormous volume of new data – this unprecedented ability to draw insights will be further heightened.

This presents governments and city leaders with opportunities to innovate and optimize in pursuit of the public good. In Singapore, for example, the government's Smart Nation programme – underpinned by a network of data-collecting sensors – aims to improve health, housing and transport in the city. The programme has been

The Internet of Things (IoT)

The Internet of Things is the interconnection via the Internet of computing devices embedded in everyday objects, enabling them to collect and exchange data.

running since 2014, and progress has been made in areas as diverse as the development of noise-reducing building materials, sustainability and testing self-driving vehicles.

Using and applying the data

But gathering data and crunching numbers is only half the story. Many smart cities go beyond looking at simply *how* data should be analysed and applied; they also look at *who* is best placed to perform that analysis and application.

By disseminating anonymized data to the public, governments are increasingly giving citizens the permission and capability to innovate on behalf of their community, government and fellow citizens. Crowdsourcing innovation in this way requires the release of as much data as possible, of course, but just as important are the platforms, which interpret and present that data in intuitive ways. **DataPress**, for example, publishes raw data and helps non-technical users analyse and understand it, while **Transitland** is a free, open platform that aggregates publicly available transport information from around the world. Platforms such as these are essential to help drive resident-created innovation, and they can ultimately lead to a stronger relationship between citizens and government.

Opening up access to data and inviting public input empowers citizens in a meaningful way, and presents a golden opportunity to increase both trust and civic capital. **Balancing Act**, the app that enables citizens to visualize city budgets, helps leaders understand the priorities of their people, and vice versa. In Mexico City, an even more inclusive approach is taken, with the government inviting input on its entire constitution. In both instances, city leaders are using their most valuable assets – their people – to tackle ingrained urban problems.

The innovations in this chapter highlight the virtues of 'opening up' data and inviting collaboration in the pursuit of smarter cities. Collectively, they herald a bright future, in which technologically enabled and engaged citizens, working closely with municipal leaders, provide urban solutions.

11

TACKLING NOISE POLLUTION THROUGH SMART-CITY RESEARCH

Singapore invests in research for sound-attenuating materials.

In densely populated urban environments, governments constantly have to come up with new and innovative ways to make cities safer and more pleasant to live in. To address some of the problems faced by residents of the sometimes noisy and unpleasant urban jungle, Singapore's Housing Development Board, in partnership with manufacturing company 3M Singapore, announced plans for the research and development of materials designed to absorb, reflect or reduce the transmission of noise between urban apartments in close quarters. The plans are part of a wider scheme for Singapore to become a wholly smart city.

The contract is worth US$10 million and other areas of development include a smart traffic light system that feeds into a wider energy-saving drive across the city-state. In terms of noise reduction, areas to be explored could include the study of suitable materials for walls, floors and windows that can absorb, reflect or reduce the transmission of noise within apartments, to create a more pleasant living environment.

The overall scheme to make Singapore smarter is being referred to as the Smart Urban Habitat Master Plan (SUHMP). The SUHMP aims to design a new strategic approach towards the deployment of smart initiatives in towns across the country, identify ground challenges for the introduction of smart solutions, highlight areas where more research efforts are needed, and explore potentially viable business models that can be adopted. This aims to provide sustainable solutions and will provide opportunities for wider partnerships with the private sector.

The initial launch of the SUHMP will take place in Singapore's Punggol Town. A new Smart Hub – the 'brain' of the Housing Development Board (HDB) estate's operations – will be developed to collect and integrate multiple sources of information, such as real-time data from sensors around estates, into a central repository located at HDB headquarters. The data collected by the Smart Hub will enable HDB to better plan, design and maintain its towns to provide a more agreeable living environment for residents.

HDB has also signed a memorandum of understanding with four parties to organize an International Planning and Housing Conference (IPHC) in Singapore in 2017. The four parties are the International Federation for Housing and Planning (IFHP), the Eastern Regional Organization for Planning and Human Settlement (EAROPH), Singapore Institute of Planners (SIP) and the Centre for Liveable Cities (CLC). This conference will bring together housing and planning experts and professionals from around the world, to foster the exchange of information and ideas. These agreements mark another step forward in HDB's journey to develop well-designed homes, sustainable towns and a high-quality living environment for residents.

HDB's chief executive officer, Dr Cheong Koon Hean, said:
'We are living in a fast-changing urban landscape, with new planning issues to tackle and new housing needs to meet. We need new partnerships and innovative ideas to keep HDB moving forward.'

Urban noise, pollution, congestion and public health are all issues at the forefront of smart-city innovation. Later in this chapter we will explore how different governments across the globe are working with innovators to address their urban problems – such as a big-data scheme employed to **manage traffic in the Philippines** and an inventive way of **tackling air pollution in Amsterdam** using birdhouses.

TAKEAWAYS

1 What other innovations could address the need to update our urban lifestyle?
2 How else could urban noise be reduced in an innovative way?
3 How can governments collaborate with tech developers and innovators to address civic and public health and safety issues?

INNOVATION DATA

Website: www.hdb.gov.sg/cs/infoweb/homepage
Contact: hdb@mailbox.hdb.gov.sg
Innovation name: Singapore's Housing Development Board
Country: Singapore
Industry: Smart cities

12

A PLATFORM TO VISUALIZE GOVERNMENT DATA FOR ENTREPRENEURS

DataPress is a platform that publishes raw data and helps non-technical users analyse and release open data.

Open data is helping to solve common problems for businesses and governments. Initiatives in the UK are starting to democratize the availability of information, but many people still find it hard to access or understand data from governments and local councils.

This is the problem DataPress is trying to solve. The London-based start-up, founded by former developers who worked on the UK Government's data.gov.uk website, transforms data from local governments into easy-to-use resources for residents and communities. The founders also believe that more open data will help encourage start-ups, with entrepreneurs using data to develop business ideas.

The DataPress cloud-based platform allows government officials to better open up complicated information and statistics. The team at DataPress works with civil servants to build data visualizations for everyday use, and to offer training to help turn public data into a public utility.

The company has worked with teams in London and Leeds to improve their use of open-source data. The platform also helps users to 'follow' data publishers in a similar manner to a blog – the developers describe their idea as a 'Wordpress for data'.

Barnet Borough Council in London was one of the first to take on DataPress to run their data portal. Their aim was to be the most transparent local authority in the UK. After launching their

DataPress platform, the council experienced a surge of web traffic and renewed public interest in open data. Originally, the council had hired a non-profit organization to build their first data portal, at a cost of £40,950, but needed a long-term sustainable solution. The DataPress hosting plan saved the council tens of thousands of pounds.

DataPress's other flagship project was known as the Leeds Data Mill. It aimed to help the city to become smarter by harnessing, interpreting and presenting open data on the city's waste, air quality, footfall and other criteria, in an effort to help decision-makers and consumers change for the better. The city is using the platform to host events and hackathons, engaging with developers and sharing raw datasets. The Data Mill relies on CKAN and WordPress. Open-source plug-ins can host event pages and integrate with Meetup.com. Developers and companies can contribute their own datasets during a hackathon, and Leeds wants to build its open-data community.

The city of Amsterdam has since enlisted DataPress to build and run its publishing platform, data.amsterdam.nl. The city required a bespoke platform that matched their visual identity and made use of technologies like CKAN and Wordpress. They were also keen to encourage more people to get involved in data publishing, so needed an interface that made it easy to publish and to view data.

Jasper Soetendal, programme manager of Open Data for the city of Amsterdam, said: 'We want to encourage data-driven decision-making in the city.' Soetendal aims to make Amsterdam smarter, more agile, transparent and efficient, using open data. The first step involved providing a clear overview of what data is available for his colleagues and partners and for application developers, researchers and citizens. DataPress enables both data and content publishing in a single platform, and is mobile-responsive and compatible with all open-data standards by default. Open data creates a dialogue between governments, councils and citizens, and helps to create smarter, safer, more efficient cities.

TAKEAWAYS

1 Could open data help improve your city?
2 What types of businesses can benefit from a platform like DataPress?
3 Could this model be applied on a national or global scale, not just in local councils?

INNOVATION DATA

Website: datapress.com
Contact: contact@datapress.io
Innovation name: DataPress
Country: United Kingdom
Industries: Government & legal / Smart cities

13

REAL-TIME BIG DATA TO MANAGE TRAFFIC IN THE PHILIPPINES

OpenTraffic uses data from a ride-share service to help government agencies manage traffic flow.

Congestion in Manila costs the Philippine economy more than $60 million per day, and commuters frequently take more than two hours to travel just 8 kilometres. Due to a lack of resources and manpower, until recently there were few concrete facts and figures and statistics on the city's congestion. Most cities in developing countries face similar issues. Traditional methods of collecting traffic data rely either on labour-intensive fieldwork, which is slow and provides low-quality data, or capital-intensive sensor data networks, which cover only a small portion of a metropolitan area.

In order to address this widespread problem, Easy Taxi, Grab and Le. Taxi, three ride-sharing companies – which, between them, cover more than 30 countries and millions of customers – are working with the World Bank to make traffic data derived from their drivers' GPS streams available to the public through an open-data licence. Through the new partnership, these companies, along with founding members Mapzen, the World Resources Institute, Miovision and NDrive, will give resource-constrained transport agencies the power to make better, evidence-based decisions that were previously completely unfeasible.

The ride-sharing services will now be using their vast swathes of data to provide real-time travel time estimates and information about traffic incidents and weather problems. The information will be available on the open platform OpenTraffic, and 200 staff at the Philippine National Police, the Metro Manila Development Authority and the Department of Public Works and Highways have already been trained to use it. The data will help to address the current issues of traffic-signal timing plans, public transit provision, roadway infrastructure needs, emergency traffic management and travel demand management.

When the idea of the Open Traffic Partnership started in the Philippines, the government approached the World Bank and asked them to help to identify and implement solutions to their traffic challenges. It was clear that they needed better, more timely data about accidents and traffic flows, as well as low-cost tools to analyse and make sense of this data.

Using data from Grab, city governments in the Philippines could, for the first time, answer the fundamental questions necessary to address safety and congestion. These are:

- Where and when is congestion most acute?
- Where and when are people most vulnerable to road incidents?
- When money is invested in interventions to mitigate accidents or congestion, do these investments work?

The open-source platform leverages open-source software and big-data partnerships to substantially reduce the cost of traditional traffic data collection and analysis, while simultaneously improving quality.

Building on the success of the Philippines pilot programme, the World Bank, along with a number of ride-sharing companies and mapping and navigation services companies, has launched the Open Traffic Partnership (OTP) to develop the global architecture for combining anonymized traffic data.

Big data has proved incredibly useful for those organizing the flow of people or vehicles. We have already seen it used for better urban planning with Placemeter in the United States, in airports and on New Zealand's roads.

TAKEAWAYS

1 Could similar initiatives work in other regions?
2 How else could existing data from location-based apps and platforms be used on a metropolitan level to address chronic challenges?
3 In what other ways could governments collaborate with developers to utilize open-source data?
4 How could your company take advantage of existing datasets that are currently not exploited to their full potential?

INNOVATION DATA

Website: www.worldbank.org
Contact: dllorito@worldbank.org
Company name: Grab Philippines
Innovation name: OpenTraffic
Country: Philippines
Industries: Access exclusive / Government & legal / Smart cities / Transport & automotive

14

A FREE, OPEN, CROWDSOURCED CITY-WIDE IOT NETWORK

The Things Network is helping to build a free city-wide Internet in Amsterdam, without the use of Wi-Fi or 3G.

Imagine a world where Internet access is free for all – where an Internet of Things (IoT) is networked by the users, for the users. Is it possible? In Amsterdam, it's already happened. The Things Network (TTN) is planning to build a global, open, crowdsourced IoT data network, and work is well under way.

In just six weeks, Amsterdam was transformed into a city-wide accessible network, without the help of any big business or telecoms companies; it has been entirely crowdsourced. TTN initiator Wienke Giezeman saw the potential in a new technology called LoraWAN (Long-range Wide Area Network) to create gateways for connecting municipal geographic zones. The devices allow things to connect to the Internet without the use of Wi-Fi, 3G or Bluetooth. It has a wide range and cheap development and installation costs: 1,500 euros for a device with a 11-km (7-mile) radius.

Pilot projects already under way in Amsterdam include a device that alerts boat owners to potential flooding of their moored vessels, and another that monitors users' bikes. The port of Amsterdam, which struggles to support the cost involved in setting up wireless networks across the whole port area, has also been contributing to the project.

After the rapid success of Amsterdam's crowdsourced city-wide activation, TTN has spread rapidly. There is now a community of 8,156 people in over 80 countries building a global IoT data network. With the LoraWAN technology, TTN will allow the IoT to change the way cities across the world function: with crowdsourcing from those who can afford to install gateways, all inhabitants will benefit from having their city connected.

There is a strong emphasis on such networks being built by us – the people. Users can contribute by placing a gateway and expanding the network. The more gateways that are placed the larger will be the coverage. At the time of writing, there are 699 gateways up and running, along with 1,489 Kickstarter gateways.

TTN hopes to support all available LoRaWAN-enabled network equipment. It currently supports three gateways: the Kerlink and MultiTech, which cost between $500 and $1,500, and their own TTN gateway, which was funded through a Kickstarter campaign.

TTN's ultimate goal is to make its network architecture as decentralized as possible and to avoid any points of failure or control. They already have a community of ten developers writing network software and equipment firmware. Users can also offer their help in building the network, for example by contributing to the open-source code, helping the network though a 'community' or network hub, or working on cases and connecting with like-minded people in TTN's 'Labs'.

Key challenges for this model include those already seen with open-source data collaboration and crowdfunded and sharing economy models: that is, can the quality and reliability of a service founded on these principles match up to the big-business equivalents we have grown so used to? And, once it passes a certain point, will the hardware, software and processes be capable of handling the system's own success?

An idea such as this depends heavily on widespread uptake. They have already reached a global network of users – predominantly those in the tech sphere – but if TTN can grow this community exponentially, through publicity, crowdsourced funding and open-source data contribution, there is huge potential to entirely disrupt the way we think about network coverage and service provision.

TAKEAWAYS

1 What other projects are possible with a Things Network?
2 What other nationwide services could be made cheaper when put in the hands of the people?
3 How could your company crowdfund hardware to help launch a disruptive model?

INNOVATION DATA

Website: www.thethingsnetwork.org
Contact: wienke@thethingsnetwork.com
Innovation name: The Things Network
Country: The Netherlands
Industries: Crowdfunding Now / Smart cities / Telecoms & mobile

15

TRIALLING A CROWDSOURCED CONSTITUTION IN MEXICO CITY

Mexico City citizens have been invited to contribute to and shape the city's new constitution through the online Plataforma Constitución CDMX.

Crowdsourcing has been able to provide useful solutions to city-wide problems, from monitoring pollution to flagging community problems that need addressing by the authorities.

Using a variety of digital tools, including Change.org and the bespoke Plataforma Constitución CDMX, Mexico City's 9 million citizens have been invited to help create an official government constitution that reflects the city they live in and its aspirations for a better future.

On Plataforma Constitución CDMX, citizens are able to comment on the first draft of the pending document, contribute written proposals for public consideration, take surveys to shape future drafts and organize formally affiliated meetings. For those who are offline, kiosks linked to the platform are located throughout the city. A citizen's petition must garner more than 10,000 signatures for it to be considered for inclusion, although there is no legally binding requirement for citizen initiatives to be considered for the final draft.

This experiment in digital democracy is not without its critics, however. For example, one of the successful proposals submitted by a citizen was that the city should guarantee a minimum amount of green space per resident. The proposal attracted some over 40,000 votes and was the first idea to be presented to the drafters. It asked for 9.2 square metres of green space per person, the minimum required by the World Health Organization.

Critics have argued that optimistic proposals such as this one are wildly unrealistic. They suggest that it is impossible to guarantee green space in a city like this without confiscating private property, businesses or land used for industry. While the constitution also states that everyone has the right to breathe a healthy atmosphere, this promise is, at least for now, completely unfeasible in one of the largest cities in the world, with a pollution problem to match.

These ideas are supposed to be aspirational, but critics argue that, without a legal system to implement all these rights, the draft document is completely meaningless. Another cause for concern is that the group that wrote the draft was selected by Mayor Miguel Ángel Mancera himself, and the whole process has been accused of being a ploy to shore up his approval ratings. Critics believe that the mayor has put the process in the hands of a small group that is unrepresentative of the city as a whole. Controversially, the document contained no guarantee of private property and proposed a capital gains tax.

Supporters argue that it is essential for tackling the city's grievous problems, and part of a long process towards making its democratic institutions more representative of the people they are there to serve. While there are unpopular passages and omissions in the text, many believe that, overall, the spirit of the proposal is good. It is an innovative constitution, and therefore would inevitably receive a mixed response.

Supporters also see it as a good opportunity to put more force behind the city's civic culture and citizen participation. Receiving input from citizens aims not only to improve the quality of the constitution itself, but also to build a feeling of citizenship and community participation. While the system may not be perfect, the idea of creating a city constitution that is directly influenced by the inhabitants of that city is surely a step towards a fairer democracy.

TAKEAWAYS

1 Could online and offline crowdsourcing provide a democratic answer for other municipalities?

2 How could this idea be reworked to eliminate political foul play and suspicion among citizens?

3 What other government systems could receive wider input from citizens?

INNOVATION DATA

Website: www.constitucion.cdmx
Contact: www.twitter.com/SomosCdMx
Company name: Mexico City
Innovation name: Plataforma Constitución CDMX
Country: Mexico
Industries: Government & legal / Smart cities

16

AN APP TO LET CONSTITUENTS HELP BALANCE THEIR CITY'S BUDGET

Balancing Act shows citizens their city's budget breakdown and lets them interact with it and hypothesize a budget according to their priorities.

In this era of information, political spending and municipal budgets are still often shrouded in confusion and mystery. But a new web app called Balancing Act hopes to change that, by enabling US citizens to see the breakdown of their city's budget via adjustable, comprehensive pie charts.

Created by Colorado-based consultants Engaged Public, Balancing Act not only shows citizens the current budget breakdown but also enables them to experiment with hypothetical future budgets, adjusting spending and taxes to suit their own priorities. The project aims to engage and inform citizens about the money that their mayors and governments assign on their behalf and allows them to have more of a say in the future of their city. The resource has already been utilized by Pedro Segarra, Mayor of Hartford, Connecticut, who asked his citizens for their input on how best to balance the $49 million budget.

The system can be used to help governments understand the wants and needs of their constituents, as well as enable citizens to see the bigger picture when it comes to tough or unappealing policies. Eventually, it can even be used to create the world's first crowdsourced budget, giving the public the power to make their preferences heard in a clear, comprehensible way.

The company lists the benefits of using Balancing Act as 'building a more educated public that understands the tough trade-offs in creating a public budget, providing an easy way to get informed input on priorities and stimulate creative ideas to improve programmes'. They also hope that the system will reach out beyond the 'usual suspects' to people who don't currently attend public meetings, and to 'cultivate relationships with residents so that when tough challenges arise in the future there will be a greater capacity to jointly problem-solve.'

Features of the user-friendly app include embedded help text, preloaded descriptions and a simple onboarding process. It has a customizable online simulation page with unique URL and ability to upload your own logo. It provides in-depth, aggregated data reports on resident budget priorities, including qualitative feedback, and is optimized for the complexity of public budgets – so is not simply a discussion forum. Users benefit from a constantly growing catalogue of background research, best practices and standards that governments can include as they wish.

Balancing Act is designed to meet the public engagement needs of governments of all types: municipalities, school districts, counties, states and perhaps, eventually, even nations. It can accommodate different world currencies and languages, so could be applied worldwide. In addition, Balancing Act's flexible interface means that its application could span much further than budget balancing for local governments. Balancing Act suggest that in the future non-profits, advocacy organizations, foundations and others can use the app either internally (such as for facilitating board discussions about a budget) or externally, to educate and get feedback from the public on an entire budget or issue.

Engaged Public, the organization behind the app, is a public policy consulting firm specializing in engagement-driven strategies. Since 1998 they have provided a link between people and policy using innovative tools and strategies. They have been involved in a whole range of policy areas, from health-care reform to education standards and water quality.

As seen previously with **Mexico City's constitution**, crowd-sourcing government legislation can be riddled with challenges, but with patience and co-operation this innovation could help governments become more responsive to and representative of the people they serve.

TAKEAWAYS

1 Could other interactive tools be used to help politicians survey the desires of citizens?
2 Would this system be popular in your locality?
3 What other areas aside from budget could use such a strategy?
4 How else could local governments reach out to those normally not interested in these issues?

INNOVATION DATA

Website: www.abalancingact.com
Contact: www.abalancingact.com/contact
Company name: Engaged Public
Innovation name: Balancing Act
Country: United States
Industries: Education / Financial services & fin tech / Government & legal / Non-profit & social cause / Smart cities

17

OPEN DATA FOR TRANSIT APP DEVELOPERS

Transitland's Mapzen Turn-by-Turn routing service
is now capable of mapping travel in more than
200 regions worldwide.

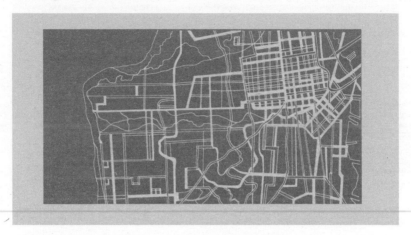

Creating effective transit apps can be difficult, given the vast amount
of city (and worldwide) data to which app builders need to have
access. Aiming to address this, Transitland is an open platform that
aggregates publicly available transport information from around the
world.

The start-up cleans the datasets, making them easy to use, and adds
them to Mapzen, an open-source mapping platform. Mapzen Turn-
by-Turn is the platform's transport planning service that, following
its latest expansion, now contains data from more than 200 regions
around the world on every continent except Antarctica. It is one of
the four pillars of the Mapzen Android Software Development Kit
(SDK) and is powered by Valhalla, a routing engine that is built on
open data from OpenStreetMap and Transitland.

Transitland encourages anyone interested in transport, data and mapping to get involved, from adding data streams to sharing new apps and analyses. Mapzen Turn-by-Turn also manages all licensing related to use of the data, leaving developers free to discover and build. The platform is available to use for free. The software provides dynamic and customizable routing by driving, walking, bicycling and using multimodal and transit options, with clear directions for manoeuvres along the route.

When users request a route, they input specific information about where they want to go, along with their own bespoke requirements for a journey such as preferred methods of transport and cost limitations. The service uses an interface called On-The-Road, which addresses client-side challenges of routing such as snapping the device location to the closest nearby road, distance calculations and turn prompting.

Mapzen Turn-by-Turn is extremely flexible. For example, if a user is planning a bicycle journey, myriad factors can be considered. Bicycle type and cycling speed can be changed, along with user preferences for paved roads, dirt paths and hills. Multimodal routes also have a wide range of options, including setting preferences for bus, rail, transfers and walking distance.

The service's route results provide details about the trip, including a summary with basic information about the entire trip and a list of legs. Each leg has its own summary, a shape, which is a line of the route visualized on a map, and a list of manoeuvres. These manoeuvres provide written narrative instructions, plus verbal alerts that can be used as audio guidance in navigation apps.

The service also prides itself on providing succinct, easy-to-read, useful guidance and narrative directions to assist users during their trip. Redundant manoeuvres are collapsed, transitions at complex intersections are simplified, and exit information on highways is clear and timely. These features aim to provide a happier and shorter trip.

We have seen a platform enable data sharing to help local communities and governments work better together in the form of mySidewalk, which was founded in the United States by city planners who recognized the potential force for change in infrastructure and city planning, contained in the communities themselves.

TAKEAWAYS

1 We've seen DataPress and Transitland, but what other datasets can be made more accessible?
2 How else could transport and mapping software be revolutionized by the free and open input of developers around the world?
3 How could your company benefit from utilizing open data?
4 In what other sectors aside from transport could open data prove useful? Health care? Education?

INNOVATION DATA

Website: transit.land
Contact: transitland@mapzen.com
Company name: Transitland
Innovation name: Mapzen Turn-by-Turn
Country: United States
Industries: Smart cities / Transport & automotive

18

FREE WI-FI FROM CLEAN AIR IN AMSTERDAM

TreeWiFi's smart birdhouses measure air quality in real time and provide free Wi-Fi when pollution levels drop.

Fresh, clean air is one of the quickly diminishing commodities most city dwellers crave on a daily basis. Based in Amsterdam, TreeWiFi's smart birdhouses let residents know about the air quality of their neighbourhood, and, if it is clean enough, they get free Wi-Fi.

Using nitrogen dioxide (NO_2) sensors to measure the amount of combustion particles in the air, the birdhouses light up with LED lights to show real-time levels of pollution. When the lights go green, the air quality has improved and the network makes the free Wi-Fi available. The Wi-Fi network itself is always available for people to connect with, regardless of the air quality, but, if the local air quality is poor, instead of free Internet it gives information and tips on how to improve air quality. The sensors measure air pollution levels emitted from combustion processes within about 100 metres (109 yards).

Right now, the company is focusing on the amount of NO_2 in the air, as the majority of it comes from smoke and exhaust fumes – two things that residents can easily influence. TreeWiFi plans to make the data collected available to researchers and several government departments have already expressed interest in the project due to its scope. Should a birdhouse be installed on every street in the city, a vast quantity of timely air pollution data will be available for analysis.

By installing a network of TreeWiFi birdhouses in a city, municipalities get better insights when it comes to air pollution in urban environments. The data is hyper-local, high quality and real time – and the bigger the network, the better the data. Founder Joris Lam says that, while broad data like this is readily available, a lack of localized data inspired him come up with the idea for TreeWiFi.

Dutch designer Lam said he wanted to find a simple and non-intrusive way to make air pollution visible to citizens in a way that they can understand on an emotional level, rather than looking at data and maps. Lam realized that the problem of air pollution is almost completely invisible to the average person because it cannot often be seen at street level. The simple birdhouse design is a benign response to what he sees as the age of mass surveillance and machines tracking our every move.

Lam launched his project at a critical time as it was revealed that air pollution levels in parts of Amsterdam break EU standards. The city was also given a very poor ranking for air quality by an environmental study, thanks in part to its failure to implement a low-emissions zone for private vehicles, as other European cities have done. Lam has raised enough money to assemble a team of engineers and scientists to refine the technology and reward system.

We have already seen air-purifying billboards designed by the University of Engineering and Technology in Peru, which deliver pollution-free air to the surrounding area, and Clean Road Mapper, which lets Toronto's cyclists avoid the most polluted streets by showing them the route with the best air quality.

TAKEAWAYS

1 How could local sustainability projects be scaled for regional or national use?
2 In what other ways could people be rewarded for sustainable eco-friendly behaviour?
3 What other environmental factors could be visualized in a similar way, and dealt with on a public scale?
4 How could your company make a serious and important issue fun and interactive for the public to tackle?

INNOVATION DATA

Website: www.heroesandfriends.com
Contact: contact@heroesandfriends.com
Innovation name: TreeWiFi
Country: The Netherlands
Industries: Nature & sustainability / Smart cities / Transport & automotive

19

ENERGY-EFFICIENT STREET LIGHTS THAT ARE ALSO MOSQUITO TRAPS

Researchers at the University of Malaya have developed street lights powered by wind and solar that attract and trap mosquitoes using a 'human' scent.

More than 1 million people worldwide die from mosquito-borne diseases every year. Mosquitos contribute to the spread of many deadly diseases, including malaria, the Zika virus and dengue fever. Controlling the growth of mosquito populations is an effective way to prevent the spread of such infectious diseases.

Energy-efficient street lights that attract and trap mosquitoes by giving off a 'human' scent are being used in Kuala Lumpur. Developed by researchers at the University of Malaya, the smart outdoor LED lamps are powered by wind and solar energy, and can function off the grid, even in flood-prone areas.

Mosquitoes react sensitively to certain wavelengths of ultraviolet light. The mosquito trap consists of an integrated weak UV light and a suction fan. Parts within the trap are coated with titanium dioxide (TiO_2). When the UV wavelength comes in contact with the TiO_2, a photo-catalytic reaction takes place that produces carbon dioxide (CO_2). This is the same CO_2 that humans exhale and is irresistible to mosquitoes. Once the mosquitoes have been attracted to the trap by the UV light and CO_2, the fan draws in the mosquitoes at the bottom and keeps them from escaping with the vacuum action created by the continuous cycle of the fan.

Developed to combat the spread of dengue fever in Malaysia, the self-powered street lights can be easily deployed in areas lacking power infrastructure, providing energy-efficient lighting as well as disease control.

The highly innovative design comprises many groundbreaking features that maximize the traps' effectiveness. The hybrid renewable energy sources consist of a solar photovoltaic (PV) panel and a vertical axis wind turbine (VAWT). The PV panel is located at the top of the system to reduce the effects of shadow and maximize the energy harness of the sun. The VAWT is covered by an omnidirectional guide-vane (ODGV), which is a wind-power augmentation system to increase the oncoming wind speed. During wind tunnel testing, researchers found that the power output for the ODGV-integrated VAWT increased by about 3.48 times compared to the bare VAWT. The rotating parts of the VAWT are enclosed within the ODGV to make it safer for the public.

The two renewable energy sources provide the power required to run the light in varying weathers, and therefore improve the system's reliability. The power generated by the green energy controls both the lighting and the mosquito trap. The long-lifespan LED lights provide brightness during the night and also serve a decorative purpose.

With increasing numbers of cases of dengue fever across Malaysia, it has been imperative to seek a solution to control the mosquito population. This is an excellent example of researchers and scientists creating innovative ways to combat disease on a macro level. The combination of lab researchers collaborating with developers and innovators as well as local governments to address widespread problems is a trend that is becoming more and more apparent. This cross-pollination is a great solution to issues that span the jurisdictions of health-care professionals, politicians, scientists and innovators.

A similar innovation is bug-trapping drones used as part of Project Premonition, which employs an autonomous drone system to monitor infectious agents and predict diseases before they infect humans.

TAKEAWAYS

1 How else could biological control systems be implemented in cities?
2 How else can researchers collaborate with governments to address widespread health-care problems?
3 How and where could this model be applied to address other mosquito-borne epidemics such as Zika?

INNOVATION DATA

Website: www.researchsea.com
Contact: chong_wentong@um.edu.my
Company name: University of Malaya
Innovation name: Smart outdoor lighting system
Country: Malaysia
Industries: Health & wellbeing / Nature & sustainability / Smart cities

20

AMBULANCES IN SWEDEN THAT CAN HIJACK IN-CAR RADIOS

Developed by three students at Sweden's KTH Royal Institute of Technology, the EVAM System uses FM radio to alert drivers to approaching emergency vehicles.

One of the many improvements constantly being made to vehicle technology is better soundproofing. Unfortunately, despite its many benefits, having a well-soundproofed vehicle makes it more difficult for drivers to hear approaching sirens. Now three students at Sweden's Kungl Tekniska Högskolan (KTH) Royal Institute of Technology have developed the EVAM System, helping emergency service vehicles hijack in-car radios to alert distant cars that an emergency vehicle is approaching. As long as the radio in the car is turned on, the EVAM System will work, regardless of what the driver is using – CD, radio or Bluetooth.

The EVAM System works by sending a voice message from the ambulance to vehicles ahead. The solution involves a radio transmission from the emergency vehicle to nearby FM tuners that are equipped with Radio Data System (RDS). The signal is sent over the FM band along with the transmission of a text message, the message interrupts whatever is playing on the car's audio system and the corresponding text message appears on the dashboard tuner display. Unlike lights and sirens, the warning system anticipates how far in advance messages need to be heard depending on the speed of local traffic. On a highway, for example, the signal will broadcast earlier than in slow-moving city traffic.

The EVAM System reaches two-thirds of all vehicles on the road, and it can also warn of accidents along the route. It fulfils three functions:

- It improves accessibility for first responders.
- It improves road safety.
- It makes the working environment in transport better for vulnerable professions.

The system began road tests in Stockholm in the first half of 2017 with a limited number of emergency vehicles. Once the system has been fully tested and approved in Sweden, the technology could be rolled out in cities across the world in a wide range of emergency vehicles. 'Often, drivers have only a few seconds to react and give way to emergency vehicles,' says Mikael Erneberg, who studies industrial engineering at KTH. 'The optimal warning time is at least 10 to 15 seconds.'

As we develop more advanced, greener and more user-friendly technology, sometimes we lose elements of safety that were formerly present – even if by accident. Not only has the better sound insulation of vehicles caused more frequent crashes involving motorists who didn't hear sirens or other vehicles, but another safety problem is posed by electronic vehicles making significantly less engine noise than petrol or diesel models. While this is a more pleasant experience for drivers and passengers and reduces overall urban noise, it is harder for pedestrians to hear them approaching, so, if they are not paying full attention, it may make them more likely to be struck.

Technology is helping to make emergency care provision swifter and more sustainable in a variety of other ways. In health care, for example, predictive sensors help prevent heart failure: a team of scientists led by Penn State's College of Medicine retrofitted defibrillators with software that predicted heart failures before they occurred. And, for climate-change refugees, innovative disaster shelters provide self-sufficient, sustainable temporary homes. A Jordanian architect designed the 'Weaving a Home', an ultra-light, temporary yurt designed to help those forced from their homes by climate change.

TAKEAWAYS

1   How else could communities use new products, designs and materials to improve emergency care?
2   Why not use this technology across all emergency services, as well as at the scene of accidents, to alert drivers that they will shortly need to slow down or stop?
3   How else could this technology or similar technology be applied in your city?

INNOVATION DATA

Website: www.kth.se
Contact: info@kth.se
Company name: Kungl Tekniska Högskolan (KTH) Royal Institute of Technology
Innovation name: EVAM System
Country: Sweden
Industries: Health & wellbeing / Smart cities / Transport & automotive

SUMMARY

Rich, open data provides a huge opportunity for cities to become more liveable, workable and sustainable. Governments have a pivotal role to play, creating the infrastructure to gather and analyse the data, and fostering an environment for innovation. Municipal leaders must then seek to disseminate this information and engage their citizens. If they do so effectively, collaboration between government and citizens will lead to more innovative urban solutions, increased civic engagement and, ultimately, trust in government.

The challenges facing today's growing metropolises are many, and are often already at a critical stage, but, by bringing citizens on board in that problem-solving process, these challenges can be transformed into opportunities. Even where data cannot be opened up to the public, the utmost should be done to engage citizens through other means. Together, the problems of today's cities are not insurmountable: the innovations in this chapter, and throughout this book, are a testimony to that.

SMART CITIES TAKEAWAYS

1 **Take data as destiny.** Smart cities depend on a host of technologies, but their beating heart is data. As the Internet of Things rapidly expands, governments have an opportunity to add layers of complexity to their datasets and garner richer insights than ever. However, the more data that is available and the more sources this data comes from, the more difficult it becomes to analyse it. The International Data Corporation (IDC) predicts that the digital universe will weigh in at a colossal 44 zettabytes of data by 2020. For governments, this means that action must be taken now to ensure that the volume does not become unmanageable. To achieve this, data should be gathered under a strategy that clearly defines the *purpose* of the analysis. Driven by this strategy, data collection should then be designed with analytics and ongoing tracking embedded from the outset, rather than tacked on as an afterthought.

2 **Watch the watchmen.** In addition to these technical considerations, we need to address human concerns when collecting data. Headlines regarding ownership rights and third-party access to data (including by security services) have fuelled public mistrust of data collection techniques. There are also justified concerns from the public over personal data being used in such a way that identifies previously anonymized information.

There are lessons here for any organization involved in data collection. An honest, transparent dialogue around the use of data, and improved legislation to regulate it, should be the bedrock of trustworthy data collection. Nicola Blackwood, Chair of the UK's Commons Science and Technology Select Committee, suggests the formation of a 'Council of Data Ethics' to address the public's concerns, and that privacy could be better protected by making the release of previously anonymized data a criminal offence.

Public consent cannot be taken for granted, and providing options to control how much and what type of data is being handed over – and to whom – will go a long way to restoring trust. Options should also be provided for the user to revoke access to their data at a later stage, to enhance further a relationship based on free and informed consent.

3 **Collaborate to progress.** Whether modelling city budgets or co-creating constitutions, citizen participation in developing smart cities is essential. While governments should retain responsibility for data collection, they must also recognize that private actors are often better at putting that data into effect.

4 **Benefit from engagement.** Wellbeing will be at the heart of the smartest cities. Not only does collaboration lead to better products, but it also creates a less anxious population. Research shows that citizens equipped with more information – about how long their train may take to arrive, say – are less stressed. The implication for government policy is that transparency and sharing leads to a more contented and trusting population.

5 **Don't forget the architect.** Throughout this chapter we have focused on the technology and data that will enable the cities of the future. This is not to say that we do not believe in the vital role that architects and creators of place are playing and will continue to play in the future city. An aesthetic that leads to an innate design-led liveability and the use of sustainable materials will spell great opportunity as we create the living spaces of tomorrow.

SUSTAINABILITY

The Global Footprint Network estimates that human consumption began to exceed the Earth's capacity in the early 1970s and that the Earth's annual 'overshoot day' – when we have used up that year's supply of natural resources – has been coming earlier each year since then. Unsustainable levels of consumption, combined with growing population levels, have created a truly global crisis, demanding global solutions. In this chapter, we'll look at the disruptors around the world looking for the answers.

Turning waste into energy

Entrepreneurs across the globe have been exploring creative ways to extract value from waste products. By transforming waste into something new, innovators can reduce the carbon footprint of production, while simultaneously limiting the amount of products going to landfill – and at the same time creating unique and profitable businesses. Their endeavours go some way towards ensuring that fewer natural resources are consumed, and there is less waste to damage the environment.

One of the most creative examples of this process in action comes from Netherlands-based **Nerdalize**. Many of the innovations described in this book make use of big data*, and all this data needs storing in data centres, which produce an enormous amount of heat, requiring large coolers to keep them running at optimum efficiency. This cooling operation is, of course, both costly and damaging for the environment. This is where Nerdalize comes in with its eRadiator server/heater, which uses waste heat produced by servers to warm homes.

77

This creative reluctance to write anything off as 'waste' is a theme we are seeing across the globe. In Bangalore, for example, Graviky Labs captures the carbon particles from car exhaust and turns them into Air-Ink pens and paints. And clean technology company Bio-bean's first consumer product, Coffee Logs, converts coffee ground waste into biomass briquettes that can be used in almost any fire-heated appliance, from pizza ovens to wood-burning stoves and BBQs.

> **Big data**
>
> Big data are extremely large datasets that may be analysed computationally to reveal patterns and trends, especially as they relate to human behaviour.

Reducing and eliminating waste

Of course, as compelling as these innovations are, reducing the actual amount of waste produced to begin with remains a top priority, and entrepreneurs across the globe are exploring new solutions that seek to eliminate waste from the start. In architecture, we are seeing a drive to produce buildings that have a minimal environmental impact. The solar-panel equipped **KODA** home from Estonia, for example, can be assembled in seven hours and produce more power than the building requires. Taking an entirely different approach, sustainable building company Larkfleet Group has developed a home on stilts that could be built on floodplains, thus reducing the need for damaging river manipulation. These two very different innovations both aim to reduce human environmental impact at source.

But these innovations are not the answers in and of themselves, and we cannot rely on other entrepreneurs to create technologies that offset our current practices. Rather, we must look all look to downscale our consumption, and there are plenty of innovations to help us achieve that.

California's dry season frequently brings drought warnings with it, meaning that residents are required to be extra vigilant with their water consumption. Helping them to achieve these cut-backs, Pandora Radio, in conjunction with the Metropolitan Water District, launched The Water Lover's Station, which exclusively plays water-related songs lasting five minutes or less. Hits included 'The River' by Bruce Springsteen, 'Waterfalls' by TLC and 'Purple Rain' by Prince, with the idea was that residents could aim to complete their shower in the time taken for one song to play.

Rewards can also be used to promote sustainable behaviour. In Medellin, Colombia, Ciclo offers top-ups on citizens' travel cards in exchange for recyclable plastic. It is similar to The Beer Turnstile in Rio, which offered free train rides home to carnival goers in exchange for empty beer cans. The turnstile saw around 1,000 users per hour, 86 per cent higher than the usual traffic. The number of drink-driving incidents that evening also dropped by 43 per cent.

Ultimately, if we are to succeed in managing the very real threat of climate change, we will need innovation in sustainable design that focuses on minimal resource consumption and waste repurposing, alongside this shift in consumption habits. The examples in this chapter help to illustrate just some of the ways in which change is already under way.

21

A GREEN COMPUTER SERVER THAT HEATS HOMES FOR FREE

Netherlands-based Nerdalize is using the heat produced by computer servers to warm the homes they are installed in.

The most ecologically sound forms of green energy are those that would otherwise have been the waste product of another process. Netherlands-based Nerdalize has created a way to use the heat produced from a cloud-based computer server system to warm individual homes.

In today's connected, computerized world, huge data centres filled with servers require extensive cooling systems to handle the excess heat they produce. As well as air-conditioning units, data centres must also provide back-up cooling units, water sprinkler systems for possible periods of excessively high outdoor weather temperatures and fire-extinguishing apparatus.

Nerdalize, on the other hand, saw the potential in the heat generated by computer data centres and found a way to make use of the substantial amounts of energy that were consistently wasted. The company's solution is to place individual servers in people's homes where the heat can be useful rather than a problem. Homeowners can lease the two-in-one heater/server from Nerdalize, which covers the electricity costs of the device. The multiple, high-performance servers create the Nerdalize Cloud, a highly distributed, sustainable and affordable computer platform, without the overheads of a traditional data centre.

Businesses can then buy the computing power they need from
Nerdalize, saving between 30 and 55 per cent on costs. The same energy
is effectively used twice, saving all parties money and creating a much
more environmentally friendly infrastructure.

One of the heater/servers can save homeowners up to 300 euros per year and eliminate the production of up to 3 tonnes of carbon dioxide. All heater/servers are protected against tampering, of both software and hardware, and, should anything be detected, the Nerdalize team can halt operations on any individual server and remotely wipe its contents.

The team points to the decentralized nature of its cloud computing service as a substantial advantage against hacks. And when a processor reaches the end of its approximate three-year lifetime, a mechanic is dispatched to replace the necessary parts.

If a server loses its connection to the Internet, the heater will continue to function. Nerdalize has built in dummy calculation functionality to prevent a heater from stopping working due to Internet connectivity. And should the temperature be too high for the homeowner to need to use the heater, Nerdalize's design sends any server heat outside.

The company continues to develop the concept of putting waste energy to productive use and recently collaborated with two Delft University of Technology computer science students to make the heater/servers even more efficient. Computer usage can now be broken up into tiny computations that can be completed by the home needing the most heat. When the desired heater temperature is reached, the computation's pieces move on to other servers, with each aspect of computer use usually using multiple servers at a time. Not only is the energy produced used most efficiently and effectively, the computing service offered by Nerdalize is faster than ever.

The company is also developing a new heater in collaboration with Eneco. Businesses and homeowners can register their interest online and will be informed when the service expands into their area.

Other ways in which waste power is being put to productive use is through Bio-Bean's transformation of used coffee beans into energy that helps to run London's coffee shops, and LucidPipes' harvesting of green energy from Portland, Oregon's water pipes.

TAKEAWAYS

1 How might local governments make better use of waste energy?
2 How could waste energy products work together to create ever lower levels of pollution?
3 Is there a waste product or process in your business that could be put to another use?

INNOVATION DATA

Website: www.nerdalize.com
Contact: hello@nerdalize.com
Innovation name: Nerdalize
Country: The Netherlands
Industries: Home & garden / Nature & sustainability / Smart cities

22

CONVERTING HUMAN WASTE INTO CRUDE OIL

The Pacific Northwest National Laboratory in the USA has developed a hydrothermal liquefaction process that converts human waste in sewage water into a crude bio-oil fuel in minutes.

Taken together, North American wastewater treatment plants typically deal with 34 billion gallons of sewage every day. Although long considered as a potential alternative energy source because of the sheer volume produced each year, sewage sludge has traditionally proven too time-consuming and expensive to use in this way. Most fuel conversion methods have focused on drying the sludge. Now, new technology from the US Department of Energy's Pacific Northwest National Laboratory (PNNL) could potentially transform sewage treatment while providing an alternative to crude oil across North America.

By mimicking the high temperatures and pressure that create crude oil naturally, the researchers developed a process called hydrothermal liquefaction (HTL) that produces in minutes what takes the Earth millions of years. The HTL process breaks organic matter down into its chemical components. This is accomplished through the use of 211 kilogram-force per square cm (300 lb/in^2) of pressure – nearly one hundred times that of a car tyre – combined with a temperature of 3,649 °C (6,600 °F).

The resulting material is a mixture of biocrude and liquids. When refined, the wastewater sludge biocrude is of very high quality and can be turned into gasoline, diesel and other fuels. The team has been working on the HTL process for six years and reviews of the process are showing it to be extremely efficient, with nearly 60 per cent of the available carbon becoming the high-quality biocrude.

'The best thing about this process is how simple it is,' says Corinne Drennan, who is responsible for bioenergy technologies research at PNNL. 'The reactor is literally a hot, pressurized tube. We've really accelerated the technology to create a scalable process.'

The first operational HTL plant is scheduled to open at Metro Vancouver in 2018 as a demonstrator facility, with PNNL hoping to convince waste management centres across the United States to adopt the system. Metro Vancouver is a partnership of 23 local governments and will provide approximately half the costs of the first plant.

Darrell Mussatto, chair of Metro Vancouver's Utilities Committee, says, 'If this emerging technology is a success, a future production facility could lead the way for wastewater operation to meet sustainability objectives of zero net energy, zero odours and zero residuals.'

PNNL's technology could produce up to 30 million barrels of oil annually, simultaneously negating the need for investment in waste treatment and disposal. It could also be applied to other waste systems, such as agricultural run-off. As well as biocrude, the residual materials produced by the HTL process could also be used, further eliminating waste. If treated with some type of catalyst, the liquids could be turned into other types of fuel. The small amounts of solids that remain could be used in place of the nutrients in other products, such as the phosphorus in fertilizers.

Turning waste products into something usable is an important strand in the fight to mitigate climate change. A floating farm located in Rotterdam Harbour uses the manure of the resident cows to power the dairy factory and visitor centre. And in Kenya, a sanitation drive by Sanivation provides homes with personal toilets and uses the waste to produce household fuels. Not only is the system nearly closed-loop but it also helps prevent contamination of local water supplies and has potential for use in disaster relief situations.

TAKEAWAYS

1 Are there ways in which your company could use its waste for a new purpose?
2 What types of waste have yet to be investigated for potential uses?
3 How could improving production processes reduce waste?

INNOVATION DATA

Website: www.pnnl.gov
Contact: Susan.Bauer@pnnl.gov
Company name: PNNL
Innovation name: Biocrude Oil
Countries: Canada; United States
Industries: Nature & sustainability

23

A FREESTANDING SMART HOME: PORTABLE AND ECO-FRIENDLY

Estonian design company Kodasema's square KODA home is assembled in seven hours and includes LED lights, solar panels and smart fixtures.

We live in an overpopulated world, where space is at a premium and it is becoming difficult, even for those in richer countries, to find affordable and environmentally sound housing. Estonian design company Kodasema has created a customizable mobile home that takes only a day to assemble.

The cube-shaped unit can be assembled on a range of different surfaces (gravel, asphalt and others) and requires only water, electrical and sewage connection points. No costly foundations are needed and the building's footprint is small – little more than 25 square metres (269 sq. ft). Each KODA contains rooftop solar panels that produce more power than the structure uses, allowing owners to earn money by selling power back to the grid. The portable KODA home is constructed with factory-made components selected for their strength and energy-efficient properties.

Air cleanliness and humidity inside the buildings are regulated and the finishing materials used are completely non-toxic. The amount and brightness of light can be adjusted to suit individual needs. Noise, dust, cold weather and summer heat are all kept outside with quadruple-glazed windows and vacuum-insulated concrete walls. The large windows maximize heat and light when required, and many components can be customized to best fit the purpose of the building. A built-in smart IT system also enables the home to learn from and adjust to its particular surroundings. Materials are also used sustainably. For example, the construction of one unit requires as little as 9 cubic metres (317 cu. ft) of concrete and, at the end of its life, components can be disassembled and reused.

Built over two levels, The KODA house comes fully equipped with bedroom, bathroom, kitchen and living room, with a clean, minimalist design of both the interior and exterior. The homes are modular, and two or more can be connected to create a larger living space. The team behind the KODA believes that the only limit to the use of the structure is the owner's imagination.

It can be difficult to make major changes to a conventional home because inconvenient and expensive repairs are often involved, or even full demolition and reconstruction. Moreover, houses and apartments cannot be moved, whereas the KODA house is designed so that it can always be relocated.

Owners of these homes are not only able to avoid the financial pressure of buying expensive property and paying for complicated building permits, but can move their house to a new location in less than a day. The building is freestanding, not fixed to the ground, and its design and structure allow it to be assembled and disassembled many times over. Dismantling and preparation for transport can take as little as four hours, sparing the neighbours and surrounding area the noise, dust and other inconveniences of ongoing construction work.

Roam is an international network of smart, flexible living spaces – where residents can access communal live-work spaces in

Bali, Madrid, Miami and many other locations for $500 a week. Architectural robotics, such as those used in micro-homes made by Ori Systems in Massachusetts, are also helping people globally live more comfortably with smaller environmental footprints.

TAKEAWAYS

1 Could these portable modular homes be deployed in your local area?
2 How could land stewardship organizations work with owners of portable homes to help alleviate the world's housing crisis?
3 How can other housing innovations begin to address problems of sustainability and affordability?

INNOVATION DATA

Website: www.kodasema.com
Contact: koda@kodasema.com
Company name: Kodasema
Innovation name: KODA
Country: Estonia
Industries: Design / Home & garden / Nature & sustainability

24

A NO-WASTE, EDIBLE EMERGENCY DRONE TO CARRY FOOD

Created by adventurer Nigel Gifford OBE, Pouncer is an eco-friendly humanitarian food-aid drone adaptable to local dietary requirements.

Getting food aid to those in desperate need as a result of conflicts and natural disasters can be extremely difficult. Access to the people affected can be restricted because of the loss of infrastructure on the ground and many other dangers. Also, traditional methods of deploying aid can be ineffective, inaccurate or just impossible to use.

Pouncer creator Nigel Gifford, of Windhorse Aerospace, is a former member of the British Army Catering Corps. Having seen how inaccurate, and thus wasteful, traditional parachute aid delivery can be, he designed a sustainable alternative – a specialist unmanned aerial vehicle (UAV) called Pouncer. This is a drone designed to be loaded with appropriate food and transported to a disaster area, where it will fly independently to its pre-planned destination and land accurately in the selected landing zone. It will thus be able to avoid all infrastructure problems, opportunities for corruption and theft and hostile groups, while saving time, money and lives.

The UAV navigates via GPS, making flight and landing extremely accurate. Its wings and body are made of empty food containers to be filled as needed, depending on local dietary requirements. The shell of the vehicle provides on-the-ground shelter and the wooden frame provides fuel.

The largest Pouncer drone is able to carry 90 kilograms (200 lb) of food, helping to increase daily humanitarian food rations from 2,200 calories per person to 3,500. The drones will be released at 7,600 metres (25,000 ft) from a C-130 Hercules aircraft and fly to their destination. Upon their release, the drones fly at 120 knots. The fuselage of each craft is 1.5 metres (5 ft), with a wingspan of 3 metres (10 ft) and a total load volume of 0.15 cubic metres (5 cu. ft). The size of the Pouncer is only limited by the carrying capacity of the Hercules aircraft used to deploy it, so future versions, using different deployment systems, may be larger.

The landing accuracy of the drone, which flies by itself with no external control, typically is as close as 7 metres (23 ft). This reduces the risk of packages being interfered with by unintended recipients, thieves or local warlords. It also reduces waste from lost or inaccessible packages.

The Pouncer has been designed to be a supplementary aid delivery system used in conjunction with other delivery systems. Many delivery systems currently in use require the host aircraft to over-fly the drop zone, but, because the Pouncer can be launched at a stand-off range of 35 kilometres (22 miles) or more, it reduces the risk to the host aircraft.

While some parachute systems can be reused, their recovery, reloading and repacking can be difficult and sometimes costly. The drone is designed to be used only once, so because it is non-recoverable there are no recovery costs. One day, the company hopes to make the whole airframe out of edible components. Future versions of the Pouncer will also have the option of an extended range with the use of a power unit.

Drones are increasingly used in emergency situations. For example, deep neural network software helps quadcopter drones identify trails and paths, and leads them to lost or injured hikers. It can also help to map terrain after a disaster: using existing smartphone sensors, the customizable UAV toolkit app gathers spatial data for mapping landscapes during crises.

TAKEAWAYS

1 What are the possibilities for combining robotics with unmanned aerial flight for remote emergency medical care?
2 How else could lightweight unmanned vehicles be used to assist remote communities, not necessarily those in immediate danger but those that are simply inaccessible via the usual routes?
3 What other design innovations could employ multi-use elements like the Pouncer's framework that can be burned as fuel to cook food?

INNOVATION DATA

Website: windhorse.aero
Contact: crewroom@windhorse.aero
Company Name: Windhorse Aerospace
Innovation name: Pouncer
Country: United Kingdom
Industries: Nature & sustainability / Non-profit & social cause

25

A FARM-TO-TABLE ORGANIC RESTAURANT THAT REDUCES WASTE

Denmark's Amass restaurant prioritizes sustainability – composting, growing on site, buying locally and finding new ways to use leftovers.

Increasing sustainability by reducing waste is a multi-faceted challenge for the food industry. In Denmark, Copenhagen's Amass restaurant takes a holistic approach to food that links the growing processes and resources used directly to the dishes that are served in the restaurant. The team is open about the fact that some of their processes are not the most technologically advanced and that they do take considerable effort, yet they are essential for as complete a farm-to-table experience as they have created.

The restaurant holds a Gold Organic Certificate, which means that 90–100 per cent of its food and drink is pesticide-free. Almost 95 per cent of the products used in its kitchens are locally sourced, and the company prioritizes partnerships with small farmers who produce speciality products such as heritage crops and breeds and extensive fruit varietals. In promoting organic practices, the restaurant hopes for 'an agricultural future not dependent on chemicals, high yields and minimal environmental protections, but one where farmers work symbiotically with nature to produce delicious food sustainably'.

Amass focuses on ethical procurement, and uses only non-farmed seafood and wild fowl caught by professional hunters who meet the company's high environmental standards. The restaurant's sustainability initiatives also extend to the saving of water and the creative use of leftovers.

Located in an industrial part of Copenhagen, the restaurant has an extensive garden, growing more than 80 different types of plant, including berries, flowers, herbs and vegetables. Almost everything grown in the garden features on the menu. The garden also contains outdoor seating, and during the summer months nightly bonfires are lit in the garden for customers to enjoy.

Because the restaurant relies so heavily on what is fresh and in season and what is available from its own garden, the menu changes regularly. The kitchen team is constantly creating new ways to use the produce while creating as little waste as possible. Cardboard packaging and any waste that is produced are used as compost for the garden. Examples of the unusual uses of food trim include dehydrating herb stems for seasonings, turning coffee grounds into crispy flatbreads, frying fish bones for snacks and using green vegetable scraps in condiments and spreads.

The restaurant also focuses on the agricultural integrity of its wine producers and, again, sources as locally as possible. Most of the drinks on the menu are European and the Amass team tries to visit each vendor that supplies the restaurant.

Furthering the principle that farm-to-table gastronomy is the future of the food industry, the restaurant also uses its garden as an educational tool. Everyone, at any level of knowledge, from professional chefs to schoolchildren, is invited to learn about the restaurant's sustainability processes. A particular success in the company's outreach programme is the Amass Green Kids Programme. The programme teaches children about the life cycle of plants, flavours, scents, harvesting and cooking, and involves participants in a full season of planting, growing and harvesting, using whatever is available.

Bridging the gaps in the food industry between what is available, when and where, takes considerable planning and creative thinking. Technology certainly helps, with a number of apps like Transfernation connecting those with leftover food to those who can help get it to people in need. Another example of reducing waste by focusing on farm-to-table experiences and nose-to-tail eating is California's Farmcation, a company dedicated to connecting interested foodies with the farmers producing their local food and drink.

TAKEAWAYS

1 How could individual sustainable solutions to food-chain processes be scaled up for industry-level impact?
2 In what ways could your brand include the customer in the product or service journey?
3 Are there examples of food waste in your local community and, if so, how could those products be repurposed for the benefit of others?

INNOVATION DATA

Website: amassrestaurant.com
Contact: info@amassrestaurant.com
Innovation name: Amass restaurant
Country: Denmark
Industries: Education / Food & beverage / Home & garden / Nature & sustainability /Smart cities

26

A MICRO-LIBRARY BUILT WITH ICE-CREAM BUCKETS

Architects SHAU Bandung's micro-library is made from 2,000 upcycled plastic ice-cream buckets that ventilate the air naturally.

Designed to be a hub for the neighbourhood, the Taman Bima micro-library in Bandung, Indonesia, is fronted with 2,000 used ice-cream buckets. Created by architects SHAU Bandung with community input, the library is one of several pilot projects aimed at reversing the country's falling literacy rate.

SHAU's mission is to rekindle interest in books by offering a dedicated place for reading and learning, by making books, other media and courses available, as well as offering a sense of identity and a source of pride for local people. The activities and teaching are currently supported and organized by the charitable organization

Dompet Dhuafa (Pocket for the Poor) and the Indonesian Diaspora Foundation. However, the ultimate goal is to enable the local people to organize the content and maintenance of the building independently.

The micro-library is located at Taman Bima, in a small square in a village near the airport. It sits between a middle-class neighbourhood and a less affluent one. The Taman Bima micro-library is the first realized prototype of a series of small libraries in different locations, which the architects plan to build throughout Indonesia.

The tiny structure is packed with multiple levels of meaning and sustainability. At street level, the space is open for multipurpose public use and has long rows of stairs for additional outdoor seating. The second level of the building is the library, which is clad in 2,000 used ice-cream buckets. This recycled wall material provides ventilation and daylight. Through a mix of open and closed buckets, the wall design spells out, in binary coding, 'Books are the windows to the world.'

The building comprises a simple steel structure made from I-beams with concrete slabs for floor and roof. The pre-existing stage on which the library was constructed was already used by the local community for gatherings, events, socializing and sports activities. The stage was reworked in concrete and a wide stair added. As the building is in a tropical climate, the architects included air conditioning to make the interior a pleasant space to be.

The used ice cream buckets that create the façade were being sold cheaply, locally and in bulk. Mounting 2,000 buckets, making the fixture and punching out bottoms of more than half of them was a time-consuming task, made simpler by the local craftsmen who fashioned their own, simple dedicated tools.

Not only does the façade give additional meaning to the building in the form of binary code, but the buckets also generate a pleasant indoor light ambience since they scatter direct sunlight and act as natural light bulbs. The buckets are affixed in between the vertical steel ribs that span the height of the building from floor to roof and that are inclined towards the outside to repel rainwater. During more extreme tropical weather conditions, sliding doors on the inside can be temporarily closed.

Increasing accessibility through miniaturization is a popular solution. Another example of this is Powerhive, which provides electricity to rural homes in Africa using microgrids.

TAKEAWAYS

1 In what other industries could going smaller bring improvements?
2 How else could an interest in literacy be reignited in the developing world?
3 What other innovations could unobtrusively slip into local surroundings while providing a useful service?
4 How could your company repurpose waste materials like the ice cream buckets seen here?

INNOVATION DATA

Website: www.shau.nl
Contact: info@shau.nl
Company name: SHAU Bandung
Innovation name: Taman Bima micro-library
Country: Indonesia
Industries: Design / Education / Non-profit & social cause / Smart cities

27

USING BLOCKCHAIN TO TELL A PRODUCT'S STORY

Provenance is an SaaS platform that enables brands to track and display their supply chain information using blockchain.

For many brands, explaining how and where products are made is one of the more difficult socially responsible tasks. Systems spread across multiple countries, and products consisting of multiple parts manufactured in different locations, make for a complex path to the consumer. Years of big brands' lip service to sustainability have also made consumers wary of businesses' claims.

Hyper-local products and services are one method of creating radical supply-chain transparency. Many companies, however, must find other options. Provenance is a software-as-a-service (SaaS) data platform that uses blockchain's★ distributed ledger technology to authenticate the processes of a product's creation and journey to the customer. The system helps companies share information about their supply chains and verify for the customer the validity of that information.

Blockchain allows Provenance to track materials and products, down to the single item level. By using the technology, shoppers, producers, non-profit organizations and businesses can be confident that the information being provided is secure, inclusive and publicly available.

Telling a story is a great way to connect with customers, and businesses can take full advantage by providing shoppers with point-of-sale information about the pieces and processes behind each

Blockchain

A digital ledger in which transactions made in bitcoin or another cryptocurrency are recorded chronologically and publicly.

product. There are three levels of Provenance membership – starter, pro and enterprise – with different amounts of administrative and communication support and a variety of item-level tracking capabilities.

The starter pack allows businesses to create a profile on the platform and includes information about the materials, people and processes behind their products. The pro plan costs £29 per month and allows companies to generate labels and unique product IDs to prove product authenticity, as well as add manufacturing stories to their e-receipts.

An enterprise account is priced on request and includes extensive item-level authentication as well as additional reporting support and options for testing and using beta developments. Provenance is also working with non-profits to find the best ways of digitizing certifications and awards in order to help provide customers with easily verifiable information.

The team says, 'We envision a future where every physical product has a digital history, allowing you to trace and verify its origins, attributes and ownership. With our technology, businesses can easily gather and verify stories, keep them connected to physical things and embed them anywhere online.'

The platform uses two types of data system. One is for traceability and one is for transparency. For transparency, images and location data are used to build a company's profile and product story pages. For traceability, items are directly tracked through the supply chain in order to confirm their attributes and identities.

Creating trust in a brand is integral to a business's success, and blockchain helps to do that by independently verifying any claims made about a product. Because it has a decentralized structure and open yet unchangeable data, more and more organizations are looking to blockchain to answer tricky questions.

Taiwan-based start-up Bitmark is using a blockchain algorithm to create distributed consensus on who owns what in the digital sphere. And in China, BlockCDN is using blockchain to create a decentralized content delivery network (CDN) to distribute online content more securely, evenly and quickly.

TAKEAWAYS

1 Who, if not you, is a leading light in your industry in terms of supply-chain transparency? What can you learn from them?
2 How might businesses partner with non-profit organizations to support sustainable initiatives?
3 How could industries that have yet to try blockchain test out its possibilities?

INNOVATION DATA

Website: www.provenance.org
Contact: hello@provenance.org
Innovation name: Provenance
Country: United Kingdom
Industries: Access exclusive / Design / Marketing & advertising / Nature & sustainability / Retail & e-commerce

28

CHARGING ELECTRIC VEHICLES FOR A DOLLAR A DAY

Energy supplier AGL is offering electric vehicle owners 'all-you-can-use' home charging for only AU$1 per day.

Australian energy company AGL recently introduced its latest sustainable offering with its home charging of electric vehicles for only AU$1 per day. In a country with some of the best conditions for taking advantage of renewable energy sources, Australia's utility companies are having to adapt to changing market conditions with significantly altered demand.

When the incentive was announced at the 2016 Australia Energy Week conference, AGL chief executive Andy Vesey said, 'The single biggest issue we have blocking this transition [the shift of Australia's energy network to a low-carbon approach and structure], from a wholesale perspective, is the fact that we have a national energy market that is overbuilt. Supply way exceeds demand.' He also said, 'We have technologies that allow us to do today things that our systems of regulation and law do not let us do, because we don't know the right policy frameworks to liberate those capabilities. But if you look around you can see it.'

The national electricity market currently in Australia has a 7,000 megawatt overcapacity, something that AGL hopes to address with its 'all-you-can-use' approach to electric vehicle charging. Owners of any brand of electric vehicle, including the popular Tesla, BMW i3 and Nissan Leafs, can take advantage of this charging plan. Customers who already own a charging station can start using the option almost immediately. Those who don't own a charging station can buy one from AGL for around AU$800. A smart meter is required in the home to track energy usage, and AGL will upgrade basic meters for free and supply digital meters for a fee to households that don't currently use one.

At its lowest, the plan will cost owners of one electric car AU$365 a year – a bargain compared to the AU$17,000 average cost of one petrol-powered car. Currently, charging an electric vehicle in Australia costs approximately AU$4.50 per 100 kilometres (62 miles).

AGL is also providing complimentary carbon offsetting of all the energy supplied by its Electric Car Plan. This is taking place through its Future Forests programme. The company will plant enough trees, or invest in other carbon-offsetting projects, to match the emissions created by its electric vehicle charging.

The company continues to look into a variety of new services to better support customers and their increasing reliance on smart appliances and devices and alternative power sources. One plan currently being trialled is the construction of micro power plants across South Australia. These plants will be housed in homes and businesses and will allow companies and individuals to buy and sell surplus solar power as needed.

Not long after AGL's electric car charging plan announcement, Melbourne property group Glenvill introduced its plans to build the country's most environmentally sustainable development. Dubbed the Tesla Town, the suburb will actually be named YarraBend after the nearby river and will come complete with inbuilt EV charging, solar roofs, Tesla batteries, high-speed Internet and a neighbourhood app that acts like a concierge. Although fairly expensive now – with the new townhouses and apartments on sale at prices from US$1.48 million – if the predictions of reductions in water use of 43 per cent, in landfill of 80 per cent and in potential energy use of 34 per cent prove true, the concept could well be adapted and scaled for wider use, helping to bring prices down.

Other projects using incentives to encourage the use of electric vehicles include Nissan and Enel's UK vehicle-to-grid smart energy trial that enables electric cars to sell power back to the national grid and a wireless electric vehicle charging lane on highways.

TAKEAWAYS

1 How and where else could incentives encourage the use of renewable energy?
2 Are there new or additional ways that renewable energy sources could be incorporated into your business?
3 How could smart cities help speed up the integration of multiple sustainable power sources?

INNOVATION DATA

Website: www.agl.com.au
Contact: evadvantage@agl.com.au
Company name: AGL
Innovation name: AUD 1 charging
Country: Australia
Industries: Nature & sustainability / Transport & automotive

29

'FEED THIS TRASHCAN FOR FREE WI-FI'

Indian company ThinkScream has created a smart trashcan, which provides 15 minutes of connectivity to people who throw away rubbish.

A New Age Media Solutions company, India-based ThinkScream, builds products that can be adapted and used in a variety of situations and to solve company-specific challenges. One of its recent successes is a smart trashcan that releases 15 minutes of free Wi-Fi when someone throws something away. The trashcans were used at a music festival to encourage responsible waste disposal rather than just leaving rubbish on the ground.

Trash is such a serious problem in the world, with predictions from 2013 estimating that the volume of waste produced could triple by 2100, that reducing it is considered essential in mitigating climate change. Trillions of pounds of garbage are produced each year, and half of the global solid waste is organic matter. Paper and plastic combine to add more than a quarter of the remainder. The majority of refuse goes into landfill, and many sites are now at or reaching capacity. Incinerators are one way of reducing the volume of rubbish, but they bring with them additional pollution concerns.

Initiatives working to reduce waste are plentiful and widespread. However, the scale of the problem means that the scale of the solution needs to be much greater than it is now. Individual industries are getting involved in waste prevention at varying rates. Some, like restaurants and retailers, are working together to help solve the food waste conundrum – how so much food can be produced and wasted while millions around the world continue to starve.

Mumbai, where ThinkScream is based, is increasingly experiencing the effects of poor waste infrastructure systems combined with a densely populated urban area. Each day, the city generates at least 7,500 megatonnes of garbage. Hazardous waste products, including electronic components, provide another challenge, for the health of citizens as well as the environment.

The city's main landfill site is overflowing, and 500 trucks line up each day to deposit another huge load of refuse. Volume reduction technology is required urgently and on a large scale. Yet when the attempts of richer countries to reduce their waste are reviewed, the prospects don't look good. Again, this situation highlights the need for rapid and connected scaling of the many workable, sustainable and innovative waste reduction projects around the world.

Helping to provide an incentive to avoid littering, ThinkScream's plastic bins have LED screens that light up with the Wi-Fi symbol when rubbish is thrown into them. The bins then provide wireless Internet for 15 minutes within a 50-yard radius.

Now that the bins have proved a success at music festivals, the founders are considering ways to incorporate the bins into Mumbai's waste management systems to help curtail the habit of the city's 18 million residents disposing of rubbish in public places. Each bin costs approximately US$1,500, and ThinkScream has been contacted by various companies that are interested in using the branding potential of the devices.

Other ways in which Wi-Fi is being used as an incentive is through **Amsterdam's Tree Wi-Fi's** smart birdhouses that measure air quality in real time and provide free Wi-Fi when pollution levels drop. In Peru, the Shadow Wi-Fi System lures beachgoers out of the sun with the promise of free Internet and educates them about skin cancer prevention.

TAKEAWAYS

1 What other amenities could be offered in a bid to encourage proper rubbish disposal?
2 How could limited experiences or access to products be used to encourage adoption of renewable energy sources?
3 How could successful waste reduction programmes be scaled quickly, sustainably and affordably?

INNOVATION DATA

Website: Thinkscream.com
Contact: contact@thinkscream.com
Company name: ThinkScream
Country: India

30

USING BLOCKCHAIN TECHNOLOGY FOR GREEN ENERGY

Australian company Power Ledger is set to trial a
peer-to-peer renewable energy marketplace.

Blockchain is the public ledger technology underpinning Bitcoin
that has since been adopted for use in a variety of other industries.
Perth-based green technology company Power Ledger uses a greener
form of blockchain technology called Ecochain. Predominantly
solar-powered, Ecochain is the world's first low-energy, eco-friendly
blockchain. Power Ledger helps households and businesses that
produce excess renewable energy to sell it on directly to other
consumers.

As the dynamics within the electricity industry continue to
change – with production, distribution and trading becoming
increasingly decentralized – Power Ledger plays a leading role in
helping Australian customers decide whether to buy, sell or swap
excess solar energy. As the company says, 'All power to the producers
and consumers.'

Selling excess energy is not new, and a number of initiatives
in different countries have a variation of the option that allows
consumers to sell back to the national grid. Power Ledger is different
because it cuts out the middleman. This allows customers to buy and
sell electricity between themselves at a price of their choosing rather
than selling it back to the grid at a minimal rate.

As a result, customers who have been able to afford to invest in
producing renewable energy will earn more from their excess.
Simultaneously, those without the infrastructure but who are still keen
to run on renewables can access energy at a lower cost. What's more, if
they want, electricity producers are able to gift electricity to whomever
they choose. Additionally, being able to earn money from renewable
energy resources represents a return on that investment for owners.

Power Ledger's co-founder Jemma Green believes that the increased possibility of earning through renewable energy will increase the take-up of solar panels. As she explains, 'Presently, if you've got surplus solar electricity you sell it back for a low feed-in tariff and buy it back [from the grid] for a high rate. Using [Power Ledger], you can sell it to your neighbour at somewhere between the two.'

The Power Ledger system works by running on Ecochain. Every unit of energy is identified from the time of generation and then followed throughout the system to the point of consumption or sale. Using local electricity distribution networks allows Ecochain to track multiple trading agreements without incurring any additional carbon emissions or costs.

The company's first project, an eight-week trial that involved ten households in the NLV Busselton Lifestyle Village, on the Western Power network, was a success. Now, a 500-site project that includes schools, homes and community groups is in development with Auckland, New Zealand's largest electricity distributor.

An example of another use of blockchain is Slock. Its smart contracts create autonomous locks to accept and unlock payments based on user crypto ID, cutting out third-party intermediaries. And helping make solar energy more accessible is Arcadia Power's new service that offers remote 'solar subscriptions' to those who want to invest in green energy but who are, for whatever reason, barred from such direct investments.

TAKEAWAYS

1 What further blockchain-supported marketplaces are to come?
2 Are there ways your business could streamline processes to give customers a more active role?
3 How else could those without direct access to renewable energy be able to take part in a more sustainable community?

INNOVATION DATA

Website: www.powerledger.io
Contact: www.powerledger.io/contact/
Innovation name: Power Ledger
Country: Australia
Industries: Financial services & fin tech / Nature &
       sustainability

SUMMARY

Scientists predict that the Earth is already on track to warm up by between 2 and 6 degrees Celsius (3.6–10.8 °F) in the next century, a rate of change approximately ten times faster than in previous periods of global warming. A global temperature increase of 2 degrees Celsius (3.6 °F) is considered the safety threshold for long-term human existence.

Campaigners are pushing governments to aggressively pursue the more difficult goal of keeping global warming to 1.5 degrees Celsius (2.7 °F). Sustained innovation and buy-in from all industries and major governments are key to achieving this, and already technology is making it easier for consumers to adapt more eco-friendly behaviours. Consider the points below in relation to your own organization, and at every turn ask whether there is more you could do.

SUSTAINABILITY TAKEAWAYS

1 **Reduce waste.** Depending on the complexity of your operations, this could be easier said than done, and you may already have a number of company initiatives in place. In either case, the next step is to look for ways to make incremental improvements. Look broadly across your operations, and don't be afraid to think small. Could you set up a printer to always print double-sided, or set aside a pile of scrap/discarded paper for employees to contribute to and reuse when printing drafts? This is an area in particular where the cumulative effects of small changes can create asignificant impact.

2 **Reduce carbon emissions.** As discussed in the Communication chapter, business travel is becoming less essential, and taking fewer flights is one of the simplest ways to reduce your company's carbon footprint. Cycle-to-work schemes are another popular option. The key here is to follow the example set by **ThinkScream's trashcan** and reward employees whenever they actively help reduce emissions.

3 **Upcycle and repurpose.** If you're producing a product, think how it could be reused once it is no longer needed or functional. Think creatively here, and remember that it usually won't be necessary for your company to actually handle the repurposing of the product. It may take only one phone call to another organization, and you may find they are more than happy to handle collection of the goods from customers, before upcycling them. The same philosophy can be applied to any waste from the production process itself.

4 **Tell a compelling story.** Knowing that goods have been produced by green and ethical supply chains is becoming increasingly important to consumers. So if you're already paying close attention to the sustainability of your supply chain, be proud of your achievements. Share the news within the company and with the public. If this is something that your brand is working to improve, then that can also be the start of a good story. Find ways to mark your progress, and don't hold back from asking for suggestions on ways to improve the cycles of production and distribution.

5 **Join 1% for the Planet, or become a B (benefit)-corporation.** Put sustainability in all senses of the word, and environmental and social purpose, at the heart of your mission. Join Springwise as a member of 1% for the Planet whose membership is growing faster than ever before. There is certainly a clear shift towards businesses and customers, in particular among the millennial generation, who care about protecting and nurturing our natural environment.

ENTERTAINMENT

In the last decade streaming services have disrupted conventional broadcasting, recommendation algorithms have become tastemakers for a generation of music listeners, and YouTube has grown into a platform for a billion independent filmmakers. Cumulatively, technology-led changes have brought about a revolution in both the production and the consumption of entertainment.

Ten years ago, if you told someone you were going to tune in to your favourite millionaire vlogger's 360-degree YouTube channel, to catch up on some behind-the-scenes updates from their latest performance on Twitch – the e-sports streaming service – they would have frowned, bewildered. If you then told them you were going to do so with a freshly released vinyl from your new favourite band playing in the background, their frown would shift to reflect genuine concern.

Each entertainment source – from film and television to music and radio – is currently facing unique challenges and evolutions, but a number of forces are reshaping the complexion of entertainment across the board. In this chapter, we'll examine these changes, and look ahead to the innovations that point to a new model of media consumption: one in which the lines between producer and consumer are further blurred; content is ever more personal; and audiences are active participants in previously one-way entertainment.

On-demand content and streaming services

Across the spectrum, three disruptive trends are apparent: conventional formats are being usurped by novel, tech-enabled alternatives; output is becoming highly personalized and increasingly co-created with the audience; and traditional ways of accessing entertainment are being upended.

With so much content now available on demand, producers are increasingly looking to push boundaries and offer innovative formats in an effort to stand out. For example, we're seeing a number of innovators creating content specifically for a few snatched minutes during a commute – such as **Pendelpoddar**, a Swedish service that suggests podcasts tailored to a users' journey time. Also of note would be the French publisher Short Édition, which prints short stories on demand – from one to five minutes' reading time – to Grenoble commuters; or Australia's Qantas airline, which commissioned fiction titles designed specifically to be read within long-haul flight times. With driverless cars soon to hit the marketplace, hands-free journeys of a set duration will become more common, meaning that time-based programming could well become more prevalent.

But while these innovations look to mould themselves around the user's context, virtual reality (VR) devices are busy totally removing them from it. Smart phone-powered VR viewers have helped the technology hit the mainstream, so that everyone from ballet performers to DJs and even news broadcasters are now taking advantage by offering tailored immersive experiences for VR audiences.

But VR is not without its issues. Dedicated VR headsets are still costly, and sustained play can induce motion sickness. To truly break through, VR needs to incorporate social elements, enabling friends to communicate and see each other's avatars in virtual space. One innovation demonstrating the potential for how that might look is **LiveLike VR**, a platform that lets sports fans watch televised events alongside friends from anywhere in the world.

Personalizing the entertainment experience

We are accustomed to streaming services recommending albums, films and books based on our preferences, but now we are beginning to see personalization in the creation as well as the curation of content. Netflix is renowned for its use of audience data to inform the creative process, notably with hit show *House of Cards*, which was commissioned once Netflix was able to find a Venn diagram intersection which demonstrated that their audience would be receptive to the concept, casting and positioning. The show's success attests to the enormous value of big data within entertainment programming, and we are seeing this reflected in the number of start-ups working in this fertile ground. MIT start-up **TVision Insights**, for example, tracks television viewers to establish who is watching what and how they are reacting, enabling broadcasters and producers to curate tailored content and attract larger audiences.

Content can also be personalized in real time: the BBC has trialled a project named **Visual Perceptive Media**, using an app to gather user data such as music preferences, gender and age, and adapting the narrative and characters in a film accordingly. A still more immersive approach comes from a German courtroom drama called *Terror – Your Verdict*, which invites viewers to act as the jury in the televised case. These interactive approaches to programming are evolving apace and – particularly as VR devices and emotion tracking are refined – we can expect audiences to become increasingly involved in the narrative of their own entertainment. The number of elements affecting the narrative are almost limitless, with factors such as the weather, the viewers' mood and even their geography all possibilities. For example, there is a radio station accessible only to commuters on **New York's Williamsburg Bridge**, and we've even seen an album released as an app by Swedish band John Moose that was listenable only in wooded areas.

In recent years the way we access entertainment has changed markedly, to the extent that consumer loyalties now lie as often with content curators and providers as with producers: we are more likely to stream a single than buy a physical album, or to scroll a newsfeed rather than pick up a newspaper.

Combined with huge quantities of free (or simply pirated) content, this has led to a number of innovations looking to offer easy access and payment options that match the flexibility desired by audiences. For instance, **PayOrShare** offers a platform for businesses to charge readers for their digital content, either with a small payment or by sharing what they've read on a social media platform of their choosing. Offering flexibility of another form, **Blendle** is a growing platform that lets readers make micropayments to access news articles behind paywalls without having to subscribe.

The ten innovations in this chapter illustrate these changes and give a flavour of what might come next.

31

A VIRTUAL-REALITY STADIUM THAT LETS DISTANT FRIENDS WATCH THE GAME TOGETHER

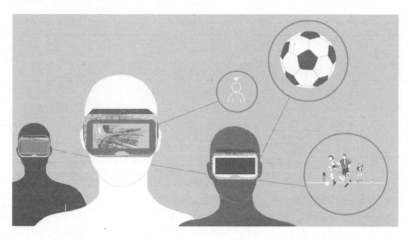

LiveLike VR enables sports fans to watch the game together with remote friends in a virtual stadium.

Most sports lovers would agree that one of the main pleasures of watching a match is the shared experience of being among fellow fanatics. Now, LiveLike is a virtual-reality (VR) platform that aims to enhance the home-viewing experience by enabling viewers to watch games together in a virtual stadium.

To begin, users download the app and create a customizable stadium. They then choose an avatar and invite their friends to join them in the virtual space. LiveLike VR is currently available using Samsung Gear VR and will soon be playable through Oculus Rift, HTC Vive and Google Cardboard VR. Users put on their headsets and are then able to chat, access stats and highlights, and choose from different angles of the field.

LiveLike VR's key strength is that broadcasters can use the service without any expensive add-ons, simply by sending the start-up the stream from one wide-lens camera. When broadcasters purchase the rights to air a particular game or league, they typically include the necessary rights for virtual reality, and LiveLike can cover a game with unmanned cameras controlled by an onsite technical team of as few as five people. Manchester City Football Club trialled the initial demo of the app in a Premier League game against Arsenal, where remote fans were placed at the heart of the action in the first broadcast of its kind in the sport.

LiveLike VR has since signed a partnership with Fox Sports to air games. It has also done tests airing tennis matches from the French Open and the famed El Clásico soccer match between FC Barcelona and Real Madrid in Spain. LiveLike has had investment from former NBA boss David Stern and a group of venture firms led by Evolution Media Partners, a joint effort of entertainment and sports agency CAA and investment firm TPG, as well as Elysian Park Ventures, Courtside Ventures, Dentsu Ventures and Techstars Ventures.

The LiveLike team had previously won a competition run by TechCrunch called 1st And Future, in which they were awarded $50,000 in cash as well as meetings with top NFL officials and Super Bowl tickets. The competition was judged at Stanford's Graduate School of Business by investor Mary Meeker and former Secretary of State Condoleezza Rice.

André Lorenceau, founder and CEO of LiveLike, believes that 2017 will be the year of VR. He equates its success and future prospects to that of the iPhone. He suggests in his blog that VR hardware growth is showing a similar path to the iPhone in its early years. He is optimistic about the future, indicating that all signs point to much steadier increase in growth from 2017 onwards, meaning good news for hardware and software developers, broadcasters and sports fans alike.

The applications for VR have proved to be incredibly far-reaching – ranging from health care and rehabilitation to education, gaming and marketing. Sports broadcasting is likely to be a medium that connects with a huge number of consumers, as well as providing lucrative and mutually beneficial links to major broadcasting organizations and sponsors.

TAKEAWAYS

1 Could other forms of entertainment such as news broadcasts or cinema use a similar set-up?
2 How else could sports be more immersive?
3 How could your company get big broadcasters or media companies to engage with technology for a relatively small investment?

INNOVATION DATA

Website: www.livelikevr.com
Contact: www.livelikevr.com/contact
Innovation name: LiveLike VR
Country: United States
Industries: Entertainment & culture / Gamification & gaming / Sport & fitness

32

PERSONALIZING FILMS TO THE VIEWER'S TASTE

The BBC is launching Visual Perceptive Media (VPM), presenting different versions of the same film, which changes to suit the viewer's unique preferences.

From podcasts to music streaming, the way we enjoy entertainment is becoming ever more tailored to our personal preferences. The BBC is now testing a system that shapes films to suit each viewer's unique preferences.

VPM is a short film produced with many separate elements, all of which will flow contiguously. First, an app will scan users' musical listening histories and ask them a series of questions to do with their personality, age and gender. This data is then used to shape aspects of the film, including the narrative, characters and music, and the film will change to please the viewer's own unique interests. For example, the software will determine which character the viewer will feel more strongly towards and will then bias the number of scenes in which that character appears. This brings an entertainment experience that ultimately maximizes viewer empathy. Broadcasting over IP enables VPM to create all kinds of new content experiences that would not be possible or scalable on 'traditional' TV or radio.

The project draws data from its companion app. In the future, it could use data from a number of services, include factors such as time of day, location and the viewer's mood, and shape the entertainment in real time.

The BBC wants to create personalized media that feels natural to the audience and exciting for the storyteller as it scales for millions of individual audience members.

Initial research conducted with a small number of people has assessed whether they perceive the film as a coherent whole or whether they notice that it is made up of media objects being delivered on the fly. The aim is to build a public prototype to test these ideas with a wider audience. The project will also test the client-side video capabilities of the browser as a platform.

Ian Forrester, who is in charge of the project, says, 'Visual Perceptive Media is made to deliberately nudge the user one way or another using cinematic techniques rather than sweeping changes like those seen in branching narratives. Each change is subtle but they are used in filmmaking every day, which raises the question of how do you even start to demo something that has over 50,000 variations?' The incredible complexity and potential of this model may be its downfall when trying to translate it from a test audience to widespread use. It may be some time before we see VPM used in the mainstream.

The system also raises the question of the ethics of personal data. How much do we really want media companies to know about us, and at what point does personalized entertainment become, or rely on, a significant invasion of privacy? In the age of big data, with governments knowing ever more about us, it may seem like a more frivolous concern, but it is valuable to constantly keep a check on who is tracking, selling, sharing and applying our personal data, whether it be governments or TV channels.

Another example of personalized entertainment is the development of a pair of headphones that play songs based on users' brainwaves. The Mico headphones, developed in Japan, monitor the user's brain activity and select songs that match their mood.

TAKEAWAYS

1 Could this model of adapting content to suit distinctive demographics be used for online video ads too?
2 Could this platform be combined with VR to create a more immersive experience?
3 How could this model be adapted to make it more scalable?

INNOVATION DATA

Website: www.bbc.co.uk/visual-perceptive-media
Contact: ian.forrester@bbc.co.uk
Innovation name: Visual Perceptive Media
Country: United Kingdom
Industries: Entertainment & culture / Film & theatre

33

A FLEXIBLE PAYWALL THAT LETS USERS CHOOSE HOW THEY PAY

PayOrShare enables businesses to charge consumers for their premium content — but lets the customer choose whether to pay in cash or social currency.

In the world of digital publishing, social media shares have a direct effect on readership figures and advertising potential — so much so that 'social currency' can be just as valuable to a site as plain old-fashioned money. We have already seen social paywall Sharewall enabling readers to unlock premium content on a share-one, read-one basis. Now, PayOrShare, from Germany, is providing an even more flexible platform. Customers are able to read the digital material first and then choose what currency to pay with — which might be in the form of a post on their chosen social network rather than money.

By sharing a post on social media, a consumer can claim a coupon for an online shop.

There are four basic steps to the process. Firstly, the user clicks the coupon and selects the option to share via social media. This prompts the PayOrShare form to appear. The user now chooses which social network they want to share the coupon campaign on. They can then choose the specific message they want to type alongside the post, to give it a personal touch and prevent it from looking like an automated post or spam. The user then posts this message to the social media site of their choice. It does not require them to leave the site on which they are shopping. Finally, the user claims their reward, which might be money off an order or credits for future business with that company. This example is also transferable to other content, such as online newspaper articles, white papers, music, videos or in-game items.

Businesses can use PayOrShare's platform to monetize their digital content – whether that be an e-commerce store promoting coupons, a publisher promoting premium content or an entertainment company sharing videos. The platform builds on Sharewall's format by acknowledging that some consumers may prefer to spend a little money rather than share content, and it has taken care not to isolate those users. By letting consumers choose how they want to pay on a case-by-case basis, businesses can benefit from increased traffic and an increase in monetary income. The system also generates useful data, through which businesses can analyse the strengths of their campaign.

PayOrShare can be integrated into an existing site in less than 30 minutes, and the team, based in Hamburg, can create custom solutions for different business models. Katharina Wolff, who has co-founded several start-ups in the media and Internet spheres, had the original idea for PayOrShare. She then teamed up with Fiona Brandes and Max Fielker to create the team that turned the idea into reality.

Several alternative payment methods already exist – Pay with a Tweet and the Hanse Ventures start-up are direct competitors – but PayOrShare stands out from its rivals in several ways. Firstly, it combines the payment and share functions in a simple form, which makes the customer experience much simpler and user-friendly. It also dispenses with the additional integration of ads and ensures that it is unobtrusively integrated into the look and feel of the client's website.

Determining the value of digital content is one of the key challenges facing the industry. PayOrShare's main focus lies in the long term on the findings for clients from their Business Intelligence scheme, which few if any of their competitors offer. PayOrSHare's vision is to offer platforms in the long term with optimized real-time pricing that finds the optimal price point for digital content.

TAKEAWAYS

1 Are there other means of harnessing the value of 'social currency' in a way that benefits businesses and consumers?
2 What other businesses could benefit from such a paywall?
3 How could your business trade consumer benefits for social currency?

INNOVATION DATA

Website: www.payorshare.de
Contact: info@payorshare.de
Innovation name: PayOrShare
Country: Germany
Industries: Entertainment & culture / Financial services & fin tech / Marketing & advertising

34

A PAY-PER-ARTICLE PLATFORM AIMING TO BE SPOTIFY FOR NEWS

Blendle is a platform that lets readers make micropayments to access news articles behind paywalls without having to subscribe.

The journalism industry is facing tough decisions on how to stay profitable with an increasingly digital audience. With so much news available for free, and such a wide variety of other content to choose from, many media outlets and newspapers are turning to paywalls to monetize their websites. However, inevitably, this can reduce the traffic and exposure of their articles, not to mention put off readers.

A journalism app is trying meet this challenge by allowing readers to pay small sums to access individual articles online. Blendle is a premium journalism platform that enables users to pay for and enjoy articles that are behind paywalls without subscribing, paying as little as US$25 cents per article. A list of curated stories is sent to their inbox and they can choose which ones to access. They can even ask for refunds if they weren't satisfied with a piece. The app has now been launched to beta users in the USA and has signed up some of the biggest names in US journalism, including *The Wall Street Journal*, *The New York Times*, *Time* and *The Economist*.

On a blog on medium, Blendle co-founder Alexander Klópping said:

'Journalism needs a Spotify, a Netflix, an iTunes – whatever you want to call it – one website that houses the best newspapers and magazines in the country.'

Klópping is a former technology journalist and he saw the need for a platform like these for journalism, where paying for content would feel like second nature. He noted how it was wrong that he had to visit many different website to read the articles he liked, only to find much of the content behind paywalls. He was frustrated by constantly dealing with pop-up ads as he tried to read the articles he did have free access to. As with so many readers, he relied on Facebook and Twitter to supply him with news and online magazine content. This raised the problem of having to sift through all the noise and clickbait and decide for himself what was real journalism.

Readers have become used to being able to access so much of their online news for free that it may not be instantly agreeable or natural for them to start paying for content again. There will have to be a transitional period, during which they get used to a small fee being the norm. It is also important that there be a marked difference in the quality and reading experience between free content and paid-for content. Once a user has paid to view an article – even if it is only a few cents – they can expect to be spared irritating ads and pop-ups that have become a mainstay of online content but make for a significantly less enjoyable reading experience.

With new platforms for journalism such as Perspecs, a news aggregation app that provides three differing views or predictions for each story, and Byline, a London-based start-up that crowdfunds independent, long-form journalism, it is clear that journalism is not extinct but simply evolving.

TAKEAWAYS

1 In what other ways could publishers generate more revenue from their content while staying independent?
2 What other subscription services or free services would benefit from a micropayment structure such as this?
3 Could your company reduce its reliance on advertising revenue using a model like Blendle's?

INNOVATION DATA

Website: launch.blendle.com
Contact: contact@blendle.com
Innovation name: Blendle
Countries: The Netherlands and United States
Industries: Entertainment & culture / Financial services &
 fin tech / Marketing & advertising / Written word

35

COULD VIRTUAL-REALITY NEWS STORIES REPLACE TRADITIONAL NEWS MEDIA?

A new platform, Emblematic, allows those consuming news to be inside the story through VR simulation.

As a society we are becoming numb to all the devastating news we're bombarded with on a daily basis. In order to react in an empathetic way to news and want to make a difference, we need to see life through the eyes of those affected by tragedy. Now, the media company Emblematic Group uses virtual reality (VR) simulation to put users in the middle of breaking news stories.

The platform is designed to help people understand what it feels like to face a natural or human-made disaster. The company's CEO, former journalist Nonny de la Peña, has developed the idea as the next frontier of journalism, explaining that 'It wasn't until I started working with virtual reality that I started to see really intense reactions from people to news stories.'

The team creates and stages room-scale VR environments that place the user inside the story, allowing them to move through the action. For example, their VR simulation of a situation in which a man has a diabetic seizure because of lack of food is intended to be an immediate way to communicate the problems facing society – more effective than real-life immersive videos and images.

Emblematic has already collaborated with media partners including *The New York Times*, Google and Al Jazeera America. In 2016 the company was awarded a grant from the Knight Foundation to produce a series of VR documentaries in partnership with Frontline, and to collaborate on crafting and disseminating best practices for virtual reality journalism.

The company has already created a piece of 'immersive journalism',
telling the story of the day teenager Travyon Martin was shot and
killed by a neighbourhood watch volunteer. The piece was produced
exclusively from real recordings of 911 calls, witness trial testimony and
architectural drawings, with an emphasis on accuracy.

There is, however, a risk that this form of reporting in the wrong
hands could be used irresponsibly. As much as we would like to think
we are being provided with an impartial recounting of events, it is
almost impossible to find a news outlet or publication without its own
biases and agendas in some form. These content providers are able to
shape the way a story comes across by the words and pictures they
choose to use. As VR reporting falls somewhere in between showing
real footage and creating a reconstruction, there is certainly scope
for this grey area to be exploited and certain biases to be interwoven
into the experience. With VR, because users are totally immersed in
what is happening and therefore emotionally vulnerable, they are
even more susceptible to manipulation and misinformation. As news
reporting evolves, so too must the system of checks and balances we
as a society have in place to ensure a free, open and responsible media.

A similar idea is the Virtual Reality Cave, which puts recovering
drug addicts in high-stimulus environments so that they can learn
coping mechanisms. Through trial and error, over the coming years
we will discover the full potential of virtual reality, the areas in which
it is useful and other areas where it is potentially problematic.

TAKEAWAYS

1 Does this use of VR mark the beginning of a change in
   the way we consume news?
2 What are the benefits and challenges of reporting
   in this way?
3 How else could VR be used to change the way we are
   informed and entertained?

INNOVATION DATA

Website: www.emblematicgroup.squarespace.com
Contact: emblematicgroup.squarespace.com/contact-us/
Innovation name: Emblematic
Country: United States
Industries: Education / Entertainment & culture

36

THE RIGHT PODCAST FOR EVERY JOURNEY

Pendelpoddar is a free service in Sweden that recommends podcasts based on users' commuting times.

Podcasts have been around for years, but their popularity has recently exploded – listening grew by 23 per cent in the United States between 2015 and 2016, and 64 per cent of podcasts are listened to on a smartphone or tablet. In Sweden the statistics are even more striking: podcast listenership grew by 50 per cent in 2015 according to the annual media survey conducted by Orvesto. Typically, the average podcast listener was found to be aged 16–35, equally likely to be male or female, with 80 per cent choosing to listen on their mobile.

As take-up increases, audiences have become more discerning about the content they choose and a number of innovations have sprung up in response to this. One such example is Denmark-based Hyvi, which analyses a user's tweets to recommend podcasts that match their profile. Now, Swedish Pendelpoddar is another recommendation service but it works using a different metric – journey time. It was found that metropolitan areas such as Stockholm and Gothenburg had the most listeners, indicating that there is a demand for podcasts that can be consumed on short, city commutes.

Based on this information, the Swedish construction and civil engineering company PEAB developed the free Pendelpoddar platform to highlight their new residential area Nya Råsunda's proximity to Stockholm. Upon landing on the website, users are prompted to enter a 'from' address and a 'to' destination. The 'from' is automatically set to Nya Råsunda by default. Users can then enter their mode of travel (walk, bike, car or public transport) and, in response, the site generates a list of podcast episodes that match their journey time. These podcasts are drawn from Sweden, the United Kingdom and the United States. Users can then click to listen to one of these matched podcast episodes on the Pendelpoddar website to get a sense of how long a commute from Nya Råsunda, for example, to their destination would actually feel.

The Nya Råsunda development is made up of 700 new residential properties alongside office and retail space, for which sales began in November 2016. And, although the Pendelpoddar platform is primarily designed to promote this development, it works just as well for journeys to and from anywhere in Sweden. Users simply need to change the default 'from' address when they arrive on the website.

In practice, the platform sometimes delivers inaccurate results – suggesting podcasts that are too long or too short to be a good match. But the premise remains a compelling one, and there is certainly potential to flesh out the idea – incorporating more countries, improving the matching algorithm and creating a standalone hosting app to support it. The commute is a huge consumption opportunity for media producers, and this will become only truer with the advent of driverless cars.

TAKEAWAYS

1 What other metrics could be used to suggest podcasts to listeners?
2 Could knowing journey time also be helpful to recommend other forms of media?
3 How could content be better tailored towards commuters in particular?
4 How else could PEAB have used media to convey Nya Råsunda's proximity to Stockholm? Could virtual reality have been employed, for example?

INNOVATION DATA

Website: www.pendelpoddar.se
Contact: hej@annehellmavold.com
Innovation name: Pendelpoddar
Country: Sweden
Industries: Entertainment & culture

37

MAKING TV VIEWERS PARTICIPANTS IN INTERACTIVE DRAMA

Germany's Das Erste TV channel aired *Terror – Your Verdict*, an interactive courtroom drama that allowed viewers to vote on the outcome of the show.

Advances in entertainment technology mean that it is no longer necessary for viewing to be a passive experience. Interactive entertainment is the future, and it is becoming more and more common – and more and more interactive.

The German network ARD broadcast an interactive courtroom drama where viewers acted as the jury. The show, *Terror – Your Verdict*, was an adaptation of a play by bestselling author Ferdinand von Schirach. It starred German big-screen actors Florian David Fitz, Burghart Klaussner, Martina Gedeck and Lars Eidinger. In the fictional plot, militants from an offshoot of al-Qaeda hijack a Lufthansa Airbus A320 with 164 people on board, intending to crash it into a stadium packed with 70,000 people during a football match between Germany and England.

At the last minute and against the explicit orders of his wing commander, a German air-force pilot shoots down the airplane before it crashes into the stadium. Having saved the lives of tens of thousands but killing all passengers on board, he now faces charges for his action in court. The viewers are asked to judge whether this pilot who shot down the plane is guilty of murder.

Viewers in Germany, Switzerland and Austria gave their verdict online and by phone. The programme was also aired in Slovakia and the Czech Republic. The vast majority called for the pilot, Lars Koch, to be acquitted. In Germany, 86.9 per cent of the 609,000 viewers who voted believed Koch made the right decision. A similar proportion of viewers backed Koch in Austria and Switzerland. Local news anchors moderated the voting process, and experts debated the law and various national rulings.

In a TV discussion broadcast after the drama, German ex-Defence Minister Franz Josef Jung argued that the lives of the plane passengers were already impossible to save and that the spectators themselves had a right to human dignity. It was a case of extra-judicial emergency, he argued. A former interior minister, Gerhart Baum, disagreed, saying that the pilot should be found guilty of murder as the fate of the passengers was not certain and human lives could not be measured against one another.

The programming chief for German broadcaster ARD, Volker Herres, said the goal was to invite the audience to be part of the plot. 'The viewer is yanked out of the passivity of television watching,' he told the *Bild* daily newspaper. 'He is actively called upon to become both an affected person and to take a decision.'

This new model of audience participation is set to revolutionize the way we enjoy entertainment – not just as passive viewers but as key players in a story's outcome.

TAKEAWAYS

1 How might interactivity be incorporated at multiple points in shows?
2 How else could audiences get involved in the shows they watch?
3 Could VR be incorporated into this model to make it more immersive?

INNOVATION DATA

Website: www.daserste.de
Contact: info@daserste.de, twitter.com/daserste
Company name: Das Erste
Innovation name: *Terror – Your Verdict*
Country: Germany
Industries: Entertainment & culture

38

USING EYE-TRACKING TECHNOLOGY FOR ACCURATE VIEWING DATA

Boston-based start-up TVision Insights monitors viewer reactions as they watch TV and provides broadcasters and programmers with in-depth viewing data.

With increasing competition from other platforms, audiences are already migrating away from traditional TV viewing. Now TVision Insights has built a device that tracks TV viewers: who is watching what and how they are reacting to it. Founded by two MIT alumni and a 2015 MassChallenge winner, the company has its headquarters in Boston, Massachusetts, with offices in New York City and Tokyo. In another round of funding, the start-up has raised an extra $6.8 million, bringing their total funding to $9.3 million.

TVision is the first company to measure actual 'eyes-on-screen' to provide advertisers, agencies and television networks with the second-by-second data required to understand the effectiveness of television advertising and programming. It uses state-of-the-art technology to collect, anonymously and passively, information on viewer behaviour, attention and emotional effects second by second and person by person from the natural viewing environment. The aim is to achieve this without compromising viewer privacy.

The company has developed a small device that sits on top of an ordinary television and can even use lasers and thermal infrared to work in low light. The technology, built on computer vision and focused on eye-tracking technology, uses sensors and algorithms capable of identifying not just who is watching in a family group, but also who is just sitting in the room rather than not watching TV, and what viewers' reactions are to the show that is on at the time. TVision's devices are already installed in some 7,000 homes that have opted in across the United States and Japan and currently provide three of the largest broadcasters with the data they need to inform their programming decisions.

As TVision's website says, 'We show you what's happening on the other side of the screen.'

Accurate viewing data is essential if television broadcasters are going to compete. Reporting shortfalls could eventually lead to advertising declines and a severe loss of revenue. With ever more inventive models of broadcasting entertainment, such as the interactive German courtroom drama discussed in section 37, perhaps traditional broadcasters can compete with the new forms of TV viewing that are expanding exponentially in their popularity.

While this is an excellent way to gather data on viewers and their preferences and viewing experiences, and the company insists that it does not affect viewer privacy, many will see it as an invasion. As a society, we are continually giving up more and more of our personal data to companies and governments looking to gain an insight into our behaviour for a range of reasons. A challenge of introducing this model will be to disassociate from the 'Big Brother' parallels that some will inevitably draw.

A similar model is the Bioanalytics platform Lightwave, which enables film companies to monitor the emotions of audience members during their viewing experience. Broadcasting and film companies will have to use new and ever more innovative ways to investigate how we view entertainment and how they can adjust their approaches accordingly.

TAKEAWAYS

1 Could this kind of in-depth tracking technology be used across other entertainment platforms?
2 How do you think people in your city/country/area would feel about having their emotions tracked during TV viewing?
3 Could your company benefit from gathering this kind of detailed user data?

INNOVATION DATA

Website: www.tvisioninsights.com
Contact: www.tvisioninsights.com/contact/
Innovation name: TVision Insights
Country: United States
Industries: Access exclusive / Entertainment & culture

39

A GAME TO UNLOCK A BONUS TRACK FOR MUSIC FANS

Artist Kaytranada promotes his debut album with an online game that unlocks a bonus track – if users get a top score.

As music consumption continues to move online, we have seen a number of musicians cashing in on the interactivity available with digital formats. There was j'viewz's music video controlled by the viewer's heartbeat, and the Freeform platform that helps artists create albums that resemble mobile gaming apps. Now, Kaytranada has embraced the gaming ecosystem too, by creating a free online game that unlocks a bonus track from his debut album, *99.9%*.

To play, fans simply visit his website and launch the side-scroller platform game. Designed by artist Ricardo Cavolo, who also created the album's artwork, the game comes with a classic arcade-style soundtrack. Players must fly a plane through a landscape of volcanoes and columns, avoiding obstacles and picking up crowns, coins and weed – all of which are worth different point values. Once a top score of 100 is reached, the player is rewarded with a free download of the two-minute bonus track 'Nobody Beats the Kay'.

The album itself – consisting of 15 tracks – features a number of high-profile artists such as Anderson.Paak, Syd Tha Kyd and Craig David. In fact, only four of the tracks do not feature guests. Released through XL Recordings worldwide and HW&W Recordings in Canada, it was well received critically: in 2016 the album won the 2016 Polaris Music Prize and was a regular on a number of 'Best Albums of 2016' lists, including those compiled by *NME*, Stereogum, *The Guardian* and Rough Trade.

While the game was designed to function as a marketing ploy for the album, the relationship between the song and the game, and the importance of the game in unlocking the full *99.9%* experience, shows an appreciation for the art form that has not always been present. In fact, gaming has historically struggled to be seen as art at all. As arcades and video gaming became more mainstream during the 1980s and 1990s, the activity was often made a scapegoat for obesity, violence and other antisocial behaviour, and, while this level of vitriol has certainly calmed, the medium is still not usually regarded as high culture.

However, this perception is changing, and indie developers are continuing to push gaming forward. Campo Santo's 2016 release *Firewatch*, for example, required the player to do little more than navigate the game's main character around a national park as the plot unfolded around him. Rather than solve puzzles or fight enemies, the player's main task was to choose the protagonist's responses during conversations with an off-screen character. The player was not required to test their gaming skills, but rather was responsible for shaping the emotional tone of the story. Such a game is a far cry from *PacMan* or early shoot-'em-ups such as *DOOM*.

What's more, gaming is the only art form that holds back content based on the consumer's ability. In role-playing games in particular, the player can find out how the story develops only by completing the challenges within the game.

Unlike other art forms, gamers essentially have to 'earn the right' to discover the next development in the plot. This establishes an appreciation for the content that is different from how we appreciate other art forms, and it is this feeling that the *99.9%* game creates for Kaytranada's bonus track. If the view from a mountain looks better once climbed on foot, why shouldn't a song sound better when it's had to be earned?

TAKEAWAYS

1 How else could gaming and music be merged for promotional purposes?
2 How could appreciation for other art forms potentially be heightened or altered by requiring the consumer to 'unlock' the experience first?
3 How else could artists require their audiences to 'earn' access to their content?

INNOVATION DATA

Website: www.kaytranada.com
Contact: info@wrcmgmt.net, www.twitter.com/
         KAYTRANADA
Company name: Kaytranada
Innovation name: *99.9% The Game*
Country: Canada
Industries: Audio / Entertainment & culture / Gamification & gaming / Marketing & advertising

40

A RADIO STATION THAT PLAYS ONLY ON WILLIAMSBURG BRIDGE, NEW YORK CITY

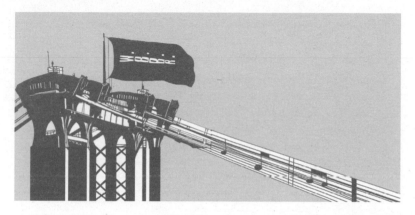

WBBR is a radio station made specifically for New Yorkers running or cycling over Williamsburg Bridge, which is the only place where they can hear it.

As every runner or cyclist knows, upbeat, motivational music can be essential to getting through the most challenging moments of a journey. WBBR is a radio station designed specifically for New Yorkers struggling over the Williamsburg Bridge – the only place where listeners can tune in. The station was created by ad agency Sid Lee in collaboration with designer/developer Eric Hu as a promotional tool for Brooklyn-based record label UNO! With the ever-changing landscape of the music industry, record labels and artists must find new and increasingly inventive ways to promote their material and reach a larger audience.

Listeners first download a free smartphone app, which is triggered by GPS to detect when users are near the bridge. Williamsburg Radio is entirely hands-free. The app starts playing music automatically once users reach the bridge. When they approach the bridge, the app plays an upbeat song to listeners as they climb up the steep initial incline of the bridge. The app senses when users have reached the peak of the climb and automatically plays a more chilled-out track for their descent. The idea is to help motivate cyclists and joggers through the tough part and then help them to relax and centre themselves after they have passed the strenuous uphill section.

The app detects a user's location roughly every second through GPS tracking and a system of beacons. The tracks change daily but are all chosen by UNO! from the pool of artists on the label, which includes Mykki Blanco and DJ Jacques Green.

Williamsburg Bridge radio earned Sid Lee a nomination for the 2016 Webby award for mobile sites and apps in the experimental and innovation category. The award focuses on the use and implementation of groundbreaking mobile technology or unconventional applications of mobile technology in mobile sites, apps and environmental situations.

This form of eye-catching innovation sets the record label apart from others whose marketing strategies are more conventional. Interest and intrigue are created by the hyper-local nature of the application, and therefore users are exposed to artists they may otherwise never have come across. Because the app is free of charge, it encourages users to try it out, with the hope that this investment will pay off later, with sales and streams of the label's music.

Swedish band John Moose's album, which is only playable in wooded areas, is another great example of a location-dependent audio product whose unique and intriguing nature attracts more curious ears. While promoting the album, this idea also encourages users to spend time in the great outdoors. A hyper-local audio experience could be used to attract users to any event or location, as well as promoting the audio content itself.

TAKEAWAYS

1 Could other forms of art and entertainment – podcasts, perhaps? – use smartphones' location capabilities to promote content by enhancing the listener's experience?
2 What other locations or events could be used as settings for hyper-local audio?
3 How could your company use hyper-local media to promote your product?

INNOVATION DATA

Website: www.wbbr.nyc
Contact: opere@sidlee.com
Innovation name: WBBR
Country: United States
Industries: Audio / Entertainment & culture / Marketing & advertising / Smart cities

SUMMARY

Audiences are moving from passive consumption to active participation in content creation. The success of games such as *Life Is Strange*, in which every player makes decisions to shape the game's overall narrative arc, are testimony to this. While most personalization to date has been through recommendation engines or audience segmentation, personalization in the future will increasingly come to involve individualized content, in which the consumer shapes their own narratives.

For businesses, success in this new paradigm means knowing your audience, crafting content that will land and then delivering that content in thoughtful and flexible ways. The innovations in this chapter speak to each of those requirements in turn.

ENTERTAINMENT TAKEAWAYS

1 **Involve your audience.** Whether it's making use of music preferences to design a recommendation engine or asking your audience to vote on the plot of a TV show, consider how audiences can be involved to help shape content. Of course, it's essential that this is done in a way that feels natural and sensible for the content in question – rather than being presented as an obtrusive bolt-on. Effective engagement means more immersive, tailored programming and ultimately a more loyal audience. Live performers, from stand-up comics to musicians taking song suggestions, can be a good source of inspiration.

2 **In a crowded market, use novel formats to stand out.** One of 2016's most talked-about releases was Beyoncé's *Lemonade*, an hour-long visual concept album that emerged on a streaming site a day before being offered for paid purchase. Later in the year Netflix released the entire first series of *The Crown* – a drama about the British monarchy – in one go. The success of these novel approaches is no surprise, as novel formatting is increasingly a way of standing out from the crowd.

3 **Understand that loyalties lie with content providers, not producers.** Yes, audiences still look out for their favourite artists, actors or writers but, increasingly, power is with the curators rather than the creators of content. Spotify's playlists can make or break careers in the same way that a top billing on Amazon Prime or Netflix can ensure a series' success. With subscription and streaming services gaining larger audience shares, expect that power balance to persist.

4 **Explore flexible payment models.** As loyalties shift, asking readers to pay for access to a single newspaper, for example, could become increasingly problematic. Many consumers access content almost exclusively from social media feeds, meaning they may stumble upon articles from a specific content provider only once or twice a year. Paywalls need to be flexible to accommodate this occasional access, without giving everything away for free. That's the logic underpinning **PayOrShare and Blendle** and it is a logic applicable to areas far beyond entertainment.

5 **Stay agile: the paradigm is still shifting.** Despite the massive changes and upheavals in both content creation and distribution channels for the entertainment space, we believe that this is only the tip of the iceberg and that change will continue to accelerate. Technological convergence, together with the dominance of a few global media players, will ensure that this discussion has a long way to run. Make sure you that don't rest on your laurels and keep your organization fresh and agile.

HEALTH

According to the World Health Organization, around 10 per cent of global GDP is spent on health care, and, despite struggles against understandably rigid safeguards and legacy systems, health care is seeing some of the most dynamic, exciting and vital new ideas of any industry. From Francis Crick and James Watson's first DNA double-helix model, through to Robert Edwards and Patrick Steptoe's work with in-vitro fertilization, medical breakthroughs have a long history of shaping our societies, with effects that resonate far beyond the walls of any hospital.

AR, VR and big data in health care

Some of the most notable health-care disruption in recent years has come from the application of augmented reality (AR) and virtual-reality (VR) technologies; the deployment of big data to draw out life-saving analysis; and the creation of applications and devices to empower patients. These innovations take lessons from beyond the medical profession and apply them to a health-care setting, driving efficiency, lowering costs and, ultimately, saving lives.

VR is being used in a number of professions to improve training, and we have already seen **VirtualSpeech** being used to coach public speakers. But it's perhaps nowhere more valuable than in the medical profession, where mistakes in a virtual world have far fewer consequences than in the real world. To that end, health tech start-up **EchoPixel** has designed an exploratory, consequences-free virtual space for surgeons to practise their skills on 3D-renderings of organs. Imagine a hi-tech, VR upgrade to Hasbro's *Operation* game, minus the light-up nose.

This chapter also contains two of the most compelling VR innovations in this book, demonstrating the true breadth of potential uses for the technology. In Sweden, the pharmacy **Apotek Hjärtat** is now supplementing traditional pharmaceutical pain relief with a series of VR outdoor scenes called 'Happy Place', while **DeepStream VR** has created a virtual-reality game called *COOL!* to help reduce pain for burn victims. Using MRI scans, the game's creators were able to prove conclusively a significant reduction in pain-related brain activity while people were using the game.

These innovations are just the start, and we expect to see a number of similar VR applications developed in health care over the coming years, for everything from pain relief to counselling. As the tools for gathering and analysing data have improved, private organizations and public services alike have sought to maximize the information at their disposal and the value they derive from it. In a health-care context, that means understanding in detail a patient's needs, progress or limitations, and using those insights to improve their quality of life.

In the United Kingdom, **Geneix** is using big data to detect patients' unique characteristics to recommend drug prescriptions with minimal side effects, while Tel Aviv-based start-up **Zebra** has developed an AI capable of diagnosing conditions in bones, the heart, liver, lungs and breasts from CT scans. Both can save vital time for already stretched medical practitioners, and potentially yield more accurate analysis, ultimately ensuring a better quality of care for patients.

Power to practitioners and patients

Of course, the most effective way to save time and reduce the stress put upon doctors and nurses is to simply reduce the number of patients they see. To that end, there have been a number of devices looking to facilitate improved self-care and more accurate self-diagnosis, such as **CliniCloud**'s FDA approved kit for heart, lung and temperature monitoring.

Like CliniCloud, many of these home check-up devices can transmit data to a local family physician or hospital for review, and if this data can then be analysed by systems as intelligent as Geneix or Zebra, it will add up to significant time savings for hospital staff. This will inevitably lead to a better standard of patient care, while freeing up time for doctors and nurses to innovate for themselves in environments such as the **MakerNurse** space. Here they can explore ways to further free up resources and improve patient care, with the potential to build more home-diagnosis kits and methodologies in the creation of a virtuous circle.

As outlined in this book's introduction, every innovation featured within these pages can be linked to another to inspire a sense of things to come. This is perhaps nowhere more true than in health care. Consider, as you read the following examples, how the ideas could be joined under one ecosystem, to create results that are greater than the sum of their parts.

41

USING DNA ANALYSIS TO TAILOR DRUGS TO EACH PATIENT

Geneix is using big data and algorithms to detect patients' unique characteristics to recommend drug prescriptions with minimal side effects.

Everyone is different, but we cannot have every single product we use tailored to our individual bodies. If it were possible, however, one of the most important industries that could benefit from such individual tailoring is health care.

Geneu is a UK company that is already using in-store DNA analysis to personalize its anti-ageing skincare products. Now, Geneix is using big data and algorithms to detect patients' unique characteristics to recommend drug prescriptions with minimal side effects. For example, if a patient has a variation in the CYP2D6 gene, they may get no pain relief from codeine.

Working with health-care professionals, Geneix has developed a platform that analyses each customer's DNA to create a digital profile, which is then accessible through a mobile app. Before prescribing a treatment, doctors can use the platform to see how likely the patient is to have an adverse reaction to it. The app uses big data processing and algorithms to show a number of metrics in a visual way to help professionals instantly make a decision, and better understand each drug to make safer recommendations in the future. The software is fully interoperable with electronic medical record software and all data is securely stored.

The system requires input of genetic data from a 23andMe* genetic test. Geneix re-analyses it using up-to-date, evidence-based guidelines and then creates and stores a validated drug response profile that doctors use to personalize prescriptions at any time in the future. Geneix specializes in drug–gene interactions, not disease risk or ancestry. Their approach is in line with current regulatory guidelines, which means they focus only on genes that have the highest level of clinical evidence. They are supported by the Chair of Pharmacogenetics for the UK National Health Service (NHS) and work with NHS trusts and the *BMJ* to implement genetics into prescribing.

23andMe

California-based company specializing in personal genomics and named after the 23 pairs of chromosomes in a normal human cell.

Once Geneix has analysed the patient's genetic data, they email the patient a drug–gene report that gives a drug response profile. It is working to integrate reports into electronic health-care systems, so that any doctor will always have this information available wherever a patient is being treated.

Geneix believes that it is no longer acceptable to treat all patients the same. A one-size-fits-all approach to drug therapy has had adverse results and become one of the biggest killers worldwide, leading to an estimated 100,000 deaths in the United States each year.

By promoting prospective rather than reactive medicine, the system helps to avoid potential adverse drug–drug or drug–gene interactions, suggesting clinically safe alternatives if needed.

The system supports prescribers so that they can offer patients the safest and most appropriate care. The unique and intuitive interface, developed with health-care workers, focuses on usability; Geneix hopes that it marks the beginning of a new approach to health care.

This is clearly the direction in which health care is moving. As we move away from a one-size-fits-all approach and towards patient-tailored medicine, we will see more and more examples of this. Later in this chapter, we will cover a new 3D-printed pill that personalizes medication doses and release timings to individual patients.

TAKEAWAYS

1 Are there ways that DNA analysis can help businesses tailor their product or service to each individual customer?
2 How else could the use of data gathering make health care more bespoke?
3 What other innovations could seek to combat widespread problems that cause hundreds of thousands of deaths a year?

INNOVATION DATA

Website: www.geneix.com
Contact: www.geneix.com/contact-us
Innovation name: Geneix
Country: United Kingdom
Industry: Health & wellbeing

42

A PHARMACY APP PRESCRIBING VIRTUAL-REALITY PAIN RELIEF

Apotek Hjärtat in Sweden is using Happy Place, a series of virtual-reality outdoor scenes, as a supplement to traditional pharmaceutical pain relief treatments.

Distracting the mind with virtual scenes of nature and calm stimuli is increasingly being found to be an effective method of relieving temporary pain. A wide range of virtual reality (VR) content has been demonstrated to reduce pain in a range of situations.

Working with start-up Mimerse, a therapeutic app developer, Sweden's Apotek Hjärtat pharmacies created the VR 'Happy Place'. Designed to supplement traditional pharmaceutical treatments, Happy Place can help alleviate aches and pains like those caused by vaccinations, toothache, menstrual cramps, tattoos and sore muscles, and even serious burns. VR technology, by definition, creates an audiovisual illusion displacing the user into a digitally created world, something one study found to be as effective as narcotics in alleviating pain.

Using a painterly style of artwork, Happy Place tracks users' eye movements, eliminating the need for extensive instructions and buttons. Users can interact with the scenes as much or as little as they like. Some people prefer to gaze at the scenery, whereas others prefer the challenge of finding the objects that, when gazed upon for a bit longer than usual, unveil new aspects of the environment.

Despite numerous research projects and companies investigating pain distraction in VR, before Mimerse developed Happy Place there was no publicly available app with this explicitly intended use. A successful pain relief VR platform has to:

- distract the person from the real world and their real body by maximizing 'presence'
- reduce negative emotion

- be accessible in terms of design, content, technology and platform
- promote positive side effects such as relaxation, calmness and feeling of awe and wonder.

The developers wanted to create something that satisfied the demands of those in pain that could be made available in Apotek Hjärtat's primary care clinics as well as free of charge. They cited their biggest challenge, besides a tight budget, as appealing to, and working for, as many different types of people, pain level and situation possible.

Immersive virtual reality pain distraction was first explored by Hoffman & Patterson at the University of Washington Seattle and Harborview Burn Center. Companies like DeepStreamVR (who also have compiled a list of relevant research literature) and AppliedVR have developed the concept further commercially. Mimerse took inspiration from this research, as well as guided meditation VR and virtual nature research, open-world games and a series of Swedish 'Where's Wally?'-style books where readers can view the densely illustrated pages time and time again, noticing different things upon each viewing.

The painterly style of the scenes found in Happy Place come from the counter-intuitive fact about virtual reality, that aiming for realism might not be the best choice to achieve maximum presence. A scene in Oculus Dream Deck (a VR demo-reel) convinced Mimerse that the popular Low Poly art style was viable for their project. Despite the lack of geometric details and textures, it felt like a very immersive place. The art style also suited the project both in terms of budget and hardware limitations.

Virtual reality is being used as a supplement to a number of different industries, from virtual crime scene re-enactments for jurors to emergency birth care education. As the technology improves and more money is invested, there should be no limit to its potential applications.

TAKEAWAYS

1 How could the technology be used ethically for personal use in less connected communities?
2 How else could pharmacies and health-care professionals collaborate with start-ups to improve patient care?
3 How else could VR be applied in health care?

INNOVATION DATA

Website: www.apotekhjartat.se
Contact: william@mimerse.com
Company name: Apotek Hjärtat
Innovation name: Happy Place
Country: Sweden
Industry: Health & wellbeing

43

STUDYING 3D-RENDERED ORGANS IN VIRTUAL REALITY BEFORE SURGERY

EchoPixel will use information from medical imaging to produce 3D VR organs, which doctors can explore before surgery.

Doctors currently rely on flat images from CT and MRI scans for pre-op information about a patient's organs. Now, however, health tech start-up EchoPixel is planning to use the information garnered from current medical imaging technology to produce 3D VR organs, which doctors can explore and inspect before beginning surgery.

True 3D uses the images that are already being gathered during medical imaging processes to create 3D-rendered body parts. These floating masses can then be examined via a VR platform called zSpace. Doctors can rotate and dissect the images of organs, including the brain and the heart, using a stylus. They can even examine a colon via a simulated fly-through.

EchoPixel hope their technology will help doctors gain an enhanced understanding of the intricacies of each organ, and enable them to go into surgery well prepared. Medical students can also use the platform as a supplementary learning tool.

There are many benefits to this innovative new system: True 3D is a real-time, interactive VR system. It moves beyond the flat screen, displaying real patient anatomy in open 3D space, with instant response and seamless interaction capabilities. Anatomical information is tailored to be procedure-specific, easily accessible and unobstructed. It provides the required visual context with no extraneous information, significantly lowering the cognitive load for doctors. Finally, it is intuitive to use. Specialized tools enable users to directly grasp, dissect and size key clinical features with one move.

Current medical visualization techniques have limitations in representing the complex 3D relationships present in human anatomy.

In order to successfully identify an area of interest from a 3D medical dataset, such as those produced by CT, MRI and other devices, doctors are required to combine a series of 2D images in their mind and mentally extract the relevant 3D relationships that define the tissue or organ of interest as well as its neighbouring anatomy. In complex cases, they must visually map two or more views of the same data to find appropriate correspondences of one view with another view to produce a match and determine if what they see is the tissue they want to evaluate.

The True 3D approach is significantly different from current 3D rendering technologies because it enables readers to visualize and interact with tissue and organs in open 3D space using a hand-directed stylus as if they were real physical objects.

Doctors and hospitals across the United States are using True 3D to increase clinical knowledge in a range of procedures and are receiving widespread positive feedback. In areas such as interventional cardiology, paediatric cardiology, interventional neuroradiology and CT colonography, doctors are using 3D interactive virtual reality to assist clinical efficacy and workflow.

Among many others, True 3D's clinical sites include the Lahey Clinic, Boston Scientific, the Deborah Heart and Lung Center and Toronto Sick Kids Hospital. In addition to clinical uses, EchoPixel's True 3D is showing enormous potential as a research and training tool. Their research and education sites include Penn State Health Milton S. Hershey Medical Center and Texas A&M Health Science Center College of Medicine.

We have already seen VR being used as a tool for pain relief. This more complex system is a great example of combining cutting-edge medical imaging software with VR capability to create a product that is greater than the sum of its parts, and that will improve training, treatment and patient care for years to come.

TAKEAWAYS

1 Could this combined technology be used in other industries too – such as mechanics or construction?
2 What other innovations could be deployed to reduce the cognitive load on doctors?
3 How else could VR be used in training and education?

INNOVATION DATA

Website: www.echopixeltech.com
Contact: www.echopixeltech.com/contact-us
Company name: EchoPixel Tech
Innovation name: EchoPixel
Country: United States
Industries: Design / Education / Health & wellbeing / Non-profit & social cause

44

3D PILL PRINTING FOR PERSONALIZED DOSES

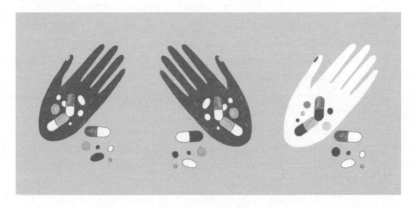

Scientists at the University of Singapore have developed a way to 3D print customized medication, which can combine multiple drugs in a single tablet.

Health care is by nature personal, and technology is making the management of it even more so. The National University of Singapore (NUS) has developed a way to 3D print customized pills, so that medication that needs to be taken at various times during the day, at different dosages, can be produced as a single tablet. The system was designed by Assistant Professor Soh Siow Ling and PhD student Sun Yajuan, of the Department of Chemical and Biomolecular Engineering at the NUS Faculty of Engineering.

Using simple computer software that does not require specialist tech knowledge, doctors input the desired release schedule and dosages of the drugs. The program then produces a custom medication mould, which can be printed by a commercially available 3D printer. The moulds are created in parts, with each shape corresponding to the types of drug being prescribed and the timing of doses. As well as printing different dosages for varying schedules, the single pills can be printed to contain different drugs.

Different types of clinical circumstances may call for different types of timed release of drugs. The key element of the new system is the ability to customize the timing and the way in which drugs are released into the body, or their 'release profiles'. Certain chemicals, such as hormones, may need to be released in pulses at regular intervals, in sync with the biological cycles of the human body. In other situations, a relatively large dose of a drug is needed initially, followed by gradually lower levels. For example, in arthritis, a large dose is required at first to eliminate pain in the morning, followed by smaller doses to keep the pain from recurring.

The drug tablet consists of three distinct components, including a polymer containing the drug in a specifically designed shape that will determine the rate of release of the drug. For example, a five-pronged shape will allow the drug to be released in five pulses over time. By adjusting the shape of the drug-containing polymer, it is possible to release drugs at any desired rate.

The use of a commercially available 3D printer in this method makes it a relatively cheap way of making personalized medication a reality, compared to conventional tablet production or other methods of making small shapes, such as photolithography. It is also often important to administer more than one type of drug to a patient at any one time. This method can be modified to include multiple types of drug within the same tablet, customized so that each drug is released at a different rate from the one tablet.

In 2015 the US Food and Drug Administration approved the first 3D-printed pill. Known as Spritam, it is a high-dosage, easy-to-swallow pill that helps prevent epileptic seizures. The advances in affordable 3D printing technology and its applications in medical science mean that the way doctors administer drugs is set to change for good. Daily pill organizers may soon be obsolete, as prescription medication becomes no more complicated than taking a single pill each day. With a more safe, affordable and personalized system in place, lives everywhere could be improved.

TAKEAWAYS

1 How else could 3D printing be used to simplify life?
2 What other commercially available technology could be applied in health care?
3 In what ways could your company collaborate with scientists and researchers to address inconvenient and outdated systems and methods?

INNOVATION DATA

Website: news.nus.edu.sg
Contact: chesec@nus.edu.sg
Company name: National University of Singapore
Innovation name: 3D prescription pill printing
Country: Singapore
Industries: Design / Health & wellbeing

45

USING BIG DATA TO PREDICT HOSPITAL ADMISSIONS

The Assistance publique – Hôpitaux de Paris (AP-HP) group of hospitals is trialling a machine-learning analytics system to improve the management of demand for health resources.

With limited resources and a growing, ageing population, hospital waiting times are going through the roof. During particularly busy periods, ER departments can be thrown into chaos as they are under-staffed and unprepared for such high patient numbers.

In order to try to address this problem, ten years of Paris hospital admissions data, plus external information including weather, patterns of flu infection and public holidays, was inputted and analysed by the Trusted Analytics Platform (TAP). For hospital administrators, predicting the number of patient visits to emergency departments, along with their admission rates, is critical for optimizing resources at all levels of staff. Ultimately, this reduces waiting times and improves the quality of patient care.

Four of the Assistance publique – Hôpitaux de Paris are trialling the new predictive system aimed at reducing hospital waiting times. TAP is an open-source analysis platform that uses machine learning to create tools and services across a range of industries.

The AP-HP project is the first to use open-source time-series analysis, and the TAP engineers who worked on the system had to build new sets of code. If the project is successful, plans are to imple-ment the prediction system through all 44 hospitals in the AP-HP group.

In TAP, the team built a browser-based user interface for hospital administrators, physicians and medical staff to easily visualize forecasted near-term hospital patient loads and plan resource allocation. In its current implementation, the application enables hospital employees to view the past 15 days of reported data for emergency department visits and hospital admissions, and to view predicted visits and admissions for the subsequent 15 days. Ideally, this will provide enough advance warning for extra staff to be made available when demand is likely to be high.

After the full dataset comprising information from four emergency departments within AP–HP was prepared and assembled, the next stage of the process involved data science research, along with the initial model evaluations. During this phase, the Intel and AP–HP teams cleaned and sampled the data and surveyed a variety of possible methods for predicting hour-by-hour visits and admissions at each site.

The team's main aim at this point was to develop an algorithm that most accurately tracked the peaks and valleys of the observed data from AP–HP. The model would later need to scale for the analysis of much larger datasets than those used in the initial project and the resulting analytics would also need to make sense to people who are not trained statisticians, that is, doctors and other health-care professionals.

Although AP–HP data provided to the Intel team was anonymized, the TAP platform is optimized for security to ensure that data and processing are protected at all stages of the process. In the future, AP–HP plans to take advantage of TAP's highly scalable model to process large datasets to increase the accuracy of predictions, and to investigate other health-care challenges that could be addressed through the analysis of big data.

Health care is embracing technology, looking for new ways to be more efficient with limited resources: An AI-powered medical information system from Kang Health in Israel provides more accurate information for people at home, and an app from Beautiful Information is being used in the UK to provide clinicians with real-time, customizable visualizations of data.

TAKEAWAYS

1 What areas of health are still awaiting a technology update?
2 How else could big data be used to improve the efficiency of health care?
3 What other industries could apply a system like this to predict future demand?

INNOVATION DATA

Website: trustedanalytics.org
Contact: trustedanalytics@gmail.com
Company name: Assistance publique – Hôpitaux de Paris
Innovation name: TAP admission predictions
Country: France
Industries: Health & wellbeing / Smart cities

46

A SNOWY VIRTUAL-REALITY WORLD REDUCING THE PAIN OF BURNS

DeepStream VR uses virtual reality gaming to help reduce physical pain in burn victims.

Virtual reality (VR) companies are constantly exploring new ways to integrate the tech into different industries, and we are seeing many applications in gaming, retail and tourism. But perhaps one of the most impressive means of applying VR is in health care. We have already seen VR flatforms being used for pain relief with Swedish start-up Mimerse's **Happy Place**. Deepstream VR has developed a similar platform with a distracting gameplay element.

Deepstream VR is a start-up formed by Firsthand Technology's co-founders, Howard Rose and Ari Hollander. The game *COOL!* creates a virtual world designed to ease pain – it aims to distract burn patients from the pain of getting their wounds cleaned or their skin grafted with an immersive first-person game, with a cute otter as a companion.

COOL! transports users on a journey through a beautiful land-scape of changing seasons. They meet and play with the creatures living there. Tasks including tossing the otters a fish and pelting them with magic orbs to transform them into fantastic colours. The land-scape holds secret puzzles, with rocks that spin and caves clustered with crystals.

During gameplay, each player can find their own mix of active fun and relaxation; they control how the game works. The gameplay can be endless; the user decides how much time they want to spend interacting with the VR environment and how they move through it, that is, in what speed and direction. Biosensors help induce a flow state in the user by controlling the intensity of the experience to maximize its benefits. The clinical interface controls the experience and tracks its outcomes.

MRI brain scans showed a significant reduction in pain related to brain activity in people using the game, and participants also reported feeling less pain. The technology has been employed by the US military in Iraq and Afghanistan, helping doctors reduce patient reliance on medication to treat pain. In a TedMed talk, Rose said it was time to 'embrace this technology and use this opportunity for health'.

There have been some concerns about the negative aspects of using VR on patients. Dr Bernie Garrett of the University of British Columbia School of Nursing describes a patient in his studies who experienced severe motion sickness from VR. Deepstream acknowledges that, unless carefully designed, virtual worlds can indeed induce motion sickness, but insist that they have years of experience building virtual worlds that are comfortable and provide a very positive experience to a wide range of people. While it's true that some people just don't react well to the VR experience, if the virtual worlds are well designed and the equipment is of high quality, problems of motion sickness can be almost eliminated.

COOL! is the latest release from the creators of 2008's SnowWorld, the groundbreaking research application that established the clinical use of VR for burn patients and wound care. SnowWorld plunged users into an immersive snowy landscape with huge icebergs, caves and snowmen, and helped to mentally distract those in severe pain from burns.

The improvement in interface and hardware quality since then means that pain relief from VR is now more successful than ever. The conclusion for health care is that VR can be very effective if it is designed specifically for the needs and challenges of the people who will use it.

TAKEAWAYS

1 How else could virtual reality be used to change the way we provide medical care?
2 What other industries could use VR in a new and innovative way?
3 What other tech could help distract patients from pain and discomfort? What about podcasts, smart lighting or visual displays?

INNOVATION DATA

Website: firsthand.com
Contact: info@firsthand.com
Company name: DeepstreamVR
Innovation name: *COOL!*
Country: United States

47

USING ARTIFICIAL INTELLIGENCE FOR IN-DEPTH ANALYSIS OF MEDICAL SCANS

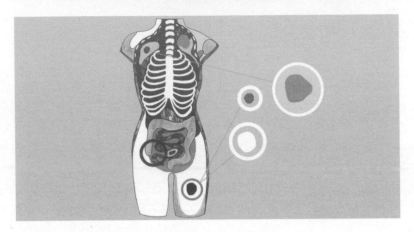

Tel Aviv-based digital health-care start-up Zebra has developed multiple algorithms to detect common conditions through AI analysis of medical scans.

With human radiologists already under pressure from growing demand, thousands of mammograms are misread each year because breast tissue can be extremely varied, and when combined with time constraints on already busy health-care professionals, this consistently adds stress to overstretched systems. Additionally, as the population continues to age, the burden on health-care provision and providers will also increase.

Israeli start-up Zebra aims to address this problem by using algorithms to detect medical conditions with AI analysis of medical scans. Users simply upload scan images to the Zebra website to receive their analysis. Currently, patients can upload two scans to Zebra for free. The company asks anyone interested in having more than two scans reviewed to contact the team.

At the moment, the service only supports analysis of CT scans. Future plans include developing the AI's capabilities for handling other types of images.

Zebra's algorithms are continually improving. The system combines an archive of millions of anonymized medical imaging scans with deep machine learning – an algorithmic technique that allows computers to analyse vast swathes of data and automatically detect patterns or features, make comparisons with new images and make predictions regarding certain conditions. So far, the AI is capable of recognizing conditions in bones, the heart, liver, lungs and breasts.

Zebra is led by entrepreneurs, health care IT and medical imaging veterans, and works with partners in patient care to explore big data and its uses in medical imaging. The company sees its service as an essential solution to an increasingly difficult situation. Making the transition towards using AI analysis, where formerly health-care professionals were required, aims to alleviate some of the reliance on human input. However, they are careful to insist that the system is not designed to replace physicians altogether, but as an initial way of identifying medical abnormalities. Zebra also make it very clear that the absence of an abnormal result does not necessarily indicate good health, and that a trained physician should always be consulted regarding any medical concerns.

We are seeing innovations all over the world that aim to rethink, simplify and improve health-care practices. Using a smartphone, for example, patients can now test for anaemia without needing to draw blood: an app by University of Washington researchers uses a smartphone's built-in camera to measure the colour of blood to check for the condition. Designed to help rural and remote communities, the HemaApp checks users' levels of haemoglobin, which carries oxygen throughout the body. Different amounts of it in the blood indicate different conditions, including childhood malnutrition and anemia.

As mentioned earlier in this chapter, a research team has developed a method for 3D printing multiple doses of medicine in a single capsule. Technological advances and new ways of looking at the way we treat patients, analyse results and administer medicine are constantly improving health care, and will surely lead to solutions to the problems faced by struggling health-care providers across the globe.

TAKEAWAYS

1 What other aspects of everyday health care could use a technology update?
2 How else could AI be deployed in health care?
3 How could your business cut down on pressure on staff by using AI systems where human input is currently needed?
4 What other solutions could we put in place to alleviate the problems of understaffed, over-subscribed health-care systems?

INNOVATION DATA

Website: profound.zebra-med.com
Contact: info@zebra-med.com
Company name: Zebra
Innovation name: Online medical scan analysis
Country: Israel
Industry: Health & wellbeing

48

A SMART MEDICAL KIT FOR HOME CHECK-UPS

Australian start-up CliniCloud has created a kit that allows patients to perform their own check-ups at home.

Visits to the doctor can be time-consuming and often, in the end, unnecessary. At the same time, a check-up can provide much needed reassurance, particularly for those with young children. Health care is big business and doctors and patients are both looking for improved flexibility and efficiency in their interactions without sacrificing quality. At Springwise we have seen a wide range of tech solutions – from the WEMU T-shirts (which can detect epileptic seizures and call a doctor) to the Peek Vision app, which allows roving doctors to give patients smartphone eye exams in the field, and telepresence consultations and pharmacies. Now, Australian start-up CliniCloud enables individuals to give themselves a medical check-up in the comfort of their own home.

The start-up, co-founded by Andrew Lin and Hon Weng Chong, uses a stethoscope, a contactless infrared thermometer and an accompanying app.

The app guides users through the process of using the equipment and also enables patients to record, store and even send data such as temperature and heart or lung sounds direct to their family doctor.

Lin, who met Chong as a medical student at the University of Melbourne, says the app aims to streamline health care, 'from people being treated quicker than they otherwise would, to unnecessary visits being avoided'. He continues: 'whole goal as a company is to bring health care to the home. We wanted to create medical devices that consumers could actually use at home, that were innovative, and allowed doctors to do more things remotely.'

The company has also been working in collaboration with Doctor On Demand, an innovation that allows patients to pay for appointments with their doctor over the phone, to build the 'first true integration of connected devices and a major telemedicine platform'. They have also been working with a number of insurers and health-care providers such as Astra Health Care, helping them to engage patients and offer affordable health care.

CliniCloud was founded in 2012 and has since grown to team of over 20. According to a CliniCloud spokesperson, the devices are registered with the US Food and Drugs Administration and Health Canada, and are available in the United States – from outlets such as BestBuy, Amazon, FSAStore and B8ta – and the United Kingdom, Canada and Australia via the online store. The next step for the company is to release their API/SDK, enabling partners to add not only CliniCloud devices to their platforms but other third-party devices as well. There are also plans to release two new products in the near future, although the company is being secretive about what these products could be. Dr Lin has said, 'We're fascinated by the potential that new technologies bring to health care and are particularly excited about the roles voice and AI technologies can play.'

This is not the first time we have seen smart home testing (we've covered various home STD testing kits before, such as the Hoope), but CliniCloud is exciting in its ability to cover a broader range of ailments and is certainly a taste of things to come.

TAKEAWAYS

1 What other innovations could be built to help better link these new technologies into traditional health-care set-ups?
2 How could CliniCloud expand to incorporate wellness tracking alongside its health data?
3 How else can technology keep costs down without compromising trust and standards in health care?

INNOVATION DATA

Website: www.clinicloud.com/en
Contact: support@clinicloud.com
Innovation Name: CliniCloud
CountrY: Australia
Industries: Access exclusive / Health & wellbeing

49

MAKERNURSE: REALIZING INVENTIVE NURSES' IDEAS

MakerNurse offers workspaces, materials and support to help nurses make more effective customized hospital equipment.

Nurses represent the interface between patient comfort and doctor treatment. This perspective often results in nurses being the first to react to each unique patient's needs, resorting to crudely customizing hospital equipment. Now in the United States, MakerNurse is an educational workspace that helps nurses build solutions to unique patient scenarios.

Founded by the director of MIT's Little Devices Lab, and a lecturer of device design also at MIT, MakerNurse acts as an educative platform – their 'makerspaces' help hospitals utilize nurses' inventiveness by providing dedicated spaces and tools for developing and testing equipment. Their blog and website community encourage the free sharing of ideas, bypassing patent-chasing companies. They believe that daily making and urgent response is what leads to better care, not 'grandiose ideas' that are incubated over decades.

Situated inside a hospital, a medical 'makerspace' provides nurses and other health-care providers with direct access to a wide range of suitable tools and materials. The makerspace is stocked with adhesives and fasteners, such as Velcro and zip ties; textiles and electronics, including sensors and microcontrollers; and a range of tools from pliers and sewing needles to 3D printers and laser cutters. The space is divided into a series of workstations, each equipped to address a specific medical challenge, such as fluid control or assistive technology.

Medical staff can use the makerspace to prototype a new tool from scratch or to upgrade a hospital device that already exists but does not exactly perform to their specific needs – for example adding a sensor to a take-home pill bottle to monitor use or customizing materials for individual patients.

While all the designs and ideas come directly from nurses working in hospitals, quality control and rigorous health and safety standards must be met before the new designs can be implemented. All devices made in the makerspaces are sterilized and tested through a quality improvement or institutional review board study before being used on the hospital floor. In order for the nurses to take credit for, document and explain how to make and use their new innovative designs, a 'selfie station' is set up in each makerspace. Users can upload their instructions, tips, photos and videos.

Founders Anna Young and José Gomez-Marquez have the perfect technical backgrounds to launch a scheme such as this. Anna has spent eight years teaching field-based prototyping workshops to health-care professionals, engineering students and industry executives across South America, Africa and Asia. She has expertise in digital fabrication and design, building networks of health technology innovators and designing clinical studies to move health technology prototypes from the lab and into practice.

José, originally from Honduras, has worked for the past decade combining health and DIY technologies. His research projects include crowdsourced diagnostics, paper microfluidics and reconfigurable diagnostics for extreme environments.

DIY medical kits, such as an initiative called iLab, developed to 3D-print medical equipment after the Haiti earthquake, are being used to solve immediate and unique medical needs. By enabling nurses to safely customize equipment and share these ideas, MakerNurse is hoping to foster a culture of innovation at the frontline of medical care.

TAKEAWAYS

1 Could other industries benefit from encouraging a DIY culture?
2 How else could companies or public-sector organizations utilize the expertise of their everyday workers to better tailor their equipment and practices?
3 How else could health care benefit from encouraging innovation from the bottom up instead of from above?

INNOVATION DATA

Website: www.makernurse.org
Contact: hello@makernurse.org
Innovation name: MakerNurse
Country: United States
Industries: Design / Health & wellbeing

50

A CHATBOT USING ARTIFICIAL INTELLIGENCE FOR MEDICAL DIAGNOSIS

China's Baidu has developed a bot that uses natural language processing to interact directly with patients, supporting doctors by speeding up the process of diagnosing.

The medical profession is under increasing pressure. A global shortfall in health-care workers will reach 12.9 million by 2035, according to the World Health Organization. And, in China, the shortage of health-care professionals is even more acute. In response to this, Chinese search engine Baidu launched a medical chatbot named Melody, designed to speed up the process of diagnosing patients.

Melody was created for Baidu's Doctor mobile app. It uses advanced deep learning and natural language processing (NLP) technologies developed by Baidu, to support doctors by speeding up the process of diagnosis and offering treatment options.

The bot works by gathering information from patients in real time through questioning and comparing their responses with Baidu's database of medical information. Wei Fan, senior director in Baidu's Big Data Lab, said, 'With Melody, our goal is to provide patients with an online experience that is close to a human conversation. We believe this natural type of interaction will help patients feel more comfortable with their doctors and result in a more beneficial patient–doctor relationship.' The bot gives highly customized and situation-appropriate responses to a patient's query. As Melody has more conversations, it will also learn and keep getting better. Its developers hope this is just the start of a much larger, AI-driven transformation of the health-care industry.

> The new AI-based medical assistant functionality will increase
> doctor productivity and enable patients to obtain faster responses
> to their health-related questions.

Baidu has built a 1,000-person team to work on AI – one of the company's top priorities. The app launches in China along with partners including doctors and health-care organizations. The company is also in talks with health-care organizations in the United States and Europe. Baidu drew on data from a number of public and private sources for Melody's artificial intelligence, including medical textbooks, medical websites and search queries and information supplied by doctors. It then applied deep learning to all that health data in order to make sense of it.

Melody is not ready to make diagnoses directly to patients. This type of technology is a long way from replacing human physicians with fully robotic doctors. The company is focused on helping to bridge the gap between patients and doctors and relieve some of the pressure, rather than replacing health-care professionals altogether.

China has already deployed chatbots in an array of roles, so Chinese consumers are already quite comfortable about chatting to AI-powered bots. However, it is hard to ignore the high-profile health-care data breaches that have taken place in recent years. In light of this, some consumers are likely to be wary of sharing too much health information with Melody and Baidu, and risk exposing their medical records to malicious parties.

We have seen some significant medical innovations that use technology to support the process of diagnosis, including a start-up called Everly that allows patients to order medical tests at home and view the results online, and a wearable chip developed at Eindhoven University that monitors sweat levels to detect whether users are ill.

TAKEAWAYS

1 What other areas of medicine could benefit from automation?
2 How else could chatbots be employed to relieve pressure on humans?
3 How could your company use advanced AI technology to learn and interact with customers?

INNOVATION DATA

Website: www.research.baidu.com/baidus-melody-ai-powered-conversational-bot-doctors-patients/
Contact: https://twitter.com/baiduresearch
Company name: Baidu
Innovation name: Melody
Country: China
Industry: Health & wellbeing

SUMMARY

The quest for optimal health is one of humankind's greatest struggles and, indeed, perhaps the most fundamental issue of all. Health and the ecosystems that surround our physical and mental wellbeing – by definition, the epicentre of the human condition – are inextricably linked to all the themes in this book. They relate to how we create the smartest, most healthy city, to the social and sustainability issues that are now so important and, of course, to how travel, shopping and other consumer industries affect the health of our bodies and our planet.

The onus to keep up the momentum falls not only on innovators like those described in this chapter, but also on national health providers, who must reinvent creaking models and create the conditions that allow those innovative ideas to flourish. If all parties play their part, we stand to gain more power and understanding over our own health; better conditions and training for practitioners; and an improved level of personalized treatment. The ten innovations here suggest all that is possible – now and in the future.

HEALTH TAKEAWAYS

1 **Consider why health care is a perfect environment for virtual reality to flourish.** From training simulators to pain relief, health care is proving the potential of VR perhaps more than any other industry. Other sectors should take note of the lessons here, and consider ways in which virtual reality can be used to provide benefits beyond simply displaying objects in a virtual space.

2 **Become your own doctor using new technology.** Doctors train for years – in classrooms and surgery rooms – because practising medicine requires an ability to accurately diagnose, prescribe, treat and operate. Some of those skills will remain off-limits, but technology means that our capacity to monitor, understand and therefore maintain our personal health is growing exponentially. Whether aided by advanced data or self-care kits, we will find ourselves requiring a visit to the local doctor less often.

3 **Connect innovations to make them greater than the sum of their parts.** We've already seen how these ten innovations could link together to form a self-improving ecosystem, but consider also how they could connect with the other innovations in this book. How could telepresence, discussed in the Communication chapter, be used alongside home-diagnosis kits, for example?

4 **Negotiate your own medical insurance policy.** With the huge rise in easy-to-access data patients will soon be in a powerful position to negotiate their own one-of-a-kind medical insurance policy. Gone will be the one-size-fits-all, high-margin policies that have driven the insurance industry over the past years. However, with this opportunity comes responsibility and, of course, it works both ways: time to go for a run!

THE WORKPLACE

'I will take it as a given that for most people, somewhere between 6 and 7 billion of them, the perfect job is the one which takes the least time.'

Tim Ferriss, *The 4-Hour Work Week* (2007)

The introduction of the Internet and email to the workplace in the mid-1990s heralded a new era of global communications that fundamentally changed the way we work. Distances became smaller, barriers to entry grew lower, and everything became faster. But future changes to the workplace are set to become even more disruptive.

While both of those developments greatly improved efficiency and speed, the developments of the near future will lead to a total restructuring of work and the workplace as we know it. We're already seeing emerging innovations that change not only the ways in which we can work but also our expectations, ethos and appreciation of what work and a workplace should be.

AI and upskilling in the workplace

Our current understanding of the impact artificial intelligence (AI) will have on society is still up for debate, but its effect on the workforce is already being felt. Many repetitive, data-driven, non-social tasks are already being automated, and it is estimated that 50 per cent of today's jobs across the globe will be replaced by AI by 2050. Roles that require lateral, creative thinking, empathy or social sensitivity are likely to be the last to be automated, but even here AI will still lead to significant time savings. How this will affect the specific day-to-day life and routine of an individual worker will vary greatly depending on their profession, but one likely outcome is that we will begin to see a diversification of job roles in the future. Time saved by new technologies will be filled with new tasks, many of which will be drawn from outside our traditional understanding of what that job should entail.

This diversification is already happening on a small scale, adding some welcome variation into the working day. **Tattoo artists in Brazil** are being trained to spot skin cancer and Finland's **postal workers** are now mowing lawns. Innovations such as 3D printing and consumer CNC (computer numeric control) devices have also led to the introduction of small-scale maker spaces in the workplace, meaning that research and development may soon become the responsibility of the entire workforce. **MakerNurse** empowers frontline nurses to prototype innovations that directly address the immediate issues they face on a daily basis. All these innovations require staff to learn entirely new skills and, for the most part, employees are more than happy to embrace this upskilling, which adds some welcome variety into their working day. (Note that many of the innovations in the chapters on the sharing economy and education also discuss an increased willingness to learn long after formal education.)

Remote working and business responsibility

The popularity of small-scale maker spaces also signposts a change in *where* employees of the future will be working. Just as trips to the workshop are now less necessary, to an extent so, too, are trips to the office. The Bring Your Own Device movement, alongside VPNs (virtual private networks), means that working from home or in remote hubs such as **Hoffice** is an increasingly common option given to employees. Today, 45 per cent of the US population is working from home or as virtual employees, and there are more examples of remote-working practices within this chapter. This movement suggests that innovations for the home environment, such as the Internet of Things, will be just as relevant to the future office as they are to domestic life.

As employees gain more choice over where they work, they are also becoming increasingly selective about who they work for, and why. Employers have come to represent more than just a pay cheque, and employees are keen for the company they work for to reflect their own values. Equality and fair treatment in the workplace are already important issues, and innovations such as **InHerSight**, which lets jobseekers assess a company's treatment of female staff, are only going to drive these issues further up the agenda.

More broadly, companies should realize that tacked-on corporate social responsibility (CSR) programmes are no longer sufficient. Rather, to attract top talent they must move to deeply integrate those CSR values into the company's *raison d'être* – much as outdoor brand Patagonia places sustainability at the very heart of all its operations. In the words of Yvon Chouinard, Patagonia's founder: 'My company, Patagonia Inc., is an experiment. It exists to put into action those recommendations that all the doomsday books on the health of our home planet say we must do immediately to avoid the certain destruction of nature and collapse of our civilization [...] Patagonia exists to challenge the conventional wisdom and present a new style of responsible business.' For Chouinard, then, sustainability is not an afterthought for a CSR programme. Patagonia might be a success as a retailer of outdoor clothing and equipment, but the health of the planet is the reason the company 'exists' in the way it does. Successful companies must look to emulate this ethos through increased transparency and fidelity to a purpose beyond the bottom line.

Both the workplace and the workforce of the future will look very different from those of today, but the ten innovations in this chapter are a real indication of the changes to come, and of the direction successful companies should be moving in to ensure that they are not left behind.

51

A CROWDSOURCED WEBSITE TO FLAG UP SEXISM IN THE WORKPLACE

A 'TripAdvisor' for the workplace lets employees anonymously review any companies' treatment of female staff.

Despite raised awareness and some progress over the past few years, inequality and sexism in the workplace are still all too common. Until now it has been very difficult to gauge in advance what the atmosphere in an office will be like, how you will be treated as an employee and what problems you may encounter in the office culture. Once an employee has worked for a company long enough to experience these problems, it is often too late and they might be afraid to leave their job or to complain.

Female jobseekers can now review the treatment of women in their potential workplace via an online platform called InHerSight. The website collates anonymous reviews from former and current employees – both male and female – so that women can find out more about the company's policies, office culture and other potential issues before applying for or accepting a job there.

A recent survey by *Cosmopolitan* magazine found that one in three women are sexually harassed at work and InHerSight enables those women to communicate misconduct and other problematic corporate policies. Importantly, they can do so without fear of recrimination or consequence, since the scorecards are entirely anonymous. Often, problems go unmentioned because employees are concerned that, if they raise issues, they will be seen as troublemakers and, at best, treated differently and, at worst, fearful of losing their jobs.

Users can complete surveys about their experience at any given company – either adding to an existing score or creating a new profile – by scoring them on 14 categories including their stance on maternity leave, flexible working hours and female representation in top positions. They can also leave a written review of the company. The crowdsourced data is then used to create comprehensive scorecards for other users to view.

By bringing individual insights together into a common framework, InHerSight provides a well-informed and representative picture of what it's really like for women in the workplace. It covers all different kinds of workplaces from offices to warehouses, wherever women work. These insights provide transparency for both employees and employers.

InHerSight's ratings help women make better-informed decisions about what companies they want to work for based on issues that are relevant to their lives, including career growth, family-friendly policies and office culture. The scorecards also allow employers to see how their policies are perceived, whether it is good, bad or neutral. Those that want to attract and retain top female talent can use the feedback and InHerSight's collective data to develop a workplace that supports women.

Both women and men have already rated thousands of past or present employers, from government agencies to household names like Amazon, Google, Coca-Cola, Walmart and Microsoft.

As with any ratings-based platform, it will be open to abuse and dishonest feedback – either from people with a personal dislike for a company or from malicious competitors attempting to sabotage a rival company's reputation. However, this problem should be addressed when the volume of reviews is large enough that any clearly anomalous ratings will be obvious as outliers.

Founder Ursula Mead envisions the site as a TripAdvisor for women in the workplace and hopes that, by holding companies accountable for their support for women, it will encourage them to review and improve their treatment.

TAKEAWAYS

1 What other experiences could be reviewed in this way, using crowdsourced data to improve working practices?
2 How else could employees find out about an employer before starting?
3 How could you make your workplace more equal and transparent?

INNOVATION DATA

Website: www.inhersight.com
Contact: support@inhersight.com
Innovation name: InHerSight
Country: United States
Industries: Non-profit & social cause / Workspace

52

FREE ENERGY AUDITS FOR SMALL BUSINESSES FROM COMPETING LOCAL STUDENTS

The Green Impact Campaign, based in Washington, DC, has launched a state-wide energy-saving audit competition – Power to Save.

Students often boast a perfect mix of enthusiasm, ambition and free time, and we have seen many initiatives aiming to give them the skills, tools and opportunities they need to put these qualities to positive use. One such initiative is the Green Impact Campaign, a non-profit organization based in Washington, DC, which trains local students to conduct free energy audits for businesses in their area. GIC launched the Power to Save competition, which saw teams of students from five universities in the capital competing to see who could help the most local small businesses save on energy.

The assessment competition was a month-long community initiative, run in association with Think Local First and Nextility. Students were trained to use GIC's mobile platform – the Green Energy Management System. The cloud-based tool enabled them to conduct free 30-minute energy audits and create customized, actionable plans for participating businesses, informing them where and how they could make savings and improve their carbon footprint. GIC have found that the average small business can make 15–20 per cent energy savings through low-cost energy-efficiency upgrades – saving themselves money and creating a greener, more sustainable business.

Student volunteers from four Washington, DC-based universities (the American University, the Catholic University of America, the George Washington University and Georgetown University) competed against one another to see who could complete the most energy assessments for local DC businesses. In Washington,

46 businesses participated, including restaurants, churches and fashion stores. Through Power to Save assessments, businesses identified 635,000 kWh of energy savings, $125,000 in energy cost savings and 268,000 gallons of water savings.

Restaurants and food service businesses accounted for 60 per cent of the participating businesses. The average energy efficiency savings identified per business was 30 per cent, or $2,655 per year. The top three identified recommendations for improving energy efficiency for participating businesses were:

- to install occupancy sensors in common areas (85 per cent of businesses were recommended this action)
- to purchase Energy Star certified appliances such as refrigerators (77 per cent of businesses were recommended this)
- to install LED exit signs (77 per cent of businesses were recommended this).

The American University won the first prize, completing 20 assessments. George Washington, the Catholic University of America and Georgetown University followed, conducting ten, nine and seven assessments respectively.

All participating students gained invaluable professional experience. Winners and runners-up teams received small cash prizes and the most impressive individual students were offered the opportunity to interview for one of two paid internships at the following energy and sustainability firms in Washington, DC: AtSite, Nextility, the Environmental Defense Fund, the Environmental Defense Fund – Defend Our Future, Citizen Energy, Lumen and Union Kitchen.

In the months following the assessment, the Green Impact Campaign worked with the participating businesses to further understand their assessment results and work with the Nextility and the DC Sustainable Energy Utility (DCSEU) to further implement recommendations. Nextility helped businesses secure lower energy supply rates and green energy through the utility. Nextility also provided solar assessments for qualifying buildings. DCSEU assisted businesses to implement energy-efficiency upgrade plans through a combination of rebates and direct installations.

This is an excellent example of taking advantage of a pool of talent in the form of students and creating a mutually beneficial outcome for them and the local businesses that saved money and became more environmentally sound.

TAKEAWAYS

1 Are there other skills that students could be taught to improve their local area?
2 Could your business become more efficient by quickly assessing its energy usage?
3 How else could students be utilized and given a reward that would help their career and give businesses access to their talents?

INNOVATION DATA

Website: www.greenimpactcampaign.org
Contact: info@greenimpactcampaign.org
Company name: Green Impact Campaign
Innovation name: Power to Save competition
Country: United States
Industries: Education / Nature & sustainability

53

A VIRTUAL-REALITY PLATFORM FOR NERVOUS PUBLIC SPEAKERS

VirtualSpeech can help nervous speakers gain confidence, by enabling them to practise in front of a virtual crowd using Google Cardboard.

Public speaking can be very nerve-racking, especially for those who have had little practice at it. VirtualSpeech is a VR platform that will help inexperienced speakers gain confidence by enabling them to practise in front of a virtual crowd using Google Cardboard.

To begin, users download the app and upload their slides and notes for their upcoming project. Then they choose a training scenario — such as a 15-person office or a 400-person conference. Next, they put on their Google Cardboard headset, which immerses them in a realistic 3D environment. The user can then practise their speech or presentation to an animated audience, input by the developers using a green screen and real people portraying a range of behaviours and reactions. They can even set varying levels of sound and visual distractions, and train themselves to be accustomed to whatever situation.

Currently available on Android, iOS and Gear VR, VirtualSpeech immerses the user in 360-degree sound using the latest Oculus audio

SDK, to provide as realistic an experience as possible. Alongside small and large presentation scenarios in offices or conference rooms, the app offers other scenarios. Users can practise a wedding speech in a specially tailored room, or enter a job interview room. This room gives the user the chance to practise for an interview in front of a small panel of people. Users select the job sector or company they are hoping to apply for, then cycle through question specifically designed for those scenarios. The platform currently provides 40 Google interview questions, 40 for Goldman Sachs, 20 for McKinsey and 20 for Tesla Motors. The developers expect to expand this to other companies (including Apple, Microsoft and Deloitte) and increase their database of questions.

The start-up outlines why its method of public speaking practice is more effective than methods currently available. For instance, they suggest that while practising in a full-length mirror will give you a good view of your body position, actually making a presentation in front of a mirror demands that you focus on two separate activities – the presentation and you watching yourself.

The VR practice experience is also more effective than just rehearsing in front of a friend or colleague. It can be difficult to find someone with enough time and patience to listen and give feed-back. It also does not give a lifelike replication of the experience of performing to a big conference room and the fear that comes from speaking to hundreds of people at large events.

VirtualSpeech, founded in early 2015, is located in Leamington Spa, England. Alongside the Public Speaking VR app, the company is also developing a Language VR, which they hope will be a more immersive way to learn languages within realistic environments. The language app is divided into several different learning areas, including sentence building, listening to audiobooks and learning vocabulary. There are sections on culture, where users can explore England, role-play scenarios, and an awards and statistics section so that a user can keep track of their progress.

We have already seen the potential for VR to be used by surgeons to help them prepare for surgery, in the form of **EchoPixel**, which uses information from medical imaging to produce 3D virtual reality organs. VR could potentially change the way we rehearse, practise and train in a huge variety of industries.

TAKEAWAYS

1 Could other stressful situations, such as other types of interview, make use of VR in a similar way?
2 What high-risk or technical procedures could be practised in VR before going on to the real thing?
3 As well as a corporate or wedding environment, in what other environments could facing down a crowd be useful? Music performance? Politics? Education?

INNOVATION DATA

Website: www.virtualspeech.co.uk
Contact: www.virtualspeech.co.uk/contact
Innovation name: VirtualSpeech
Country: United Kingdom
Industries: Gamification & gaming / Workspace

54

TRAINING TATTOO ARTISTS TO SPOT SKIN CANCER

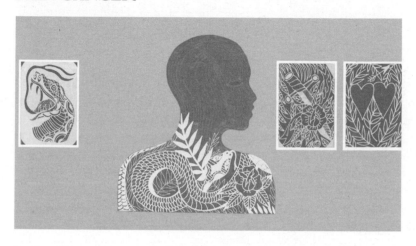

In Brazil, a project called Tatuador Consciente has been teaching tattoo artists how to detect signs of melanoma and other skin cancers while they're inking.

Brazil is famed for its beaches, but days spent soaking up the sun's rays can carry serious risks for Brazilian beachgoers if they don't use the necessary protection. There are 140,000 new cases of skin cancer in Brazil every year, and it's the most common cancer for the country – more than breast and prostate cancer combined. What's more, young people in particular believe that skin cancer checks are more for the elderly. In order to get through to the youthful demographic, a project called Tatuador Consciente (which translates as Conscious Tattoo) has taught tattoo artists how to detect signs of melanoma and other skin cancers while they're at work.

Initiated by Ogilvy Brasil in 2014 for 'The Sunscreen Brand for the Youth' Sol de Janeiro, the project initially trained up 200 certified tattoo artists from across Brazil with help from the A C Camargo Cancer Center. The students were taught how to identify marks on the skin that can be signs of the presence of skin cancer or of potential risk from harmful UV rays. One customer, Hanna Martins, said, 'It was my tattoo artist who pointed out that a mole I had appeared irregular. We later discovered that it was a mole that could turn into skin cancer.'

The idea was that the tattooists, while inking their customer, would also be able to give them a quick check that could help them catch cancer early – the kind of check that would usually require a trip to a specialist dermatologist. The initiative was also available online, where over 250 further artists completed their diploma at no cost, and the website enabled young people to find a qualified tattoo artist near them.

As a result of the project, some customers were advised against getting tattoos over specific moles which needed to be left exposed for monitoring, or were encouraged to take extra care if they had fair skin. Some customers were even made aware of early signs of skin cancer thanks to the course. With 450 trained tattoo artists seeing an average of six clients a day, there were approximately 18,900 people being checked for cancer every week as a result of the initiative.

Of course, Tatuador Consciente is not the first innovation to use tattooing to help cancer patients, and we've already seen the P.INK campaign offer women with breast cancer scars some creative ink ideas to cover them up.

Unfortunately, the Tatuador Consciente website has now been taken down, and this was always designed as an awareness campaign rather than a long-term initiative. But there's plenty of scope for this idea, and ideas like it, to be established on a more permanent basis.

TAKEAWAYS

1 What other jobs would be well suited to incorporate additional health-care services?
2 How else could tattoo artists broaden their skill sets to incorporate new services into their offerings?
3 What other professions would be well suited to medical training to encourage young people to engage with serious health issues, as an alternative to traditional authority figures?

INNOVATION DATA

Company name: Sol de Janeiro
Contact: www.ogilvy.com.br/#!/contato
Innovation name: Tatuador Consciente
Country: Brazil
Industries: Beauty & cosmetics / Education / Health & wellbeing / Non-profit & social cause

55

APARTMENT PODS THAT CAN MOVE BETWEEN CITIES

Kasita is creating movable, smart homes that can be easily inserted into desirable urban neighbourhoods.

As rents increase with a neighbourhood's desirability, the metropolitan lifestyle is becoming less and less accessible to millennials. But Kasita could pave a way for the democratization of urban living, with its modern, stackable, movable apartments, which are affordable but comfortable alternatives to conventional luxury apartments.

Kasita is creating simple apartment block 'scaffold shells', which are easy to build on small lots of urban space generally classified as not developable. Essentially a 20-square-metre (208-sq.-ft) box of glass and steel, each apartment can literally be picked up and moved by a truck whenever required. Users can even do this by requesting a move through the companion app, without dealing with the usual moving stress.

Though compact, the apartments are comfortable, with smart tech throughout that will control air conditioning, music and bring out the foldaway bed, all by voice recognition. A unique tiling system allows users to customize walls towards their personal storage needs.

At the South by Southwest conference in March 2016, the company unveiled its first dwelling: the 30-square-metre (319-sq.-ft) Model One house. The mobile structure is a rectilinear pod clad in metal and glass, with one side featuring a cantilevered glazed box. It slots horizontally into an engineered steel frame, or 'rack', which can include many units stacked high and wide. Other tech features include a smart thermostat by Nest and a voice-controlled Echo speaker by Amazon. The design also includes a wireless LED lighting system and electro-chromic windows that automatically turn from opaque to transparent, depending on the outdoor lighting conditions. The open-plan interior has ceilings 3 metres (10 ft) high and the kitchen offers all standard appliances such as dishwasher and cooker, and the sleeping area is fitted with a queen-sized mattress.

Austin, Texas received the first Kasita homes in 2016, and users will soon have a host of other cities across the United States and beyond to pitch up whenever they feel like a change of location. Priced at around $300 per month, Kasita are redefining what a home can be for an emerging consumer base that prefers location over large, settled family homes.

The company was founded by Jeff Wilson, who began his career at the height of the Internet boom in the late 1990s. After three years working in the high-pressure environment of Silicon Valley, he began to feel oppressed by its lack of real innovation. Wilson retreated from the corporate world and began down a more entrepreneurial route. After earning a PhD and becoming a professor, Wilson became interested in minimalism. He sold most of his possessions cheaply and spent his summer breaks travelling abroad with nothing much more than the clothes on his back. After moving to Austin, Texas, his love for minimalist living culminated in an educational and social experiment where he lived in a used 3-square-metre (33-sq.-ft) dumpster for an entire year.

This style of living led Wilson to reimagine what a comfortable home could be – especially in a growing city in need of affordable, urban housing. He took all the best elements of living in a small and compact way – more from less, beautiful design, and smart technology – and conceptualized the Kasita home.

The company hopes to attract developers who will purchase multiple units and stack them up to ten storeys high. With the right investment and compliance with town-planning laws, this model could completely revolutionize cheap urban living.

TAKEAWAYS

1 Could pop-up restaurants take a similar approach?
2 Would it be possible to deploy these homes in your city?
3 Could your company save money by using a mobile, compact unit as its primary headquarters?

INNOVATION DATA

Website: www.kasita.com
Contact: hello@kasita.com
Company name: Kasita
Innovation name: Kasita movable smart homes
Country: United States
Industries: Design / Home & garden / Smart cities

56

FREE CO-WORKING SPACE IN EXCHANGE FOR ONLINE CONTENT

Berlin's Blogfabrik is a co-working space and publication where freelancers can work rent-free in exchange for monthly content contributions.

Two hugely valuable commodities in the modern working world are great content and affordable working spaces. Marrying the two is Blogfabrik, a co-working space and publication in Berlin that invites freelancers to work on their personal projects there rent-free, in exchange for monthly contributions to the blog.

Blogfabrik, which translates as Blog Factory, has been operating since 2015. It is a spacious co-working environment of 555 square metres (6,000 sq. ft), complete with a photography studio, event space and meeting rooms. It currently houses 30 freelancers, who contribute two pieces of content each month to the company's online magazine *DailyBreadMag*, which in turn promotes the working space and the events hosted there. Freelancers pitch content ideas to creative director Claudio Rimmele and are also required to organize one event per year and promote the magazine and its home using their social media channels. Rimmele was part of the founding team of I Heart Berlin, one of Berlin's most popular culture blogs.

With its 30 desks, conference room, video-editing technology, photo studio, lounge and kitchen,

---

Blogfabrik is a fully equipped space designed to be ideal for communication and collaboration.

Content creators in this light, airy industrial space in the heart of Kreuzberg describe the atmosphere as cosmopolitan and say that it encourages creativity, innovation and professional development.

The space is dotted with quirky details to give inspiration and a creative, unique feel. Walls are covered with chalkboards and there are stacks of vintage suitcases in the foyer.

With workshops, readings and networking events that are all open to the public, Blogfabrik doesn't limit its use to content creators, but strives to be a place all Berliners attend, learn from and be inspired by. The online magazine sees itself as a think tank that primarily reflects the lives of the Blogfabrik freelancers, while also addressing topics like digital culture, accessibility, feminism and terrorism. The target readership consists of 18–35-year-old digital natives as well as 'open-minded people from other fields'.

Apart from their work for *DailyBreadMag*, freelancers have the opportunity to work with Blogfabrik's affiliated agency, Kiosk, for which they're paid separately. Because of the intrigue created by this unique system, Kiosk has been able to bring in extra work from companies attracted to the idea of having a pool of talent comprising an interesting and diverse group of talented individuals working under one roof.

Blogfabrik also aims to offer another way of contributing, with 'flex' desks. These offer a part-time co-working option that can be booked in exchange for one contribution to DailyBreadMag per month. And while the magazine had been published primarily in German, the site began running articles in English in 2016.

While it may seem like a start-up-based environment, Blogfabrik is not in fact an independent company. The concept was developed and is funded by Melo, a media and logistics company based in Munich, which specializes in distributing print and digital press. Melo originally wanted to invest in Blogfabrik to learn more about content creation and disruptive publishing models that could be tested and implemented in Germany. Journalism has suffered endlessly in the digital age, pay is low and good work is scarce. Blogfabrik is a response to the need for journalists and media organizations to rethink their approach, to incorporate all the changes this new world has brought.

TAKEAWAYS

1 What other valuable skills could be exchanged for rent in co-working spaces?
2 What other disruptive structures could help journalism adapt to the digital age?
3 Could your company benefit from offering co-working space for freelancers?

INNOVATION DATA

Website: www.blogfabrik.de
Contact: kontakt@blogfabrik.de
Innovation name: Blogfabrik
Country: Germany
Industries: Entertainment & culture / Home & garden / Marketing & advertising / Workspace

57

OPENING UP HOMES AS COMMUNAL OFFICE SPACES

Hoffice is a crowdsourced network of free working space, set up in the homes of its users.

As cloud computing becomes more mainstream, it's now possible for a large portion of the population to work from home, either as freelancers, remote employees or self-employed citizens. But working alone can be, at best, a little lonely and, at worst, completely unstimulating. Endless distractions and a lack of interaction can make even the most disciplined worker unproductive.

Swedish platform Hoffice is hoping to offer a solution by crowdsourcing a network of free working spaces in the homes of its users – effectively bringing the sharing economy to office space. Hoffice worker Mårten Pella says, 'Often when I am alone, I can work focused for a couple of hours but then [I am] very easily distracted. The help of others makes me so much more disciplined.'

Users begin by signing up to the Hoffice community via Facebook, which links them with other home workers in their area.

They can then either choose to host a Hoffice event in their own home or attend a pre-existing one. The idea is to provide a loosely structured workday, in a sociable working environment that encourages productivity without ignoring other human needs. Members are encouraged to start the day with meditation or relaxation exercises, for example. Work time is split up into 45-minute segments with 15-minute breaks – for exercise, conversation or games – in between.

At every event, a facilitator is in charge of keeping the structure, but members are welcome to ignore it and work at their own pace.

Workspaces are always free to use but members may be asked to contribute towards costs. Hoffice is a growing network with most groups so far operating in Scandinavia. Potential members from unserved areas are encouraged to start their own group and invite local people to join.

Outside Scandinavia, the Hoffice concept has at times proved problematic. No background checks are carried out on new Hoffice members – be they hosts or attendees – which has led to security concerns in certain areas. In India, in particular, hosts feared they could potentially be robbed during a meet-up. In Stockholm, these fears are simply less prevalent.

Spacehop and OfficeRiders are two other notable players in this area, enabling members to rent office space in a host's property. Founded in England and France respectively, both give insurance policies that cover theft and damages for hosts. But, to an extent, offering insurance policies feels at odds with Hoffice's founding principles of gift giving, community and trust.

In an interview with the Swedish reporter and lecturer Agneta Lagercrantz, Hoffice founder Christofer Gradin Franzen explains that the movement was inspired by Gandhi's social philosophy of the Sarvodaya movement, which is based on Buddhist principles: 'It is Sri Lanka's largest people's movement and has spread to 15,000 villages. Its base lies in voluntary work called Shramadana ("to donate effort"), or gift economy, where the volunteers help people to help themselves and then each other to, in the first place, get food, drink and shelter. Thereafter, they help each other in improving the village's communications, environment and schools and creating possibilities to provide cultural/intellectual stimulation.' There are obvious similarities here with the Dugnad movement (see the chapter on the sharing economy).

With hubs now available across the world, Hoffice is beginning to gain traction. The São Paolo Facebook group has over 1,890 members, while the original Stockholm Facebook group has over 1,850 members. Frankfurt's group is smaller, with just over 80 members, and it's clear that Hoffice's success is heavily influenced by the different working cultures of these cities. In Sweden, workplaces tend to operate under a low-level hierarchy, and there is a large amount of trust from managers with respect to flexible working, making it an ideal birthplace for the Hoffice movement.

TAKEAWAYS

1 How else could people's homes be used as a shared facility?
2 Where would you expect Hoffice to succeed, and what cultural changes would be required elsewhere to help it realize the same level of success?
3 How else could remote workers be brought together during the working day to optimize their productivity and help combat any feelings of isolation?

INNOVATION DATA

Website: www.hoffice.nu/en
Contact: info@hoffice.nu
Innovation name: Hoffice
Country: Sweden
Industries: Non-profit & social cause / Workspace

58

POSTAL WORKERS WHO ALSO MOW THE LAWN

Throughout the summer, employees of Finland's postal service Posti will offer a weekly lawn-mowing service during their regular delivery rounds.

In face of the decline of physical post, Finland's mail service Posti is expanding its services to include lawn mowing – the latest example of an unusual but convenient job overlap. Throughout the summer, Posti's employees offer a lawn-mowing service on Tuesdays, since this is the least demanding day of the week in terms of deliveries. Customers can sign up for a 30- or 60-minute session online from 65 euros per month, and they must provide their own lawnmower. The postal workers fulfil the service while making their regular delivery rounds, creating an efficient workday around the neighbourhood.

The idea for the lawn-mowing service came from mail delivery employees themselves, who recognized lawn mowing as a tedious job that many customers would jump at the chance to avoid doing.

As well as being a chore that many able people would like to avoid, it can be one which is too physically demanding for many elderly or less able people to carry out on their own. Postal workers realized that, with their declining business and the quieter Tuesdays, they could helpfully and efficiently perform this basic task.

Orders for lawn-mowing services will be taken into account in the planning of mail delivery routes. In the event of rain on the day of intended service delivery, the lawn will be mowed at another time. The lawn-mowing service is tax-deductible for domestic costs.

The work of mail delivery employees in Finland has become increasingly diverse. Posti currently delivers some two million meals to Finnish homes annually. As part of the development of new home services, Posti is also partnering with the South Karelia Social and Health Care District Eksote in the provision of home care and services for people with disabilities by assisting customers with eating and daily chores. Posti is also partnering with Securitas to perform security services in a pilot being conducted in the Finnish towns of Muhos and Ylivieska.

The company has acquired home care company HR Hoiva, which produces home care and personal assistance services for municipalities, joint municipal authorities and private customers. HR Hoiva's net sales in 2016 were approximately 2.5 million euros and the company will continue its operations as a subsidiary of Posti. HR Hoiva will provide Posti with care professionals and the capability to address customers' home-care needs. HR Hoiva currently produces services in approximately 30 localities. HR Hoiva is part of the HR Yhtiöt Group. Ilpo Marttila, CEO of HR Yhtiöt, believes that Posti will help to deliver essential services to municipal customers as well as improving the cost-effectiveness of the municipalities involved.

We have seen other examples of dual job efficiency, with **tattoo artists** trained to spot skin cancer as seen earlier in this chapter, and cashiers in Dutch supermarkets keeping an eye out for signs of loneliness or neglect in older customers as part of the Super Care initiative.

TAKEAWAYS

1 What other potential job overlaps could help those in need?
2 What other public services have experienced a decline and could be diversified?
3 How could companies change the services they provide according to the seasons?

INNOVATION DATA

Website: www.posti.com
Contact: www.posti.com/contactus
Company name: Posti
Innovation name: Posti lawnmowers
Country: Finland
Industry: Home & garden

59

USING BIG DATA TO PREDICT COURT DECISIONS

Predictice is an app that provides lawyers with statistics and data on the likely outcome of commercial and social disputes, based on previous court decisions.

More and more sectors are using the power of predictive technologies to be able to preemptively adjust their processes and get a better idea of the outcomes they are likely to achieve Offering a similar application of big data to the legal services industry is Predictice, a French start-up that uses machine-learning techniques for case law, allowing it to extract a statistical analysis of the outcome of litigation.

The world's largest law firm, Dentons, has partnered with the start-up to develop software that helps to predict the likely course, cost, length and outcome of litigation based on historical court decisions.

It allows advocates to know in advance the probable outcomes and make strategic adjustments accordingly. This can aid decision making such as prioritizing certain arguments or adjusting the compensation claimed.

Predictice, which specializes in data analytics and predicting court decisions, is leveraging the legal knowledge of lawyers in Dentons' Paris office, who are providing user feedback to refine the platform. The platform provides legal professionals with the statistical probability of success of a case they are pleading. It allows lawyers to optimize their strategy, by identifying and prioritizing the key points that will help to positively influence the resolution of a dispute in their favour, based on the track record of a particular legal mechanism. Predictice also delivers an estimate of benefits that were achieved through previously judged, similar lawsuits, and a map of the most favourable judgments, depending on the type of problem. This could help lawyers adjust their pricing according to these statistics.

This unique and flexible innovation was conceived as a mutually beneficial pilot project between the law firm and the Paris tech start-up, and is agreed on a non-exclusive basis. Predictice benefits by receiving first-hand feedback from the legal professionals trialling the system, while Dentons' lawyers gain direct experience in legal innovation and also have their say in influencing how the tool develops.

Marie Bernard, Dentons' director of innovation, said the system allowed the lawyer to price according to risk, and would benefit clients and law firms alike: 'Predictability is one of the many fields we are committed to exploring. Predictice suggested a sensible approach and our feedback so far is really positive. It's a good match, which enables us to understand predictive technology better and to consider our adoption options early on.'

Across a huge range of different fields, whether it is business, engineering, health care or education, a common pattern we are seeing is collaboration with tech start-ups. With their technological expertise and fresh perspectives, they are able to assess a system or model and disruptively come in and solve chronic problems these antiquated systems and models face.

Legal tech and law firms must collaborate to develop the next innovation in legal practice. In the United States, the start-up Legalist uses an algorithm to vet commercial lawsuits, with a view to providing finance to those with potential for success.

TAKEAWAYS

1 Will this technology be adopted in other countries?
2 What other industries could use this predictive tech? Finance? Entertainment?
3 Could your company collaborate with a tech start-up to address chronic problems?

INNOVATION DATA

Website: www.dentons.com
Contact: www.dentons.com/en/whats-different-about-dentons/
contact-us
Company name: Dentons
Innovation name: Predictice
Country: France
Industry: Government & legal

60

A SMART EMPLOYEE BADGE TO IMPROVE STAFF EFFICIENCY

Humanyze is a smart employee badge using wearable sensors and data to help businesses improve the productivity of their staff.

Humanyze is a tracking tool in the form a smart employee badge that combines a microphone, an accelerometer and other sensors. It collects massive amounts of behavioural data from employees, which businesses can use to analyse and improve the productivity of their workforce.

Each badge is worn by an individual employee and collects over 40 pieces of data daily – including how much they move around, the tone of their voice and if they leaned in when speaking to co-workers. This data is uploaded to the cloud, where it can be fed into other business metrics via a dashboard, enabling companies to gain insight into how behaviour affects overall company performance. The company can then begin to make adjustments to its employee relations and see how effective their changes are through A/B testing*.

The start-up behind the big data wearable – Humanyze – was launched from the MIT Media Lab. It has already worked in a partnership with a number of organizations, including the Bank of America, where the system was tested out on some of its 10,000 employees, with interesting results. For example, having noticed that employees interact most with one other during the overlap of their lunch breaks, the company experimented with giving one set of employees a group lunch while keeping another on the staggered schedule. They were able to ascertain that the group lunch had an

A/B testing
A controlled experiment using two variables, A and B.

overwhelmingly positive effect on the employees' performance: it reduced stress – measured by tone of voice – by 19 per cent and it significantly increased staff efficiency, with call completion time rising by 23 per cent.

All data is privacy protected and participating companies are not able to access an individual's data. Furthermore, Humanyze insist on an opt-in agreement, meaning that businesses cannot use the system without their staff signing up.

While the technology may appear intrusive, there is already a precedent set for such systems in the sporting world. Today, a number of professional sports clubs require their athletes to wear a GPS and/or heart-rate monitor. In the United Kingdom, Leicester City Football Club's players wear Catapult Sport's OptimEye S5 device, which can collect 800–900 data points per second relating to direction, acceleration, position and the impact of collisions. Heart-rate monitors enable coaches to ensure that athletes are training to their maximum without risking over-exertion and injury.

In the workplace, systems such as Humanyze could be used in very similar ways to ensure staff wellbeing. Managers could be given a warning if their staff's heart rate was too high for too long – indicating a prolonged period of stress. Actions could then be taken to ensure that staff don't burn out.

Inevitably, Humanyze will encounter resistance from staff who feel that the technology is overly invasive, but with benefits available to both employers *and* employees, it may not be long before systems such as this gradually start to become more commonplace.

TAKEAWAYS

1 What other businesses could make use of big data in this way?
2 How could Humanyze market their product to employees to address concerns over privacy?
3 What experiments could you run to improve productivity if you had Humanyze in your office?

INNOVATION DATA

Website: www.humanyze.com
Contact: info@humanyze.com
Innovation name: Humanyze
Country: United States
Industries: Fashion & wearable tech / Workspace

SUMMARY

Unlike previous revolutions in the labour market, strong arguments suggest that this current sweep of changes is fundamentally different. When workers lost their jobs to the mass mechanization of the Industrial Revolution, many sought out new professions that machines were ill suited for. Today, as AI encroaches further into traditionally white-collar professions, there may be little room for humans to 'move up the food chain' and find alternative sources of employment. The outcome is likely to be either a utopia – in which the jobless are supported by alternative means such as universal basic income and invest their new-found free time in creative pursuits – or a dystopia – in which a few super-rich tech giants look down on a struggling and impoverished jobless populace from silicon towers.

Regardless of the outcome, flexibility will be the governing force for the journey. If automation and ever-improving AI are going to lead to further job cuts over the coming years, job roles will need to become increasingly diverse in often surprising and creative ways. For example, in addition to melanoma-spotting tattoo artists and a lawn-mowing postal service, it's now a legal requirement for beauty stylists in Illinois to be trained to recognize signs of domestic abuse among their clientele.

Employees will increasingly find themselves with ever more diverse job descriptions, which most people will see as a very good thing. Few will see learning new skills and having a more varied working day as anything other than an exciting opportunity, and rightly so. For their part, employers will need to be flexible around a mobile workforce that demands increased transparency and a sense of purpose beyond the bottom line from its employers. For employers, too, this should be seen as nothing but an opportunity – a chance to position the company as more than a company and transition into becoming a genuine force for good.

WORKPLACE TAKEAWAYS

1 **Make time to think creatively.** There's a natural temptation for employers to focus on reducing costs by automating tasks. But equal priority should be given to considering how saved time can be reinvested. Think creatively about what other tasks certain individuals or positions within an organization would be well equipped to take on. Staff are usually more than willing to learn new skills.

2 **Put purpose at the heart of your organization and culture.** Corporate social responsibility (CSR) programmes are to be applauded, but for many employees this won't cut it anymore. CSR should be embedded into a company's very existence, reflected in everything from who the company works with, who provides its webservers and what reward schemes it offers employees. Do not underestimate the increasing importance of a culture of innovation and transparency. Great brands of the future will have these core precepts as their foundations.

3 **Always be flexible; it is a two-way street.** Just as staff should be flexible in embracing more diverse roles, so, too, should employers. Infrastructures should be built to accommodate an increasingly mobile and remote workforce, using new technologies to ensure that everyone remains connected. The office will increasingly become a central 'hub' to check into depending on project requirements, rather than a required workplace for a daily nine to five. Embracing this can be tricky at first, but employees will appreciate the flexibility and the opportunity to work at a time and in an in environment where they can be most productive. Employers will also reap the

benefits when they next recruit new staff, with the ability to cast the net over a much wider geographical area in search of the best talent.

4 **Keep it human.** Remember that technology is primarily an enabler, a means rather than an end. As the workforce of the future evolves, the role of the human being will evolve with it. It is tempting to focus solely on robots, AI and other tech innovation but the wisest will consider and come to understand the best way to integrate the tech with the human.

COMMUNICATION

Technological innovation has fundamentally changed the way we interact with others. Every day, approximately 205 billion emails are sent and hundreds of millions of hours of YouTube videos are watched, while communication platforms such as Slack continue to change the way we work. It's now hard to call to mind a time before email and mobile phones, and how different the pace and style of communication was. Even as recently as the 1990s the pager was considered the height of technological sophistication – a device that seems impossibly basic by today's standards — although we can be grateful for model names such as the 'Pageboy II' and the 'Scriptor Jazz Flex'.

Smart devices, social robots and us

Over the years at Springwise, we have seen innovations improving methods of communication in a number of incredibly worthwhile ways. Many of the most inspiring ideas have not only improved communication between individuals but also opened up conversations that were simply impossible before. For example, stroke and autism are two life-changing diagnoses that have the potential to leave sufferers feeling disconnected from the world. But the mobile app **I.am.here** is now helping some of the millions of people paralysed each year by a stroke close that divide. Employing a brain computer Interface, the app translates emotional data into language, enabling family, friends and carers gain a greater insight into the patient's state of mind. For those diagnosed with autism, the wearable **Autism Glass** uses Google Glass and machine learning to read emotions and help the wearer practise their understanding of social cues.

Health care is also an area where we're seeing another communication innovation – telepresence – used to great effect. Telepresence is a broad term to describe any technology that creates the illusion or effect of someone being in a physical location they are remote from. In the United States, for example, HealthSpot stations use a video conferencing set-up to provide remote health-care check-ups and e-prescriptions, while in **Ghana** teachers in Accra use a similar set-up to broadcast daily lessons to underserved schools around the country. And, as we've seen with **360i'S** first 'robot internship', the evolution of this technology could have an impact in the workplace beyond common video conferencing set-ups. The addition of a robotic 'body' for a remote worker to 'inhabit' opens up a wealth of new possibilities, enabling interactions with co-workers and equipment in the physical environment. We have even seen the same set-up used to enable disabled viewers to tour museums and galleries remotely. It is not appropriate for every scenario, but it has great potential to enhance collaboration and facilitate remote attendance.

The Internet of Things

However, even a cursory glance at communication innovation in the present day reveals a much more fundamental movement. One of the biggest technological developments of the last few years has been the advent of the Internet of Things (IoT), which has altered how we interact with the everyday objects around us. Communication in the twenty-first century is as much about human-to-object relationships and object-to-object relationships as it is about human-to-human relationships.

The Internet of Things is a convergence of information and operational technologies that allows everyday physical objects to send and receive data, and there are notable examples in both the Retail and Smart cities chapters of this book. In the home, it means that lighting, for example, can be set to react to the weather or even in response to a phone call. Objects will be able to perform actions and make 'decisions' based on context, without human input.

The American IT research and advisory firm Gartner is predicting that the number of connected devices (excluding PCs, smartphones and tablets) could reach 26 billion as soon as 2020, which, along with their greater convenience, bring real risks. Everyday IoT items will be open to cyber attacks, as will any connected driverless cars, which is already having ramifications in insurance and how we legislate to tackle data anonymity and security. If TVs are listening to conversations, the data needs protecting.

But the benefits are too compelling to be ignored. **Jibo**, for example, which functions as a friendly interface for humans to interact with their IoT devices, can also act as a family cameraman or order food on its owner's behalf. Smart hearing aids by **Oticon Opn** allow wearers to set bespoke alerts and tasks that could range from turning on the coffee machine when the aids are activated to providing an in-ear alert when the doorbell rings. Birmingham City University's **connected clothing** project hints at a future where apparel becomes an integral part of the Internet of Things, perhaps presenting outfits based on downloadable colour combination presets, or in response to the weather. For now, the project is able to suggest infrequently worn items for donation.

As with every chapter in this book, the innovations presented here do not stand alone, and developments in communication will affect other industries in profound ways. Travel, for example, could become exclusively a pleasurable pursuit, with telepresence conferences becoming the norm in the interests of sustainability. As you read through the following ten innovations, it's worth considering what the wider implications could be in other sectors.

61

AI GLASSES THAT HELP CHILDREN WITH AUTISM READ FACIAL EXPRESSIONS

Autism Glass is a wearable, behavioural aid that uses machine learning and real-time social cues to help those with autism interact with others.

Autism affects more than one in 100 people and is a lifelong condition. In the United States more than a million children suffer from autism. In the United Kingdom the figure is 700,000. These children find it difficult to recognize emotions through facial expressions, making social interactions very challenging. While patients can gain an understanding through behavioural therapy, this can be both time-consuming and expensive. Autism Glass is a wearable aid from researchers at Stanford University that uses Google Glass, machine learning and real-time social cues to provide those on the autism spectrum with another option.

To use Autism Glass, patients put on the wearable glasses, which incorporate an outward-facing camera. Then, the system uses machine learning and artificial intelligence to understand the facial expressions of people the wearer encounters, and provides cues about their companion's emotions in real time. The system records the amount of eye contact that takes place, which can provide insights into the wearer's interactions. The glasses are connected to a smart-phone app so that the patient, their parents and medical professionals can monitor and understand their progress and even watch back their interactions.

The Autism Glass Project is an interdisciplinary effort bringing together some of Stanford's leading minds in psychiatry, behavioural science, human–computer interaction and AI. It is based out of the Wall Lab in the Systems Medicine division of the Stanford School of Medicine Pediatrics department and was founded by Stanford scholars and researchers Catalin Voss and Dr Nick Haber. Their mission is to use their expertise in computer science and machine learning for a cause close to both their hearts: improving the lives of people with autism and others who experience difficulty with social functioning and communication. With a donation of Google Glass units from Google, the founders have been able to make this project a reality.

Research is still ongoing after a successful 40-person pilot study, and the developers are currently seeking participants on the autism spectrum aged 6–16 for the second phase of their research. This entails a 100-person at-home study that will consist of 80 children with autism spectrum disorder and 20 children who are neurotypical. With these participants, they aim to study long-term behavioural progression over a four-month period. The study will allow families of children with autism to use the device at home, with scheduled, periodic in-lab visits.

Future work will allow researchers to improve the software and techniques – using a widening set of data. If the results are positive, the product could be commercially available within a few years. While Google Glass never really took off as a commercial enterprise for myriad reasons, this is a great example of how an existing technology can be repurposed for the clinical good.

This cutting-edge technology has the potential to change the lives of children with autism all over the world.

In the past, we have seen an app that gives users friendship advice by monitoring their heart rate: Pplkpr is an app synched to a wearable device, which monitors users' responses to their acquaintances and acts on their behalf. Smart wearable technology has a huge range of potential clinical applications and will continue to be at the forefront of communication innovation.

TAKEAWAYS

1 Are there other new technologies that could help people with autism better understand the world?
2 What other failed commercial enterprises could be repurposed to help those in need?
3 How could your company use machine learning and wearable tech to help with communication?

INNOVATION DATA

Website: www.autismglass.stanford.edu
Contact: autismglass@stanford.edu
Company name: Stanford University
Innovation name: Autism Glass
Country: United States
Industries: Education / Fashion & wearable tech /
                   Health & wellbeing

62

SMART HEARING AIDS USING IFTTT FOR PERSONALIZATION

The Oticon Opn is an Internet-connected hearing aid that works like stereo headphones with surround sound.

More than 35 million Americans and 11 million Britons suffer from some form of hearing loss. Innovations in hearing assistance range from real-time theatre captioning to hearing aids that double as fashion accessories. Now, through customization and connectivity, hearing device specialist Oticon's latest creation, the Oticon Opn, uses a microchip system to recreate realistic surround sound. The hearing aids are also Internet-enabled, allowing wearers to connect to the If This Then That (IFTTT) system for custom sound management.

The left and right devices communicate, providing wearers with accurate spatial awareness of where sound is coming from. Via Bluetooth, the hearing aids also act as stereo headphones. Wearers can answer phone calls, listen to the TV and radio, and chat via Internet applications. With IFTTT, users can set up bespoke alerts and tasks. These can range from an in-ear alert when the doorbell rings to linking a baby monitor to the system or turning on the coffee machine whenever the hearing aids are activated. They can also link to smoke detectors in case of an emergency. This means that a signal from a smoke alarm can be sent directly to the Opn instruments, letting the wearer know that the smoke alarm has been activated.

The core, everyday purpose of this hearing aid is to make it easier for wearers to handle noisy environments in which there are multiple speakers.

This is one of the key functions of the human ear and one that is most difficult to overcome during hearing loss. The smart hearing aids do this using machine learning to seek out sounds they recognize as voices, typically within certain frequencies, and by dulling all other background sounds. Inside each hearing aid a Velox sound processor powers the firm's proprietary BrainHearing technology. This alters only the parts of the signal that the individual ear doesn't hear well, boosts softer speech and voices, and removes feedback.

Each hearing aid can also be customized to the user's skin tone and fashion requirements, and the specific sound profile can be acutely tailored to address only the areas of hearing loss they suffer from. Child versions are also available, and the Oticon ON app lets users manage settings via their smartphones.

As well as simply assisting with day-to-day tasks, it has been proven that there are wider benefits from improving your hearing through hearing-aid technology. A new study shows there is a higher risk of accelerated cognitive decline due to withdrawal from social activities for individuals with hearing loss who do not actively use hearing aids. The study documented hearing loss and cognitive decline among a group of nearly 4,000 volunteers over a 25-year period.

According to research, by far the single most important thing we can do to maintain our brains as we age is to stay mentally engaged, through an active social life with friends, family and business associates. Healthy hearing is a key part of staying involved with people and the world around us. The study showed that people with hearing loss who used hearing aids and were socially active experienced cognitive decline at a rate similar to those without hearing loss.

By helping to restore communication abilities, at least partially, hearing aids may help improve mood, increase social interactions, and enable more participation in cognitively stimulating activities and thereby slow cognitive decline. With these benefits and the practical and safety implications, this smart, customizable technology is the future of hearing assistance.

TAKEAWAYS

1 How could specialist smart devices be adapted for more widespread use?
2 What other health-care-related technologies could benefit from being Internet-connected?
3 How else could chronic health problems like hearing loss be alleviated with smart wearable tech?

INNOVATION DATA

Website: www.oticon.com
Contact: peoplefirst@oticonusa.com
Company name: Oticon
Innovation name: Oticon Opn
Country: United States
Industries: Audio / Entertainment & culture / Health & wellbeing / Internet of Things

63

AN INTERACTIVE ENCYCLOPAEDIA OF THINGS USING OBJECT-RECOGNITION SOFTWARE

Sense is a cloud-based platform that looks to enable interactions with its crowdsourced 'encyclopaedia of objects'.

In 2011 the application IFTTT — If This Then That — seemed little more than an algorithm with vast potential. Since then, new cutting-edge devices have been powered by IFTTT, such as Smappee, which enables users to program limitless actions within their digital environment — with tangible, real-world results. Sense, developed by British Cambridge-based start-up Neurence, came on to our radar in early 2015, with the potential to become the next building block in the connection between real-world objects and online intelligence through highly advanced object-recognition software.

Sense is an exciting but unfinished platform — a growing cloud-based brain populated by the input of its users. In essence, it is a Wikipedia of objects — built from programmer and user-inputted image data.

Users can currently contribute to the library by uploading an image of any object they wish to add. They must then enter the name and brief description of the object, and add tags (such as 'book' or 'film').

Finally, there is the option to add suggested 'interactions' to the object. For example, if the object in question is a book, a suggested interaction could be a link to the book's page on Amazon. Or a DVD could link to the relevant IMDb page or Wikipedia entry. Anyone can create a new entry, and anyone can edit an entry.

Using this database of information alongside image-recognition technology, the platform then enables other users to identify and call up information on real-world objects – from books and buildings to pieces of food – by simply viewing it through their smart device's camera.

Sense will then present the user with any 'interactions' associated with the object. This could be simply informing a user about the history of their chosen object, or guiding them to the relevant e-commerce page where they could purchase it. A film poster could trigger the relevant video trailer or information on the next local screening.

Neurence's aim was to create the next generation of search engine – one that doesn't require reading and writing and that can be seamlessly incorporated into the consumer's life. For companies or programmers that incorporate the technology into their offerings, they are effectively able to 'outsource' all the heavy information processing to Sense's cloud, and gain access to its wide pool of knowledge.

In February 2015 the company received $4 million in funding from Cambridge-based VC vehicle Invoke Capital. But, following a successful launch, during which time Neurence was working alongside six device developers including Google and Samsung to experiment with Sense's potential uses, it would now appear that the library has unfortunately failed to gain the buzz and momentum such a crowdsourced project requires to truly take off. The death of Google Glass – a device for which Sense was perfectly suited – won't have helped.

However, this may not be the last attempt we see to create an encyclopaedia of things. Current iterations of artificial intelligence remain narrow by nature, finding the unstructured environment of our human world hard to comprehend. Until AI becomes more capable and general, there will probably be many more attempts to structure this world to make it fit for artificial comprehension. Such projects will necessarily be ambitious in scope but, if successful, would open up an almost limitless world of possibilities for interaction between the online and offline world.

TAKEAWAYS

1 What are the most intriguing potential uses for the platform?
2 How could contributors be encouraged to add images and data to the library?
3 If such a library were populated to a truly useful extent, how could the platform be used in relation to some of the other themes discussed in this book?

INNOVATION DATA

Website: www.neurence.com
Contact: info@neurence.com
Company name: Neurence
Innovation name: Sense
Country: United Kingdom
Industry: Education

64

CONNECTED CLOTHING THAT DONATES ITSELF IF NOT FREQUENTLY WORN

Birmingham City University researchers have created an Internet of Clothes where items will request donation if left unworn for long periods of time.

Retrofitting unconnected items is one useful method of reducing waste through the Internet of Things. Using radio frequency identification (RFID), washable, wearable tags now allow networks of clothes to communicate.

Created by researchers at Birmingham City University's Future Media team, the smart wardrobe system sends messages to clothing owners. The messages depend on the weather and how regularly each item is worn. If items of clothing are rarely worn, they will contact a local charity to ask to be donated. The charity will then send an envelope to the owner to make it easy to give the item away.

The research team wants to encourage more ethical consumption of fashion, possibly leading to a system where ownership is unnecessary. The project was shortlisted for a European Network for Innovations in Culture and Creativity award. Future developments include creating a virtual stylist to provide ideas for outfits and tagging items from point of sale.

As a society, we own four times as many clothes as we did 20 years ago, but regularly wear only about 20 per cent of them. The average American buys 64 items of clothing a year and UK shoppers buy 2.15 million tonnes of clothing and shoes annually. UK citizens have an estimated £30 billion worth of unused clothing sitting in their wardrobes.

Overconsumption of clothing is a problem for both the environment and exploitation of the people who produce them. Clothing production is highly damaging to the environment, from the petrochemicals used in synthetics to cotton growing, which uses more pesticides than any other crop. The processes of bleaching, dyeing and finishing add even more pollutants to the environment and use considerable energy resources. Figures show that clothing manufacturing is among the most exploitative industries in the world. Workers in clothing manufacture – 85 per cent of whom are women – are among the worst paid in the world.

Birmingham City University academics hope to develop their working prototype into a network of many open-source wardrobes – or an Internet of Clothes. Garments will compare and share their usage to others in the network with their own story about where, when and who wore them, as well as being able to offer individual items up to someone else.

Future innovations for the technology could also see the creation of a 'style matcher', which will encourage greater usage of clothing by making wardrobe combinations easier to find. Furthermore, Birmingham University's academics would like to see garments tagged at the point of retail, meaning that clothing labels could also let buyers know details such as the exact origin of the item, who made it and how much the worker was paid to make it.

Mark Brill, Senior Lecturer in Future Media at Birmingham City University, is behind the project. He suggests that, as well as ensuring that unused clothes go to charity, the Internet of Clothes could also automate the options for selling our own clothes, meaning that underused items are automatically posted to selling sites like eBay, ASOS Marketplace or Depop.

The project was made possible by Maker Monday, an open innovation project from Birmingham City University that brings artists and technologists together to create new concepts. This collaboration could spark innovations in a huge range of disciplines and help us to be more sustainable and ethical consumers.

TAKEAWAYS

1 Where else could new networks provide sustainable solutions?
2 What other used items could you retrofit with smart technology?
3 How else could we ensure that our underused items are not left to go to waste?

INNOVATION DATA

Website: www.bcu.ac.uk/internet-of-clothes
Contact: enquiry@filmfutures.me
Company name: Birmingham City University
Innovation name: Connected clothing
Country: United Kingdom
Industries: Access exclusive / Fashion & wearable tech / Internet of Things / Nature & sustainability / Non-profit & social cause / Retail & e-commerce

65

REMOTE PATIENT–DOCTOR RELATIONSHIPS USING TELEPRESENCE ROBOTS

InTouch Health's RP-VITA telepresence robot enables doctors to monitor and attend to patients in a different part of the hospital.

Connecting patients with doctors virtually is territory that start-ups such as Hello Health and Carena have already stepped into through video calling. Now, InTouch Health is taking that concept back into the hospital with its RP-VITA (Remote Presence Virtual and Independent Telemedicine Assistant) telepresence robot, enabling doctors to monitor and attend to patients elsewhere in the building.

The robot – made with InTouch's AVA telepresence broadcast tech and Massachusetts-based iRobot's autonomous navigation and mobility technology – includes a camera and a screen, allowing for two-way interaction between patients and doctors. Controlled through a specially created iPad app, the RP-VITA robot can be directed by a medical practitioner to specific points in the hospital, using state-of-the-art navigation technology to move around buildings while avoiding anyone around it. This makes it viable for use on busy hospital floors, and InTouch Health has received clearance from the Food and Drug Administration to bring the device into hospitals.

Using the system, doctors can remotely check up on patients to see how they are doing and provide assistance if necessary.

The robot is well suited for a range of assessments, from cardiovascular, prenatal, neurological, psychological and critical care. The patient can see the visiting physician on the robot's screen, while their vital signs can be sent alongside their own video feedback to the physician.

The robot was specifically designed to make these interactions feel as similar to a human interaction as possible. The robot is 1.7 metres (5 ft 6 in) tall, so when a doctor's face appears on the robot's screen they will be at roughly the patient's eye level. In conversation with MedTech Boston, Youssef Saleh, general manager of the remote presence business unit at iRobot, explained, 'We made it very natural so that after 30 seconds of your first interaction with the robot, you're no longer feeling like you're talking to a robot. You're talking to the specialist. You're focusing on the body language.'

The InTouch Telehealth Network is currently supporting more than 1,500 clinical sites with over 19,000 encounters every month in more than 130 health systems. Through InTouch Health's TeleStroke and TeleICU platorms, patients can also gain access to experts in their field of care, who can guide them through necessary exercises and actions for recovery. If required, the system allows for conference calls so that multiple medical staff can interact with the patient at the same time.

The RP-VITA could make dealing with urgent patient consultations easier for health professionals, or to ensure that necessary specialist care is on hand even from hundreds of miles away, potentially saving lives in the process.

TAKEAWAYS

1 Are there other industries that could benefit from telepresence devices?
2 What other features could the RP-VITA incorporate to broaden its potential uses?
3 How could future iterations of the robot be designed to make interactions feel as human-like as possible, to emulate the comfort of a real face-to-face conversation?

INNOVATION DATA

Website: www.intouchhealth.com
Contact: www.intouchhealth.com/contact/
Innovation name: InTouch Health
Country: United States
Industry: Health & wellbeing

66

THE FIRST ROBOT INTERNSHIP USING TELEPRESENCE

New York advertising agency 360i is recruiting for a robot internship, so remote graduates can get valuable work experience in the Big Apple.

With telepresence technology, the possibility of undertaking a huge range of experiences remotely is now possible. Ad agency 360i is using the technology to create a 'robot' intern. For five hours a week, one successful internship applicant will be present in 360i's offices using the BeamPro telepresence robot from Suitable Tech. The mobile 1.2-metre (4-ft) high robots enable the remote intern to shadow employees and communicate via the two-way screens for meetings and presentations.

The agency wants to create a 'robot' intern to enhance career opportunities for those unable to afford to live in expensive cities with valuable work opportunities. The aspiring ad creative awarded with the internship will have the opportunity to beam into the ad agency's Los Angeles office via beam robot to work with the creative team on client briefs, attend internal meetings, present work and manage special assignments. In all, the internship spans four weeks.

The inspiration behind the scheme is the notion that every young ad student should have the opportunity to intern at a high-profile ad agency. On i360's site they acknowledge the fact that often, through financial or logistical barriers, it can be difficult for aspiring ad professionals to attain internships at the top agencies. These agencies are often based in expensive cities such as New York and Los Angeles, so not everyone has the ability or means to take advantage of the opportunities available, which are already limited and, in a highly competitive field, difficult to grasp in the first place. 360i realizes that young talent living in remote parts of the United States may also be limited by local responsibilities they can't leave or financial challenges that would make covering temporary living experiences too difficult.

The robot internship eliminates all such barriers and opens up the opportunity to anyone, anywhere, with the passion to create. The company posted the call for applicants on their social media channels and over several weeks set a series of exercises to challenge applicants and allow them to show their skills and capabilities. Finalists to the internship position are selected and interviewed via the beam robot itself.

The company does not require applicants to have any previous robot experience or any ad school or advertising experience. According to the job advert, applicants simply need to be excited to learn about new technologies, social media and advertising. The whole experience is captured via Snapchat on an account created just for the robot intern.

The remote workforce is growing as more companies offer employees the flexibility of working from home or make the most of freelancers in the gig economy. From Slack to blockchain (which was used by Nasdaq's Estonian stock market to allow shareholders to vote remotely), start-ups are coming up with easier ways to communicate and interact remotely.

TAKEAWAYS

1 How else can the experience of working from home be made more efficient and convenient?
2 How else could high-profile agencies reach and recruit talent from distant small towns?
3 How could your company use telepresence to become more efficient and effective?

INNOVATION DATA

Website: www.360i.com
Contact: www.360i.com/contact
Company name: 360i
Innovation name: robot internship
Country: United States
Industries: Marketing & advertising / Telecoms & mobile / Workspace

67

AN APP TO HELP PARALYSED STROKE VICTIMS COMMUNICATE EMOTIONS

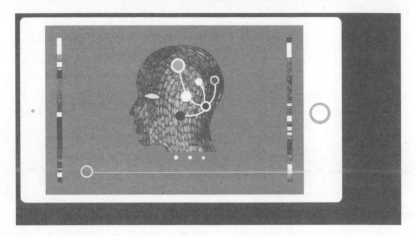

I.am.here is a mobile app that uses a brain computer interface to translate paralysed victims' emotions into simple statements of feeling.

Every year, almost 15 million people worldwide suffer a stroke and 5 million are left permanently disabled. Often, victims lose the power of speech and vision and many experience paralysis – leaving them isolated and unable to communicate with friends and loved ones. Now, a mobile app called I.am.here is using a consumer brain computer interface (BCI) to translate paralysed victims' emotions into simple statements of feeling, such as 'I'm so happy' or 'I feel bored'. In doing so, it seeks to go some way towards re-establishing or deepening the connection between stroke victims and their friends and families.

I.am.here was created by the Russian stroke foundation ORBi and software developers Yarr! in collaboration with Moscow-based digital communications agency AdWatch Isobar. The system uses a brain computer interface (Emotiv EPOC+ 14-channel EEG headset) to gather raw data about the wearer's brain activity. This data is then transmitted to a mobile device or tablet, where the free I.am.here app analyses and maps it on to human emotions that can then be translated into words. These words display on the screen, on top of matching graphics and colours, to communicate the stroke victim's emotional state to friends, family and loved ones. The app also stores a 30-day history of all communication, which can be useful for checking trends in a stroke victim's wellbeing, for example. Daria Lisichenko, President of the ORBI foundation, says, 'In most cases the brain fully retains its function, so we can discover the emotional state of the person.'

Alexey Fedorov, creative director at AdWatch Isobar says: 'We believe that technology can unite people and bring them closer to each other. All it needs is the right idea that would connect different disciplines and thus bring the impossible into reality. Today, millions of people can think and feel, but cannot physically express themselves because of a stroke. Today, millions of people want to hear back from their loved ones, but to no avail. Combining two very different technologies (apps and brain signal readers) together with years and years of scientific research, we came up with a way to connect those people, giving back an ability to communicate to those who've lost it. However, we believe that we've just scratched the surface. We believe that the product we've developed is just the first step along the great road of discovery, and we hope it will inspire others to join us in search for solutions that could help people bring back something they've lost.'

I.am.here is available to download for free from the App Store and Google Play.

TAKEAWAYS

1 Could this technology be used to help others who struggle with communication, such as people with autism?
2 Could the technology have potential applications for people who do not suffer from communication difficulties – to enhance rather than enable an experience?
3 How could the 30-day record of data be used to further enhance a stroke victim's wellbeing?

INNOVATION DATA

Website: www.iamhereapp.com
Contact: hello@yarr.cc
Company name: ORBi
Innovation name: I.am.here
Country: Russia
Industries: Health & wellbeing / Non-profit & social cause

68

A COMMUNICATION SYSTEM FOR HEALTH-CARE PROFESSIONALS

Carecode is a digital communication system for medical practitioners and patients, complete with virtual waiting rooms.

In the medical profession, there is an abundance of vital information that needs to be transferred between patients and different personnel. Now, Carecode is an all-encompassing communication system for health-care providers – enabling virtual waiting rooms, remote group messaging, real-time video and more.

To begin, health-care facilities set up an encrypted environment that all employees can access. Then, communication groups are set up between different parties including individual patients and their team, or nurses and doctors who need to share information or documents about specific cases.

Carecode can then be used to facilitate remote consultations for patients in care homes or those needing long-term care, or enable specialists to provide expertise to generalists.

Users communicate through messages, video appointments, photos and other attachments. The service notifies users about new messages, so that they can return to the case when suitable. This helps users manage their workload and focus on the task at hand. The virtual waiting room format means that clinicians can easily manage patient cases efficiently and can be sure to direct a case to the right person. This helps the entire organization communicate in a more organized way.

The designers of Carecode had a strong focus on user-friendliness. The service does not need to be installed and learning to use it is simple. The system's intuitive interface means that managing large numbers of users is easy for administrators. The software is designed to work independently of an organization's patient record system, so does not require integration. Carecode can be used on a computer, a tablet or a smartphone. A network connection is all that is required. Sending and receiving messages in Carecode is secure. Closed cases are automatically deleted from the service.

Users of this innovative system have noted its many benefits over more traditional organizational tools. Messages are stored for as long as required, and it is possible to add photos and other attachments for support. Because this efficient way of communicating frees time from unnecessary delays and waiting, health professionals have more time for patient care. As the platform can be used anywhere and at any time, it decreases the need for health professionals to move between places. Some patients don't need to come in for appointments, which shortens the queue in the waiting room. Streamlining the communication process between professionals helps prevents delays, miscommunication and complications.

Another benefit of Carecode is that implementation is extremely quick and easy. It creates a secure encrypted environment for an organization's communications, and is ready in just a few days. Upon set-up, users help to create the user groups the organization needs, whether they are professionals or patients. Due to the nature of the system, importing even large numbers of users is easy. Only very brief training for professionals is required – usually just a 30–60-minute group training session. Carecode also offers clear steps and ready-made templates for marketing the new service.

We have seen many examples of systems that are helping to digitize and streamline the communication process between health-care providers and patients. Examples include Bright.md, a tool for automated appointments, and a digital check-in system called Queue, which reduces patient waiting times. Antiquated systems, prone to delay and error, are being phased out, and health-care professionals and patients are benefiting from the new wave of smarter, more intuitive systems.

TAKEAWAYS

1 Could any other industries make use of this type of communication platform?
2 What other old and slow systems in health care and other industries need to be replaced?
3 Would your company benefit from an any-time-any-place communication system?

INNOVATION DATA

Website: www.carecode.fi
Contact: info@carecode.fi
Innovation name: Carecode
Country: Finland
Industries: Health & wellbeing / Workspace

69

JIBO, A SOCIAL ROBOT FOR THE HOME

Jibo is a friendly robot that uses facial recognition and natural language processing to offer personal assistance in the home, and perhaps become a new member of the family.

Smart homes are becoming big business, and there is a real need for a single interface to control and interact with the plethora of smart, Internet of Things devices now appearing on the market. Both Amazon and Apple have their own offerings (the Alexa-powered Echo and the Siri-powered Apple TV), but even their biggest fans would admit that neither device is particularly characterful. Jibo, on the other hand, is a friendly robot that uses facial recognition and natural language processing to offer assistance in the home with a strong emphasis on character and personality. Jibo might say things like, 'Hey, my name's Jibo, but between you and me I've always felt more like a Sagittarius. Or maybe a penguin.'

Created by social robotics pioneer and MIT professor Dr Cynthia Breazeal, the robot looks similar to Pixar's animated lamp and is designed to elicit the same fuzzy feelings. Behind its circular face are two hi-res cameras, 360-degree microphones, a speaker, an on-board computer, and Wi-Fi and Bluetooth connectivity. Jibo learns what its owners' faces look like, as well as their voices, so it knows who is speaking to it and who it's addressing in its Siri/Alexa-like natural voice. It can also sync and interface with other smart appliances and learn homeowners' preferences and daily habits.

The robot has been designed to be social. Users can call on it to take photos or video of special family moments and it tracks body movement and facial expressions to make sure that everyone's in the shot and looks happy. It can also give out personalized reminders depending on who's in the room, and read bedtime stories complete with sound effects and matching graphics. Significantly, it can also place orders for food and goods on request. Jibo is responsive and uses its swivelling base to make sure that it faces family members before speaking. While many companies and labs have been working on humanoid robotics for decades, Jibo is notable for these anthropomorphic behaviours.

Jibo raised just over $3.7 million on Indiegogo in 2014, with a scheduled release date of 'Holiday 2015'. However, production appears to have been problematic and in August 2016 it was announced that orders from all customers outside the United States and Canada were to be cancelled and fully refunded. The reason offered for this was that there were 'more issues with Jibo's ability to understand accented English than we view as acceptable'. They also point to 'rapidly changing consumer-privacy laws' as a reason for the cancellations and delays, which are obviously pertinent for an always-on device equipped with cameras, microphones and access to smart devices around the home. Since work began on Jibo, the European Union's Safe Harbour data transfer agreement has been scrapped and replaced by the EU–US Privacy Shield, and new data protection rules (GDPR) have been agreed for 2018.

The team proposes that the solution is to create 'fully localized' versions of the robot, with local servers, and they 'plan to expand to some international markets in late 2017', although followers of the project are understandably sceptical. However, following an investment of $25.3 million in Series A funding in January 2015, the project received a further $11 million later that year from a number of Asian investors to facilitate delivery to Taiwanese, Japanese, Korean and Chinese markets. This may mean that there are still real plans to expand into Asia in the near future.

Production issues and delays aside, the original Jibo Indiegogo project had over 7,000 backers, and there remains a real demand for a home assistant that is more than purely functional. It is hoped that Jibo can still deliver on its original promise in the United States and beyond but, if not, is it only a matter of time before someone else does?

TAKEAWAYS

1 Are there other ways to make technology more friendly?
2 How can tech companies work to address privacy concerns surrounding smart-home devices?
3 How could your own products or services be made more personable?

INNOVATION DATA

Website: www.myjibo.com
Contact: info@myjibo.com
Innovator: Dr Cynthia Breazeal
Innovation name: Jibo
Countries: United States
Industries: Entertainment & culture / Home & garden

70

CITY SENSORS TO MAKE BILL PAYING EASIER AND TRACK URBAN HEALTH

Two projects improving Chicago are tracking trash allowances for pay-as-you-throw bills and measuring the city's environment via Array of Things sensors.

The way we run our cities is changing. As seen in the Smart cities chapter, we are improving life in urban environments with smart solutions to urban noise, pollution and overcrowding. Now the city of Chicago is implementing two new initiatives: the first to make waste collection smarter; and the second to track the city's health by measuring a huge range of environmental factors and releasing the data as an open resource to the public.

Some of Chicago's residents, who pay for trash collection by volume, now have their bills automatically generated. New trash carts containing radio-frequency identifier (RFID) chips allow Lakeshore Recycling Systems to quickly link collections to the correct household. A device on the garbage truck reads the implanted chips, which link the trash cart to a particular customer and address. The system is currently being used in the Highland Park area, where about 3,900 residential customers are opting pay for trash service by volume rather than enrol in a subscription service with higher monthly fees.

For residents who split their time between Highland Park and another locale, the volume-based service keeps down costs during the times when homeowners are away and not generating any garbage. Before Lakeshore's new system was implemented, customers who paid by volume had to purchase waste stickers for $2.45 apiece and affix one to their 35-gallon refuse cart when they took it to the curb for collection. They also paid a monthly service fee of $5.29.

The firm's recycling carts are also equipped with RFID chips, which could eventually be used to monitor participation in recycling programmes, although the firm has no plans to use the technology to trace recycling participation to individual households.

In wider use throughout the city are the Array of Things sensors developed by a team of scientists from the University of Chicago, the Argonne National Laboratory and the City of Chicago. Installed on lamp posts and the sides of buildings, the sensors track the city's general wellbeing. Temperature, traffic patterns, air quality, vibration and other aspects of city life are measured. Each sensor contains a camera, and all of the collected data is available to the public as an open resource.

Array of Things is designed as a 'fitness tracker' for the city, collecting new streams of data on Chicago's environment, infrastructure and activity.

The hyper-local, open data can help researchers, city officials and software developers study and address critical city challenges, such as preventing urban flooding, improving traffic safety and air quality, and assessing the nature and impact of climate change.

In the first phase of the project, 50 nodes were installed. These nodes contained sensors for measuring air and surface temperature, barometric pressure, light, vibration, carbon monoxide, nitrogen dioxide, sulfur dioxide, ozone and ambient sound intensity. Two cameras collected data on vehicle and foot traffic, standing water, sky colour and cloud cover. A total of 500 nodes will be installed across Chicago by the end of 2018, and additional nodes will be shared with cities across the United States and in countries such as England, Mexico and Taiwan.

Open-source data are increasingly valuable, and companies are helping the public make use of it. From transit planning apps to visual representations of government information, local authorities are more transparent than ever.

TAKEAWAYS

1 What other public services could benefit from increased levels of access and citizen engagement?
2 Could these initiatives be launched in your city?
3 How else could RFID chips be used to track and communicate data in a civic setting?

INNOVATION DATA

Website: www.uchicago.edu
Contact: infocenter@uchicago.edu
Company names: University of Chicago; Lakeshore Recycling Systems
Innovation names: Array of Things; RFID tagged trash carts
Country: United States
Industries: Government & legal / Internet of Things / Nature & sustainability / Smart cities

SUMMARY

Communication in our digital age moves at lightning speed. There is no more fertile area for the disruption of the linear and the arrival of the circular. Every day the Springwise editors battle with the volume of information communicated to us from across the planet via our spotters and other numerous sources. Much of our discussion is around what to leave out, what not to communicate, and we firmly believe that our critical role of editor, of curator, will become only more important as the clutter increases and it becomes ever more impossible to see the wood from the proverbial trees.

Innovation and technology can help, as we have seen in this chapter. Having built on the radical upheaval brought about by Internet and email, intelligent, connected devices are producing a new, contemporary wave of transformation. Despite current hesitancy over the use of the Internet of Things, its capabilities are growing at such a rate that it is likely that, in the near future, so called 'smart-connected' devices will become the norm. The relationship between human and machine will evolve continuously and these technological advancements must ultimately remain focused on placing improved human connections at their core.

This theme that runs throughout this book and many of the innovations featured in the chapters on the sharing economy, smart cities and travel feed into this discourse, highlighting technologies that seek to bring us together rather than supplement human relationships. The future of communication is here every day and, in a disrupted and dysfunctional world of 'fake news', the hand of the ethical editor has never been so important.

COMMUNICATION TAKEAWAYS

1 **Think inclusively.** Which of your services or products could be offered with an additional level of support for people with a disability? Take a close look at the diversity of your employees. If teams are fairly homogenous, maybe recruitment communication is where you could begin your inclusivity campaign. If teams are a fairly good representation of what has become our global community, ask them for suggestions for improving company communications and offerings.

2 **Reconsider business travel.** What are some of your main expenses other than staff wages? If business travel is high on the list, consider using telepresence services. If business travel is not applicable to your company, could telepresence be used to better support and include remote workers? And if remote working is not a part of your brand's culture, maybe telepresence could be introduced as a way of making flexible working manageable.

3 **Strengthen internal collaboration.** Thinking beyond telepresence, what other aspects of connectivity could help make the working lives of remote employees easier and, ideally, more enjoyable? It may be worth considering whether cross-department collaboration is as strong as it could be. If not, how could cloud services such as Slack or Carecode be used to reinforce the company approach to innovation and service?

4 **Connect more.** Although the Internet of Things is still in its infancy, the range of devices available is steadily growing and mainstream adoption will quickly follow. How could connected devices be incorporated into your company's offering? Or, if not applicable, how could they help streamline processes within your office?

EDUCATION

Around the world, innovation in education is bringing fundamental changes that have ramifications far beyond alterations to syllabuses and course content. We're seeing disruption in how lessons are being taught and delivered, who is doing that teaching, and what skills and areas of expertise are now considered essential. This change provides opportunities, and we now have more tools and knowledge than ever before.

Virtual, creative and connected: new ways of learning

Rural, remote and often very poor communities are benefiting from increased connectivity in all parts of the world. Great distances and treacherous terrain are becoming less of a barrier, and virtual lessons, such as the fantastic **Making Ghanaian Girls Great!**, can be tailored to specific communities, traditions and circumstances. Streaming platforms like **Livecoding.tv** are showing professional developers at work in real time, letting people pick up new skills and a better understanding of what the job entails. Furthermore, a wealth of open-source (rather than proprietary) material is further contributing to the online learning movement.

But of course, while Internet access continues to improve, it still remains far from ubiquitous. More than 50 per cent of the global population does not use the Internet, either because they have no access to it or because they cannot afford to connect. These are the challenges that initiatives such as Mark Zuckerberg's Internet.org are trying to address, and the success of these programmes will directly lead to the creation of even more virtual education initiatives, at an ever-increasing rate.

It would be remiss to portray virtual education as relevant only to those in remote areas, however. Its development will also benefit citizens in well-connected areas who are no longer in formal education. Many professionals are now retraining later in their career, and anyone of any age or level of ability can be a student or a teacher – and may often be both. In Lisbon, **LATA 65** acts as an extreme and wonderfully vibrant example of this. The project links experienced street artists with senior citizens, teaching them how to help beautify the city with contemporary murals. 'Education' is no longer exclusively for the young.

LATA 65 is also a good example of the increasingly popular peer-to-peer learning model that exists outside formal educational bodies. These exchanges of information and time allow a more diverse citizenship, including previously marginalized groups, to take on active social and economic roles. Sharing skills allows time-rich, cash-poor people to participate in, and benefit from, these new outlets. The **NaTakallam** platform is another example, offering Syrian refugees the opportunity to earn money by conversing online with Arabic-language students.

Although levels of education and rates of literacy are increasing (83 per cent of the world's population is now literate), there are still significant shortages in professional qualifications, and it is broadly recognized that there are more science, technology, engineering and mathematics (STEM) jobs available than there are qualified candidates. Development in these areas has been so rapid that take-up of necessary fields of study has in fact been stunted, as both students and teachers are uncertain about what curriculums remain relevant. Worsening the situation further, traditional teaching methods are often not effective, or simply incompatible, with new material.

Programmes such as Andela, the talent accelerator that pays promising students to train to become remote software developers, are going some way towards filling the gap between what is needed and what is available to employers. But the challenge remains substantial.

Further efforts have looked to address the gap by improving the number of women working in science, technology, engineering and mathematics (STEM). Working women are more likely than men to have a bachelor's degree, yet fewer than 30 per cent of the world's researchers are female. Professionals have realized that interest in STEM must be sparked and the gender imbalance redressed, from a young age. Once again, new technologies can help stimulate this take-up, and the virtual reality school bus **Field Trip to Mars** is a brilliant example of this. From programmable friendship bracelets to build-it-yourself speakers, new technologies are embracing fun to promote learning, with the long-term aim of enthusing more children, and in particular girls, about a future in STEM.

Big data: new ways of teaching

As new teaching methods emerge – such as the **CoWriter** project, which sees pupils act as a teacher to a humanoid robot to improve their own learning – traditional teaching roles are also broadening out to incorporate new data-driven insights. In the United States, for example, Panorama Education uses surveys to help schools measure abstract aspects of a student's daily life, such as feelings of personal safety. Knowing more about a student's motivation, and his or her underlying levels of wellbeing, improves a teacher's ability to interact and teach, and to better tailor lessons to their students.

Education is changing – from how we teach, where we teach, to whom we teach and who does the teaching – while big data is helping us to better understand students and to better tailor lessons to different learning styles and abilities. The reality is that there is a still a long way to go to improve global literacy rates, and ensure that every child on the planet has education as a basic human right.

The innovations on the following pages are a testimony to the people around the world striving to improve these statistics, hinting at a brighter future for all.

71

PEER-TO-PEER CODING WORKSHOPS RUN BY HIGH-SCHOOL STUDENTS

Math and Coding is a non-profit organization that runs peer-to-peer coding workshops for secondary schools.

As with languages, young people are often able to pick up coding more easily than adults, so it is no wonder we have seen a huge number of initiatives that teach kids as young as five about coding and programming. There are coding delivery boxes, coding story-books and even programmable bracelets for children.

Math and Coding is an NGO run by schoolchildren, which is furthering the cause through peer-to-peer workshops. Based in San Francisco's Bay Area, Math and Coding was set up by 15-year-old school friends Nikhil Cheerla and Vineet Kosaraju. It has already provided hands-on training for over 1,000 students. The charity recruits teachers aged 13-plus to teach their peers Java programming, visual programming, robotics and more. Through free courses and workshops, students can learn the skills they need to produce websites, advanced games and smartphone apps. Math and Coding are also inviting students elsewhere in the United States to launch chapters in their community, for which the charity provides all the resources.

The first class was held at Mountain View Public Library and was a coding for kids workshop for elementary school students. After the huge popularity of the class spread by word of mouth, many others began to invite Nikhil and Vineet to host workshops in their libraries.

After realizing that they could not be present in all the libraries at once, they decided they needed to recruit and teach more teenagers to train others. Over the course of three years, they expanded their team from two to 50 volunteers. The volunteers helped them expand and add many more workshops. The pair have received commendations from the mayors of San Jose and Cupertino for their efforts to teach kids coding and other technology skills.

The programme makes an effort to reach out to underrepresented youth from minority neighbourhoods. As part of this effort, workshops were offered in libraries in less privileged areas such as at the Alum Rock, Biblioteca Latino Americana, Bascom and East Palo Alto libraries.

As part of a collaboration with LinkedIn, Nikhil and Vineet went to its campus to introduce young kids to coding. More than 250 students attended their six-hour-long workshops across two campuses. They have since been invited once more by LinkedIn to prepare a curriculum to teach in its outreach programme for secondary school students from low-income neighbourhoods.

Math and Coding also operate extremely popular summer coding camps. Each summer it organizes more than 20 summer camps, each with three to five sessions that include day camps, technology days and weekend camps.

Although most of their workshops teach coding, Nikhil and Vineet also conduct periodic maths camps for underrepresented youth. Their Green Math camp at the Alum Rock Library taught maths to a group of first to fourth-grade students from the East San Jose neighbourhood. The camp used a fusion of online maths and worksheets to get maximum productivity.

Using Google Chat and WebEx, the pair trained librarians and young volunteers from outside the Bay Area who were unable to attend training in person. Libraries in Fortworth, Gilroy, Roseville, Mendocino and Atlanta started coding for kids programmes with training from Math and Coding.

The incredible initiative shown by these two youngsters has demonstrated the power of peer-to-peer learning and the huge interest from young people in coding and computer programming.

TAKEAWAYS

1 What other skills could be taught to youngsters by their peers?
2 How else could young people be introduced to coding?
3 Could your business use peer-to-peer learning to spread knowledge and expertise?

INNOVATION DATA

Website: www.mathandcoding.org
Contact: mathandcoding@gmail.com
Innovation name: Math and Coding
Country: United States
Industries: Education / Non-profit & social cause

72

FREE ACCOMMODATION FOR STUDENTS AT A DUTCH CARE HOME

Humanitas Residential Care Centre gives free accommodation to students in exchange for 30 hours of voluntary work in the home every week.

A nursing home in the Netherlands is offering university students rent-free accommodation in return for their daily interaction with their elderly co-inhabitants. Alongside their residents, Humanitas Residential and Care Centre in Deventer, Holland provides free accommodation to six students, in exchange for 30 hours of voluntary work in the home every week.

In 2012 the Dutch government withdrew funding for the continuous care of over-80-year-olds who were deemed not to be in desperate need. This meant that a number of elderly citizens who had previously been able to stay for free at homes such as Humanitas were left struggling to find funds. This, in turn, led to a drop off in the number of people seeking long-term care, and Humanitas was forced to find new ways to fill beds and reinject some much needed energy, vitality and new skills into the home. The answer was students.

The arrangement is mutually beneficial. Money-poor young people who are struggling to afford increasing student rents benefit from the free accommodation, while elderly residents benefit from the extra company.

Isolation and loneliness have been linked to mental decline and increased mortality, and while most care homes encourage visiting volunteers, the arrangement at Humanitas has a much more significant effect on those living there, since they are able to forge meaningful relationships with young people. As CEO Gea Sijpkes says, 'The students bring the outside world in; there is lots of warmth in the contact.'

Students earn their keep by spending time with the elderly residents and teaching them skills such as how to email and use social media, as well as assisting staff. It's even been known for the students to teach the elderly citizens beer-pong and how to create a bit of graffiti, which, as with **LATA 65**, could well be set to be the new knitting. They also help keep conversations fresh, reporting back from their days at university to their elderly co-residents, some of whom are rarely able to get out. It's not uncommon for conversations about sex to take place over a jigsaw puzzle. Rather than discussing aches and pains, elderly residents can feed off the energy these students bring in, which engenders a sense of fun and vitality.

Humanitas is not the only care home to adopt the intergenerational model, but it is the first to offer rent-free accommodation to the students. Since Humanitas opened its doors to students, two more nursing homes in the Netherlands have now followed suit, and a similar programme has been set up in Lyons, France. We have also seen other companies using students as a resource for caring for the elderly. Lift Hero, for example, was an 'Uber for the elderly', offering transport with friendly care. The peer-to-peer lift service used trained or studying medical professionals to drive the elderly safely to their destination.

The Humanitas initiative is a true win–win, with staff, elderly residents and students all benefiting. And, of course, it's not just free lodgings that the students get to enjoy. While educating their neighbours on the virtues of thrash metal, they're sure to pick up some life lessons coming the other way, from those who have seen it all before.

TAKEAWAYS

1 How else could young people help out in the local community while receiving an education and tangible benefits in return?
2 Where else could students stay for less and help the communities they live in at the same time?
3 How else could people in a community creatively assist the elderly?

INNOVATION DATA

Website: www.humanitasdeventer.nl
Contact: www.humanitasdeventer.nl/contact
Company name: Humanitas Residential Care Centre, Deventer
Country: The Netherlands
Industries: Health & wellbeing / Home & garden / Non-profit & social cause

73

REFUGEES EARN AN INCOME BY TALKING TO STUDENTS OF ARABIC

NaTakallam's platform connects students of Arabic with Syrian refugees, who receive an income for having an online conversation.

The Syrian refugee crisis has produced some innovative initiatives, such as a start-up incubator in Finland and a real-time translating social app in Sweden. Now NaTakallam is providing refugees with a source of income when they chat with a stranger.

Through NaTakallam (which means 'we speak'), students of Arabic can have Internet-based conversations with native speakers who are refugees, and pick up some of the more colloquial subtleties of the language. The Syrian speakers will receive payment for the service they provide. Currently setting up in Lebanon with support from Sawa, a non-profit organization, NaTakallam aims to expand to all countries along the refugee migration routes.

In the United States, Arabic is the fastest-growing area of foreign-language study, and its popularity has doubled over the past decade. The growing need for people to communicate with Arabic-speaking refugees is quickly becoming more urgent, as conflict continues to unfold in the Middle East. Academic and language institutes tend to teach Fusha, formal literary Arabic, but students are increasingly interested in Ammiyyah, the local dialect and primary spoken form of Arabic in a given region.

The best way to learn a language is to practise it with native speakers who talk like real people, not like a textbook. However, because of the conflict in the Middle East, there are few opportunities to learn and practise the language with native speakers, especially the Levantine dialect, spoken in Syria, Jordan, Lebanon and Palestine. Damascus, which used to be a hub for Arabic learners, is no longer accessible.

The Syrian conflict has triggered the worst refugee crisis since the Second World War. Even if Syrians manage to flee the violence and obtain asylum abroad, many of those displaced have few work opportunities, often because of language barriers and local labour restrictions. Many Syrians today find themselves stuck in neighbouring Lebanon, Jordan, Egypt, Iraq and Turkey, and need desperately to find an opportunity to work.

NaTakallam pairs displaced Syrians with Arabic learners around the world for language practice over Skype. The platform offers affordable, flexible, tailored Arabic practice with native speakers. For the Syrians, NaTakallam offers a valuable income primarily for those in Lebanon, but also in Turkey, Egypt, France, Brazil and Germany. The result is that users and Syrian conversation partners engage in a powerful cultural exchange, often developing transatlantic friendships between worlds that sometimes feel a million miles apart culturally, socially and politically.

The initiative was set up by graduates of Columbia's School of International and Public Affairs, who have extensive experience in language learning and teaching. Their interests lie in economic and political development, human rights, humanitarian affairs and journalism. All core members of the team are originally from the Middle East.

NaTakallam's work is being partially facilitated by Lebanese NGO arcenciel, and is being housed and supported by Columbia University's Start-up Lab at the WeWork space in Soho, New York City. NaTakallam is a member of TrustLaw, the members-only service of the Thomson Reuters Foundation, which offers NGOs and social entrepreneurs an easy way to request free legal assistance from lawyers around the world.

Previously, we have seen travellers being able to trade **conversation in their mother tongue for lodging** when they travel. Conversation with native speakers is a valuable commodity and, if it can be used as a source of income for those displaced by conflict, so much the better.

TAKEAWAYS

1 How else can start-ups empower refugees through making the most of their skills?
2 How else can the commodity of conversation with native speakers be leveraged?
3 How could this simple model be used for people across the world to gain income?

INNOVATION DATA

Website: www.natakallam.com
Contact: info@natakallam.com
Innovation name: NaTakallam
Countries: Lebanon; United States
Industries: Education / Non-profit & social cause

74

SURVEY TOOLS HELPING SCHOOLS ASSESS THE CLASSROOM EXPERIENCE

Panorama Education helps schools to conduct affordable surveys that measure the more abstract qualities of a student's school experience.

It could certainly be argued that educational bodies tend to look to test results and attendance records perhaps not because these are the most important achievements of a school, but because they are the easiest to measure. However, a new dashboard tool from Boston, Massachusetts start-up Panorama Education could enable schools to measure the previously 'unmeasurable': the data analytics company helps educational institutions to conduct regular, affordable surveys measuring the more abstract qualities of a student's classroom experience. It asks questions such as 'Do you feel safe at school?' and 'Do you think anyone would notice if you were not there?'

Panorama Education believes that these additional aspects of a student's life should be tracked – not only because they are important in their own right but also because they directly correlate to a child's performance in tests. 'In school there are many things that help students succeed. It takes strong relationships, deep engagement with content and teaching, and positive social emotional skills to help students thrive as twenty-first-century learners. It also takes passionate, well-supported teachers, and families and communities that are actively engaged. These are the things that matter for schools, but sometimes these things are hard to measure.' The company's methodology was developed under the leadership of Harvard Grad School's Dr Hunter Gehlbach and covers a range of metrics – from a student's sense of belonging to their interest in a subject.

The company is focused on improving K–12 (primary plus secondary) education by helping schools to measure these more abstract

metrics and understand the underlying reasons for any student problems. They collect feedback from teachers, students and parents via
their carefully designed surveys. Panorama Education uses a paper-
based system – as this works best with participants – and scans and
digitizes the results using a unique algorithmic method. The response
data is then converted into comprehensive reports, focusing on four
key areas:

- the student's perception of the school's teaching and their
  learning
- the student's social-emotional learning (the mindsets, skills
  and attitudes required for success)
- the school's climate and culture
- family–school relationships.

To help educators understand and learn lessons from the results, the
reports contain National Benchmarks. In a social-emotional learning
report, for example, a school can compare its students' levels of grit,
social awareness and sense of belonging against a national average.
The reports can also break down analysis based on subgroups — to
look at performance based on race/ethnicity, gender, grade level and
more – and offer actionable resources for educators to help improve
results. Speaking to *The New York Times*, one teacher, Leila Campbell,
said, 'The surveys have been transformational in how I operate. I've
grown tremendously from this data.'

The company, founded by three Yale graduates, is already
serving 6,500 schools across America. Their new dashboard, which
has been tested at 300 schools, helps to streamline the process,
enabling principals to access changing metrics online anytime they
need to. The system offers schools an affordable and transparent
alternative to expensive consulting companies, while providing the
same detailed analysis that can lead to happier students, achieving
better grades.

TAKEAWAYS

1 We've already seen variations of this model used in the office setting (for example Leo the Slack bot), but where else could it apply?
2 Could teachers be better trained to understand the many factors that affect a child's performance and how they influence learning?
3 What other innovations described in this book (for example **The CoWriter Project**) could Panorama Education partner with and incorporate into their results?

INNOVATION DATA

Website: www.panoramaed.com
Contact: contact@panoramed.com
Innovation name: Panorama Education
Country: United States
Industry: Education

75

BRINGING EDUCATION TO DISADVANTAGED COMMUNITIES IN GHANA

Making Ghanaian Girls Great! is a project delivering expert education from the country's capital to remote places using virtual teaching in the classroom.

Deprived regions in Africa often lack the money or resources to offer students basic education, and initiatives such as Ideas Box are already providing disconnected communities with books, e-readers and tablets. Taking a different tack, Making Ghanaian Girls Great! (MGCubed) is delivering expert education from the country's capital to remote locations using virtual teaching in the classroom.

MGCubed was created to address the challenges of teacher absenteeism, teacher quality and poor student learning in Volta and Greater Accra in Ghana. The United Kingdom's Varkey Foundation turned to video conferencing technology to offer a solution. The pilot, funded by the UK Department for International Development (DFID), which began in 2013 and scheduled to operate until 2017, is Ghana's first interactive distance-learning project.

MGCubed lessons are broadcast live to multiple classrooms by six master teachers from two teaching studios in Accra.

Every day, using basic video conferencing and microphones in the classroom, students receive two hours of interactive, two-way education in maths and English. The project has equipped two classrooms in 72 Ghana Education Service primary schools, helping around 8,000 girls gain access to an education they otherwise couldn't get. The project has especially focused on young girls aged seven to 16 living in deprived communities.

The participating schools are equipped with a webcam, computer and satellite that mainly run on solar energy to minimize costs. On location, there's a local helper with teaching and computer skills to provide guidance for the kids. Over 144 facilitators were trained in modern teaching techniques to support the programme. After school, there's also a special 'Wonder Woman club' broadcast for to up to 50 marginalized girls per school, where female role models are featured and students get the opportunity to participate in a question and answer session.

The initial results from the pilot are very positive: between 2014 and 2015, average attendance for girls at MGCubed classes increased from 54 per cent to just under 80 per cent, and all the girls surveyed thought positively about the teaching they received.

As a result, Innovations for Poverty found that the project had significantly improved the girls' learning, with the most significant progress made by girls in the lowest grade. MGCubed's own data confirms the improvement, with an average increase of almost 25 per cent in mathematics test scores. Progress in English was less substantial, but there was still an improvement in the words per minute reading measure for the lowest-performing students, and on reading comprehension for students overall.

The project, and especially the Wonder Woman club, has also helped improve the girls' self-esteem. In an analysis of over 130 girls' feedback, more than half of them proactively identified that these after-school sessions had had a major effect on their confidence and self-respect, their desire to avoid early marriage and pregnancy, and personal hygiene.

Girls who attended the Wonder Women sessions were also significantly more likely to disagree with the statements 'I think that I am a failure' and 'I do not have much to be proud of'. When asked, 'If a mother wants to buy school items for her children but their father does not agree, should she go ahead and buy them?' they were more likely to answer 'Yes'. The girls were also more likely to express a desire to attend university or gain higher education.

TAKEAWAYS

1 Through the power of the Internet, the MGCubed project enables remote villages to access quality education for their children in a way not possible before. Are there other ways in which technology can be used to deliver education in resource-scarce locations?

2 Could a similar project be used in already high-achieving schools to improve performance even further?

3 To improve performances in other areas, how could a programme of regular video conferencing sessions with an expert be used outside the education system?

INNOVATION DATA

Website: www.varkeyfoundation.org/content/
making-ghanaian-girls-great
Contact: www.varkeyfoundation.org/contact-us
Company name: GEMS Education Solutions
Innovation name: Making Ghanaian Girls Great!
Countries: Ghana; United Kingdom
Industries: Education / Non-profit & social cause

76

INSPIRING CREATIVITY IN ELDERLY CITIZENS THROUGH STREET ART

Portugal artists' collective WOOL creates stencil courses that connect well-known street artists with senior citizens.

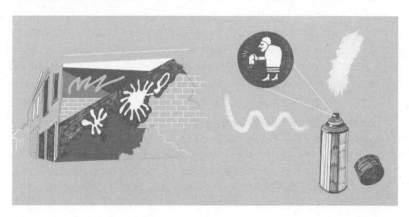

The elderly are often invisible to the rest of society and so they frequently do not receive the social and creative stimuli they require to make the most of later life. LATA 65 is a community art project offering graffiti workshops to the elderly that aims to establish and strengthen connections between generations and inspire creativity at all ages, while at the same time destigmatizing the practice of street art.

Designed in partnership with WOOL – the Urban Art Festival of Covilhã and Cowork Lisboa – the urban art workshop is the brainchild of two Portuguese artists: architect Lara Seixo Rodrigues, who also runs a local street art festival called Wool Fest, and Fernando Mendes, a designer and co-founder of Cowork Lisboa. For Rodrigues, the idea for the project originated at a city street art festival in Covilhã, Portugal, in 2011, where she noted that those who were the most receptive and interested in street art techniques, materials and history were older people.

LATA 65 combines Rodrigues's twin passions for graffiti and the local history of Covilhã, which is closely linked with the textile industry. WOOL urban arts festival began in 2011, aiming to use contemporary art as a tool for the social, cultural, economic and urban transformation in the community. Since then, this idea has been taken up in many other places, both within Portugal and globally.

After observing the interest that the elderly had in the art festival, Rodrigues was challenged by Mendes to make a workshop for seniors. After the first workshop in 2012, which was very successful, entirely self-funded and free of charge, Rodrigues decided that she wanted to expand the project. To fund it, she applied to, and was awarded, the Participatory Budgeting of Lisbon Council 2013. LATA 65 was then invited to a festival in the Azores and has since taken workshops to a number of small villages across Portugal. Today, the team works with groups of elderly people all over Portugal, and has plans to expand to other countries, too. The average age of students in the workshops is 74, but they have had students as old as 92.

LATA 65 is a two-day workshop that takes place over four hours each day. It is normally attended by a group of 15 people. Each workshop starts with a brief theory class on graffiti and street art history, and an explanation of the main differences, key players and techniques in graffiti, street art and mural making. After this, a practical session begins, where the elderly students are taught the techniques they need to begin taking to the streets, where they use their spray cans to decorate run-down parts of the city.

Much of the current innovation in aging focuses on health care and communication, such as the connected systems for messaging among family with Bloom, a trio of connected devices that aim to enhance the quality of connections between remote family members. However, with many senior citizens now active for far longer than previous generations, health care is not always the most pressing concern, and intellectual stimulation and social connections are becoming more important.

TAKEAWAYS

1 What other personal skills could be redeveloped for use in the later years?
2 How could your company or organization reach out and engage with the elderly?
3 How else could the arts be used as a medium to inspire and help sections of society that are in need or often ignored?

INNOVATION DATA

Website: www.woolfest.org
Contact: info@woolfest.org
Company name: WOOL
Innovation name: LATA 65
Country: Portugal
Industries: Education / Entertainment & culture / Fine art / Non-profit & social cause

77

A SURPRISE VIRTUAL-REALITY ROAD TRIP TO MARS FOR CHILDREN

Field Trip to Mars rigged an entire school bus with virtual reality screens, providing an immersive Martian experience for the schoolchildren on board.

Many schoolchildren (and also many adults) dream of one day becoming an astronaut. The idea of going into space and to other planets ignites a sense of wonder and curiosity that regular science topics such as physics or chemistry may lack. That is why incorporating space exploration into the classroom is a fun way of getting schoolchildren interested in learning about science.

Field Trip to Mars is a school bus equipped with VR windows that give the children on board a lifelike Martian bus ride. The project, based in Washington, DC, was a collaboration between aerospace company Lockheed Martin, McCann New York, and visual effects company Framestore. Thinking they were being taken for a field trip to the Science and Engineering Festival, the children were surprised when the lights dimmed and their windows showed passing images of the Red Planet.

To simulate the experience of a bus driving on Mars, the teams used Unreel and Game Engine to integrate the physical with the virtual: when the bus was driving along the road, the screens displayed a Martian landscape at the same speed; when the bus came across a bump or turned left or right, the screens moved according to what the passengers were experiencing. The bus even had speakers that simulated a sandstorm when it drove through one.

The team created a 650-square-kilometre (250-sq.-mile) drivable area, and mapped every street in Washington, DC on the virtual Mars. Wherever the experience began in the real-life street, it would begin at the equivalent point in the road grid drawn out in the virtual Mars landscape. To simulate driving on the surface of Mars, the developers used a combination of GPS, a three-axis accelerometer, a magneto-meter and a laser surface velocimeter. This last piece of apparatus employs a laser, pointing to the ground from the outside of the bus, which simply gives accurate data as to how far forwards or backwards the vehicle has travelled.

To turn the transparent windows into high-definition moni-tors, the developers had to custom-design a box to be fitted to each window, which contained a 4K high-definition display and a layer of switchable film that can turn from clear to opaque. This was a brand-new system designed especially for the purpose, not available anywhere else in the world. The special screens were hand-built in China and South Korea.

The project explored the potential for group VR to be an immer-sive and social experience without the need for goggles or headsets, where users can communicate and interact in 4D. With this innova-tive system, it is truly a group experience – children are able to view the passing landscape together and point out the features they are seeing to their friends.

We have already seen a start-up Ardusat enabling students to conduct experiments in space. Field Trip to Mars shows the capa-bility of group VR to inspire the next generation of scientists and astronauts.

TAKEAWAYS

1 What other industries or sectors could use group VR?
2 How else could innovations such as this be used to revolutionize the way children learn?
3 How could your company use VR in a way previously not seen?

INNOVATION DATA

Website: fieldtriptomars.com
Contact: dan.nelson@lmco.com
Company name: Lockheed Martin
Innovation name: Field Trip to Mars
Country: United States
Industries: Education / Entertainment & culture

78

A PLAYFUL DIY COMPUTER SCREEN FOR KIDS

Kano's DIY coding kits teach users how to build computers, screens, cameras, speakers and pixel kits using storybook-style instructions.

Kano's do-it-yourself educational devices use Lego-style building kits to teach coding and more. With 8.2 billion devices worldwide connected to the Internet, and with most of us carrying a powerful computer around in a pocket or bag (smartphones), coding has never been more important.

Yet only around 50 million people in the world, professionals and amateurs combined, have the knowledge to speak to, interact with and control the outputs of these ubiquitous devices. Kano's team hopes to change that by reinjecting fun and creativity into an industry too often held back by educators' focus on vocation and profit: 'Build an app, make millions.'

Kano's first product was a computer that was fun to build, to meet the challenge given by a six-year-old who wanted to build one that was 'as simple and fun as Lego, so no one had to teach him'. Following the success of that computer, the company introduced its screen kit and is now developing camera, speaker and pixel board kits.

Building a Kano device involves putting together the pieces using the storybook instructions and then connecting to any monitor using the HDMI port. Makers then use the Kano Blocks coding arena to start customizing.

Coding starts out as easily as dragging and dropping code blocks, giving users instant gratification in seeing the changes reflected in their device. And it's not just children who appreciate the bright colours and unlimited creativity available through the kits. James Vincent, reporter for multimedia platform The Verge says, 'It brings coding off the screen and into the physical world. Seeing this happen in real time is genuinely delightful.'

The code blocks are not only colourful, easy and fun to use; they can shape the actions of the connected device, beat challenges set by the Kano team and connect to games including **Minecraft**, allowing gamers to not only play but also to create the game anew. Once a maker is ready to move up to writing code themselves, a Javascript-based learning window helps users turn their ideas into actions. Each device can contain up to three custom apps at a time, allowing makers to mix and match the capabilities of their devices.

Kano's operating system is Linux-based, and each kit comes with the most up-to-date version of the open-source Raspberry Pi hard-ware. For educators, Kano kits provide full curriculum support, training and resources. The curriculum support includes lesson plans, design challenges and how-to coding lessons for teachers, along with regular phone support from the Kano team and membership to the Kano Educator Community network.

The computer and screen kits each cost $150, with custom bundles available to those buying in bulk. Anyone wanting to donate a kit can buy-one-give-one for $299. The soon-to-be-released Pixel Kit costs $130, and the camera and speaker kits are still in development.

'It brings coding off the screen and into the physical world. Seeing this happen in real time is genuinely delightful.'

By presenting complicated engineering in simple, engaging and accessible formats, products such as Kano's can be used to help children get a head start. Making education more accessible is a central tenet of the international sustainable development goals, and Foldscope Instruments' $1 portable, origami paper microscope is helping students anywhere afford scientific study. Woodenwidget is another company contributing to the popularity of the learn anywhere maker movement, offering illustrated how-to guides for building a wooden bike, boat or caravan.

TAKEAWAYS

1 How could you change a passive learning experience into one in which students learn by doing, thus creatively directing their own education?
2 How could the hackathon model of solving problems with creative technology be used locally?
3 How could other complex subjects use the creativity of play to teach by doing?

INNOVATION DATA

Website: http://uk.kano.me/products/screen-kit
Contact: help@kano.me
Company name: Kano
Innovation name: The Screen Kit
Country: United States
Industries: Design / Education / Gamification & gaming

79

LIVE-STREAMED PROFESSIONAL CODING SESSIONS FOR ALL

Livecoding.tv hosts live-streamed videos of experienced programmers coding, while encouraging viewers to ask questions and give feedback.

Livecoding.tv has something for everyone involved in the coding industry, from amateur enthusiasts and beginners to experienced professionals and recruiters. More than 21,000 projects are available in a wide range of programming languages, and the site has already attracted 40,000 users from 162 countries.

Peer-to-peer networks with a variety of purposes continue to grow in strength and numbers, and Livecoding.tv helps create a community of coders.

Viewers can watch developers build games, mobile apps and websites, and the site is free to use and watch and encourages socializing and active learning.

Users follow other members and are notified when they start a new stream. When a project is live, the audience may ask questions and give feedback, including contributions to the work being undertaken at that time. All participants benefit from access to the User Directory, a fun and easy way to network with people based on location, programming language and professional background. The messaging capability on the site allows viewers and broadcasters to chat, publicly and privately, as well as take part in group conversations.

Projects on the site are categorized according to programming language and difficulty level. The difficulty levels are beginner, intermediate and expert, and beginners are likely to be encouraged by the huge number of beginner projects and channels. Visitors to the site can search the Project Discovery section and the Streaming Schedule to find relevant topics and set alerts for future streams. Coders working on a live-streamed project benefit from the enhanced concentration that is created by knowing they have an audience.

There are three different types of accounts on the site – Free, Pro and Recruiter. Most live-streams on the site are automatically archived as videos for additional, later viewing. Certain account levels have the option to set videos as private or to choose not to archive content that has been streamed.

- A free account provides unlimited access to the broadcasts, videos and playlists, and viewers can be matched with a code mentor to help accelerate their development. Since the videos are streamed live, viewers gain more insight than they would watching an edited YouTube tutorial, which is likely to cut out a lot of the trial-and-error problem solving that can be very valuable to beginners. Free account holders may also broadcast.
- Pro accounts cost $9.99 per month and give subscribers the option to set up team or private channels. Pro broadcasters can download up to 100 videos a month and can choose whether or not to archive their projects or to set them as private.
- A recruiter account costs $100 per month and gives prospective employers first-hand knowledge of a candidate's proficiency. Recruiters can post jobs on the site as well as access the search capability to choose from users' profiles.

Coding is now an incredibly valuable skill across a multitude of fields, and we have seen a number of online platforms springing up to offer free tutorials. Asciinema is an open-source coding archive which enables users to record coding sessions directly from their terminal for other users to learn from, while Free Code Camp is an organization letting anyone learn to code for free by working on projects for non-profit organizations.

TAKEAWAYS

1 Is there something you or your organization could provide or offer to the public in a similarly interactive way?
2 Could other creative skills be taught like this, with live-streaming encouraging a more honest portrayal of maker processes?
3 How else could an online community of learners and professionals improve access to jobs as well as education?

INNOVATION DATA

Website: www.livecoding.tv
Contact: partnerships@livecoding.tv
Innovation name: Livecoding.tv
Country: United States
Industries: Education / Gamification & gaming

80

A ROBOT TO HELP CHILDREN IMPROVE THEIR HANDWRITING

In the CoWriter Project, a humanoid robot is the least advanced pupil in class – giving struggling students someone to learn with and teach.

Research in AI tends to focus on developing robots that are more capable and efficient than humans, but a study at the École polytechnique fédérale de Lausanne in Switzerland sought to create just the opposite. They created a robot that is always less competent than the child it is interacting with.

It is widely understood in pedagogical research that when children teach their peers they gain motivation and self-esteem – and ultimately improve themselves – all without realizing it. To harness this teaching technique, the CoWriter Project created a robot classroom assistant that is less advanced at handwriting than the most struggling students – giving those pupils someone to learn with and teach.

Scientists from the Computer–Human Interaction Lab at EPFL used the likeable humanoid 58cm NAO robot in its research with schoolchildren aged six to eight, over a two-year period in four different schools. To begin, the child created a word from small magnetic letters and the robot wrote out the word on a tablet screen. The robot was programmed to reproduce common handwriting errors, which it learned from a database of examples based on common mistakes. The child then identified any errors the robot had made and corrected them using the tablet's stylus, either by rewriting the whole word or by correcting specific letters. In doing so, they were teaching the robot how to write while improving their own writing in the process.

The robot then repeated the task, using algorithms that learned from and emulated the child's corrections, leading to gradual improvement. Once the child was satisfied, they moved on to another word. The robot could even be made to adopt a child's specific writing difficulties – such as the letter f or h.

When a child feels they are the worst in their class at something it can be demotivating, leading to a drop-off in effort. They may also become self-conscious and try to avoid practising for fear of embarrassment. The 'learning by teaching' method used by the CoWriter Project is effective because it counters these feelings through something called the 'protégé effect'. Rather than becoming demoralized for being the worst in their class, a child, in their role as teacher, feels a sense of responsibility for the robot's performance, and so makes a concerted effort to understand what is difficult for the robot and where it is going wrong. In doing so, they also become more confident, develop their own metacognitive skills and reflect on their own errors. This self-reflection can be a more effective learning process than being told they are making mistakes by someone else, and although the primary objectives for the research were to explore whether the child would accept and engage with the robot and the methodology, case studies form the research do show handwriting improvements among the children.

The robot was designed not to replace handwriting teachers but to help them, and it was very well received throughout the research. (Note that the version used in the research required a supervisor at all times due to the 'level of expertise required to deploy and operate our system', and an adult was required to guide the student through their role as teacher.) Deanna Hood, project co-supervisor, explains that 'It is not just a simple tool, and not a replacement for teachers, but rather a partner in learning. We believe there is a new role for robotics being created, and that the CoWriter Project is just the beginning.'

TAKEAWAYS

1 Are there other applications for a robot that enables children to teach the skills they are struggling with?
2 Would there be appetite for an adapted version of the CoWriter system to be made publicly available to educators?
3 How else could the learning by teaching method be used in the classroom and beyond?

INNOVATION DATA

Website: chili.epfl.ch/cowriter
Contact: accueil@epfl.ch
Company name: Computer–Human Interaction Lab at EPFL
Innovation name: CoWriter Project
Country: Switzerland
Industry: Education

SUMMARY

'Education, education, education' has long been a rallying cry of Western politicians. While it is much easier to say the words than to follow them through, education is a priority for a modern, functional and sustainable society. The urgent need to radically disrupt and transform much of the current educational system remains in stark contrast with the rate at which transformation is actually happening, in particular among high-school groups. To succeed in our new disrupted economies, education must become a lifelong quest – more a state of mind than a task to complete.

Today, almost anyone can be a student and, with new technologies and emerging peer-to-peer models, almost anyone can become a teacher, too. This phenomenon will only gather pace and, as the knowledge economy grows and fragments, the opportunities seem boundless. More interesting, perhaps, is the opportunity this new, more flexible style of learning will inevitably present to people living in developing economies. Offering the gift of education to every human being on the planet must be a worthwhile goal for the age of disruption.

As these changes in education advance, we have the potential to begin fulfilling employers' needs for new combinations of professional skills. The agility and ability of students to design their own learning pathways bodes well for a future where many jobs have yet to be created. The ideas in this chapter could provide the spark to send all of us, whether as a teacher or student, on an exciting new path of discovery.

EDUCATION TAKEAWAYS

1 **Make education more accessible.** Who is currently being taught, and why? Be creative and find new angles that could interest entirely new groups of students. Are there ways in which you could use new technologies to overcome barriers faced by potential students?

2 **Combine subjects that relate to each other.** The advances in mathematics, science, technology and engineering, to name but a few, are moving at such a pace that it is inevitably almost impossible for educators to stay up to date. When crafting lessons and curricula, think about how strands from a multitude of disciplines may be drawn out to bring the topics to life – much like what we are doing in this book.

3 **Find alternative methods of teaching and learning.** Perhaps experiment with a peer-to-peer model even in a classroom environment. Or do you have specialist knowledge that you could swap yourself for something else in a bartering economy? If students are willing and able to teach their peers, teachers should also be willing to take up the role of student once again.

4 **Measure all the data points.** Start small. You never know what the numbers will reveal. Often, several sets of small measurements create a very interesting bigger picture. If you're a student, how do you measure success? What would help make your work easier? If you're teaching, how could you tweak your measures of success to make them more inclusive and diverse? What other conditions could you measure and track to complement more traditional progress reports?

5 **Understand the importance of lifelong learning.**
An overarching theme in any chapter on the future
of education must mention the growing importance
of lifelong learning. Indeed, many of the innovations
mentioned in this book relate to the wish and need for
us all to continue to learn every day. With the pace of
change, this has never been more important: we need
to realize that the formal education we receive at the
start of our lives is just the beginning of the process.

RETAIL

Conventional wisdom, until recently, showed a direction of travel for retailers from bricks and mortar to online. In the face of online competition from the likes of Amazon, more than half the independent bookshops in the United States and the United Kingdom have closed down over the last 20 years, and grocery purchases in the United Kingdom are now twice as likely to be made online as they were in 2010. Click-and-collect services are increasingly common, with Argos recently pairing with eBay to provide the service at hundreds of stores.

The appeal of online is well documented and easily understood: there are no queues or strict opening hours, discounts abound, and the range of products available to browse is almost limitless. Shopping online also means that social media is just a browser tab away, opening up opportunities for immediate validation from peers, helping push uncertain consumers towards that purchase. Research shows that 43 per cent of social media users have purchased a product after sharing or 'favouriting' it on Pinterest, Twitter or Facebook.

From online to offline and beyond

Conversely, physical shops can do something better than any website. They are able to create an evocative, almost tangible atmosphere, conjuring up a strong sense of brand and identity, spraying a unique scent and curating beautiful displays. They also have dedicated, knowledgeable staff on hand for face-to-face interactions and guidance, and online cannot recreate the experience of trying on clothes, listening to headphones or testing out a chair. For the foreseeable future, physical stores will remain on our high streets and, despite the growth of online shopping, bricks-and-mortar shops are still where the vast majority of consumers' cash is spent.

While playing to these strengths, innovative physical stores are also now attempting to replicate the best aspects of the online experience. Enabled by new technologies, physical stores can now begin effectively 'borrowing' established best practices from their digital counterparts. **The Physical Cookie** is an excellent example of this. It enables data collection on consumers in a physical mall environment, just as a cookie would online, thus opening the door to an exciting new period for bricks-and-mortar retail. Amazon Go replicates the convenience and speed of an online checkout that has remembered the shopper's payment details. Ultimately, VR experiences such as Innisfree's **Jeju Flying Bike** experience may represent a perfect fusion of both online and offline environments.

Home as a new retail channel

Considerable attention has been paid to omni-channel, a sales approach that provides customers with a seamless, holistic experience across wearables, desktops, mobiles and stores. Judging by the innovations we see on a daily basis at Springwise, the physical home environment is now rapidly becoming one of the most important of these channels.

Consumers can already purchase specific items at the touch of a button from within the home, using devices such as the Amazon Dash, a Wi-Fi-connected button that can be placed anywhere in the home and pressed to immediately order an item from Amazon. The button essentially functions as a convenient shortcut, removing the need for the consumer to pull out a smartphone or laptop … though it still requires human input.

As smart Internet of Things devices make their way into an increasing number of homes, we're beginning to see the introduction of products with the ability (and permission) to make purchases on the owner's behalf. Internet of Things devices already gather data and recognize habits to better cater for their owners' needs, so it's a natural evolution for them to begin ordering items accordingly. **Jibo** is able to recognize family members and interact with them according to their previous behaviours, making it capable of suggesting a takeaway based on the time, day and what it knows about its owner.

Smart devices often know when they needed refilling or repairing. Already we have seen innovations such as **Voltaire**, a coffee grinder that monitors the beans within it and reorders a preferred brand when they begin to lose their freshness. In South America, families that rely on propane gas for power can use the Mabe smart scale to automatically order refills before the tank is empty. The **FridgeCam** alerts users when food expiration dates are near and automatically compiles shopping lists.

These developments follow the pattern of minimizing consumer effort in the retail process, with the ultimate aim of making purchasing decisions as close to subconscious as possible.

Conventional supply models disrupted

Lastly in this chapter, you will also find innovations that address a disruption to conventional models of production, supply and delivery – making systems more flexible while improving transparency for the consumer. New production methods such as 3D printing represent an opportunity for brands to switch to a leaner, more efficient and more sustainable model, manufacturing certain goods on the shop floor, or even outsourcing manufacture to the consumer.

London's **Opendesk** platform sells designer furniture but outsources the burden of manufacture. Customers can buy access to a design file and then either make the piece themselves or take the blueprint to a local workshop. Such networks help new and small creative businesses focus on design without the financial pressures of production and shipping. Meanwhile, 3D printing is offering consumers the chance to customize, purchase and then print their own products. Over the last year we have seen companies offer everything from 3D-printed electric bike accessories (EET Industries) to synthesizer parts (Teenage Engineering).

For retailers searching for the magic elixir of success, the challenge lies in finding the particular concoction that brings a brand to life – connecting with consumers in a meaningful way by providing high-quality product with unique experience. The ten innovations highlighted here show some of the ways businesses are reacting to, and shaping, the current changes in retail by creatively embracing interactivity.

81

TRANSPARENCY IN THE PRODUCTION OF HANDMADE FURNITURE

Argentine designer Alejandro Sticotti and Sudacas.com provide true transparency in the production of their wood furniture by live-streaming each item made by hand in their workshop.

The origin of goods is increasingly important to consumers trying to buy responsibly. Argentine designer Alejandro Sticotti showcases the beauty of artisan-created pieces meant to last a lifetime.

In partnership with e-commerce platform Sudacas.com, the Sticotti workshop live-streamed production of its products during its recent Kickstarter and indigogo campaigns. The Sticotti bookshelves and Sticotti coat racks were available for pre-order for the duration of the live stream 'at a fraction of their retail value'. The campaign surpassed its funding goal of $100k within a few days. Modular and handmade, wooden Sticotti bookshelves and coat racks are flatpacked, easily assembled and shipped worldwide for free.

Both of these crowdfunded pieces have a simple, modern aesthetic. The Sticotti bookshelf is a wall-mounted piece using high wooden brackets to support vertical slats with interlocking shelves, and requires no additional nails. Intended to be infinitely expandable and adaptable, it's the sort of design that would look at home next to a mid-century Scandinavian dining set or in an ultra-modern loft. The modular possibilities are endless and can go as big or as little as your space requires; its minimalist design would fit in a small hallway as well as in a lofty space. Each piece is created only once it is ordered, so there is no waste. It took Sticotti ten years to develop and perfect his modular shelving system, billed as 'the only bookshelf you will ever need'.

The Sticotti coat rack is more unusual in appearance, with its odd angles and quirky pegs. Inspired by Japanese carpentry techniques, the self-sustaining joints mean that it's easily assembled without the use of screws, brackets or hand tools.

Sticotti operates a workshop in Buenos Aires and has a team of workers who handcraft wood. With a grandfather who was a carpenter and a father who had a workshop in the house, Sticotti grew up around natural materials like wood, and his family valued craftsmanship. An architecture graduate of the University of Buenos Aires, a quarter of a century ago he founded NET, his own bespoke furniture line.

Sudacas believes in the integrity of South American wood, and the long-lasting characteristics of beautiful wooden furniture. He creates his pieces using sustainable South American wood – lapacho, cedar and Brazilian pine – and he employs local artisans and craftsmen to help realize his vision, preferring to leave the wood as it is, its colour and grain on show.

With decades of design experience, Sticotti's work has been published by major design companies globally. But he always felt as though he was removed from his consumers. This time, though, he wants to engage potential buyers in the process. They aim to take transparency to the ultimate level by live-streaming the creation processes of their South American craftsmen. Sticotti wants people to be able to watch the hard work that goes into crafting furniture.

In the past we have seen a SaaS platform use blockchain to help brands tell a product's story. As we take more and more interest in sustainability, craftsmanship and the provenance of our possessions, this important connection between the consumer, the products they buy and the craftsmen who make them will become an ever more popular trend in retail.

TAKEAWAYS

1 How else can tech be used to showcase production transparency?
2 With what products could your company share the production process?
3 How could the crowdfunded live-streaming model be used to promote and showcase other products and services?

INNOVATION DATA

Website: www.sudacas.com
Contact: hola@sudacas.com
Company name: Sudacas.com and Alejandro Sticotti
Innovation name: Live-streaming workshop production
Country: Argentina
Industries: Access exclusive / Design / Nature & sustainability / Retail & e-commerce

82

VIRTUAL REALITY THAT LETS SHOPPERS PICK BEAUTY PRODUCT INGREDIENTS

South Korean beauty brand Innisfree uses virtual reality (VR) to take consumers on the Jeju Flying Bike experience to collect its products' natural ingredients.

Brands constantly have to think of new and innovative ways to connect consumers to their products. Consumers are increasingly interested in the origins of the products they buy and the brand's journey through conception to production. We have previously seen a manufacturer giving consumers a unique experience that shows them the provenance of their product, with the South American **Sticotti** workshop live-streaming production of bookcases and coat racks.

Brands are also increasingly using tech to provide intrigue around a product and offer a unique experience that draws consumers and attention to a store or product launch. VR is a perfect platform to deliver an immersive escapist experience in a retail environment.

South Korean beauty brand Innisfree is using VR to solve the question of how to take customers on the same journey taken by the brand. Powered by in-store bicycles, customers escape the four walls of the company's new Shanghai Disneyland store by pedalling on the Jeju Flying Bike, which travels around the UNESCO-protected island of Jeju.

Jeju is a volcanic island with a rich diversity of plant life, growing many of the ingredients used by Innisfree in its products. The Jeju Flying Bike, created by PostVisual, 'flies' consumers from the 16.5-square-metre (178-sq.-ft) store to the 1,650-square-kilometre (637-sq.-mile) island, a popular vacation spot for honeymooners and a World Heritage Site for its breathtaking landscape.

By mounting a bike and donning the VR goggles, consumers fly to Jeju at a speed that matches their pedalling. Descending from above the clouds and skimming the sea to fly around the island, they can 'collect' natural ingredients such as canola blooms, green tea leaves and nutmegs, using eye-tracking technology.

To create the 360-degree airborne and underwater surroundings, PostVisual spent three months producing the content, which included building a VR drone camera in house. The creative director of PostVisual, Hyunbok Jung, explained that the key challenge of the project was to break the limitations of the small space provided by the shop floor and build a unique brand experience that could deliver the Innisfree story. Through the medium of interactive play, the Jeju Flying Bike lets consumers experience the brand through their entire body and drives home the brand essence in a fun way that will be memorable and create buzz and talk around the brand and its products.

Since the Jeju Flying Bike arrived at Shanghai Disneyland, thousands have enjoyed the virtual ride to Jeju. The concept is being rolled out this year to flagship stores in Hong Kong, Indonesia, Singapore, Vietnam and the United States.

Exploring new worlds is a key attraction in the use of VR, and projects are using the technology for everything from health care to criminal law. For example, a new game is teaching emergency birth care, and crime scene re-enactments are being used for jurors.

Using VR endlessly increases the scope of the scenes and worlds in which you can place a consumer. It can create an experience never before possible from inside a store, a conference room, a restaurant or an office. Combining VR with product promotion is already a prevalent technique – from gaming to skiwear to sports and climbing equipment – and will continue to change the face of retail.

TAKEAWAYS

1 How else could VR be used to present different options in education and business?
2 In what other innovative ways could tech be used to create intrigue around a product?
3 What experience could your company provide to consumers through VR to share the story of your brand?

INNOVATION DATA

Website: www.innisfreeworld.com
Contact: support_world@innisfree.co.kr
Company name: Innisfree
Innovation name: Jeju Flying Bike
Country: South Korea
Industries: Beauty & cosmetics / Health & wellbeing / Marketing & advertising / Retail & e-commerce

83

THE IOT COFFEE GRINDER THAT KNOWS WHEN TO ORDER MORE BEANS

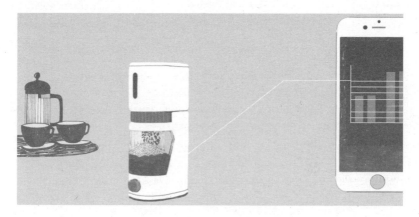

Voltaire is a portable, smart coffee grinder that monitors the beans and orders more when it needs a fresh supply.

There are dozens of products that can help amateur baristas perfect their coffee-making at home. But the one thing that makes the most difference to a good home brew is the freshness of the beans. Voltaire is an IoT portable coffee grinder that monitors the beans and reorders the user's favourite kind when they need a fresh supply.

Once they are roasted, coffee beans begin to lose their flavour in a matter of days. Many factors can affect this process, so it is impossible to predict their exact best-before date. To get around this, the Voltaire grinder uses a built-in sensory platform that accompanies either the grinder or the Airvault coffee storage accessory.

The platform is an array of electronic sensors that measures bean freshness, using an algorithm that takes into account everything from roast date and bean variety to gas concentration, temperature, humidity and bean mass. It connects to a smartphone app and tells the user when the beans are beginning to degrade. Users can choose either to receive notifications or to have their beans automatically reordered before they go bad. The platform also has Wi-Fi, linking to the Internet of Things for displaying its information in colourful graphic charts and messages via the smartphone app, and can reorder coffee from select sources automatically if a user so chooses.

The algorithm and the sensory technology is all open-source, encouraging developers to modify the equipment to track other items such as fruit, grains or even cupcakes inside the containers. As more users contribute more data and the company continues to refine the algorithm, the idea is that the entire system will get 'smarter'.

The platform itself does need to be plugged in for continuous power, and is built into a removable base that attaches to both the Airvault and the grinder, doubling as a battery-charging dock. This is because of the large volume of data being collected and transmitted to the cloud on a continuous basis, as well as the operation of an onboard fan that extracts the air samples used for monitoring.

The smart grinder is currently crowdfunding on Kickstarter, where at the time of writing it has surpassed its $100,000 goal by 50 per cent.

GIR CEO Samantha Rose consulted with Scott Heimendinger, Director of Applied Research at Modernist Cuisine, as well as several baristas in New York City and Portland, Oregon. The company initially introduced the Voltaire to consumers in order to be able to train and refine its learning algorithm against a broad set of data including roast types and environments; but with a new, larger, non-portable version of the Voltaire grinder that uses a similar configuration and sensing capabilities, they hope to tap into a commercial market by the end of 2017.

Other innovative coffee-making products include the IKAWA Home Roaster. It is a digital micro-roaster that lets users roast small batches of coffee beans at the touch of a smartphone button. Technology such as this could make possible a new level of quality control for baristas.

TAKEAWAYS

1 Could similar sensing and recording systems be used for other food and drink items?
2 What other innovations could revolutionize food and drink quality control?
3 What consumer items could your company adapt to suit a commercial setting?

INNOVATION DATA

Website: productofgir.com
Contact: hello@productofgir.com
Company name: GIR
Innovation name: Voltaire Grinder
Country: United States
Industries: Beverage / Food & beverage / Home & garden / Internet of Things

84

PERSONALIZED CUSTOMER SERVICE FROM AN APPLE WATCH

Employees of True Religion use Apple watches to provide loyalty account members with truly customized service, any time they walk into a store.

Band by True Religion is the retailer's latest advent in its Endless Aisle technology project. Band combines the True Religion app for shoppers with Apple watches worn by sales associates to provide highly personalized, concierge-style customer service.

When a loyalty account member who has opted into the app walks into a store, the Apple watches worn by the sales team use haptic technology to alert staff to the VIP's presence. With one tap on the watch's screen, a store associate can access a rich vein of customer data. Social media integration provides sales teams with the customer's profile pictures, allowing the individual to be greeted by name.

Associates can see at a glance a customer's buying history, their communication preferences (that is, email or text) and additional details like what silhouette of jean he or she tends to prefer. Once a customer has been engaged in conversation, the associate can access the label's current inventory and project products on to the store's digital sales floor – 42-inch LED touchscreens that allow team members to highlight new products and help customers find exactly what they are looking for.

The touchscreens also help customers find products that are available from the brand but not necessarily stocked in that particular store. Associates can use their handheld mobile point-of-sale checkout terminals to order the product and arrange for free delivery.

John Hazen, the brand's head of omni-channel, says the company's Endless Aisle technology project is designed to make staff more efficient and effective and provide new methods for engaging with customers. 'With this,' he says, 'it's a moment where we can actually look at things together. I can showcase and put on a show for you with this solution.'

The Band watches, combined with the mobile checkout terminals, free sales team members to interact with customers at any point in the store. And, something that is particularly important in Hazen's opinion, for achieving buy-in from staff, is that the combination of technology allows each sale to be directly credited to the relevant associate. Noel Goggin, CEO and culture leader for Aptos, says that True Religion 'clearly understands this opportunity to unite its digital and physical retail environments to support unified commerce and seamless experiences that inspire brand loyalty and customer engagement'.

Initial predictions were that 10 per cent of the brand's loyalty customers would opt in to the app, and early reports show that the new combination of technologies is proving successful. Since introducing the app, True Religion says that 'in-store customer engagement and conversion rates are higher and the number of Endless Aisle transactions has increased significantly'.

Additionally, through the Endless Aisle project, the brand's buy-and-ship business has doubled, where customers pay in store and receive the product at home. Band was created in partnership with Aptos and Formula 3 Group and first uses of the watches were in the company's flagship store in New York City's SoHo neighbourhood and Los Angeles' Beverly Center mall. They are now being extended to a further 30 retail spaces.

Further development of the Endless Aisle technologies includes incorporating text messages to customers alerting them to new products, and any responses, into the overall profile stored within the Band app. This will further enrich the options available to sales associates for improving individuals' customer experiences.

Unifying on and offline shopping experiences with an added dose of customization is the retail industry's current holy grail. From Cornershop's on-demand personal grocery shoppers who deliver within 90 minutes to Sephora's in-store YouTube make-up tutorials, brands are finding interesting, creative solutions to a complex challenge.

TAKEAWAYS

1 Are there ways your teams could be made more mobile, thus giving them more freedom to interact with customers?
2 How could customer data be put to more effective use by your brand, particularly for improving personalization?
3 What would help provide a particularly resonant local experience to further your brand's capability for customization?

INNOVATION DATA

Website: www.aptos.com
Contact: kmiller@aptos.com
Company name: Aptos
Innovation name: True Religion
Country: United States
Industries: Access exclusive / Retail & e-commerce

85

THE SMART CAMERA THAT MONITORS FRIDGE CONTENTS

London-based Smarter's latest product, the FridgeCam, is a connected camera that prevents waste by alerting users when food expiry dates are near.

Smarter began in 2013 with the introduction of the world's first Wi-Fi-connected kettle. Founder Christian Lane's goal is to find new ways to make connected kitchens an affordable reality. Being based in England meant that the company's first product, the smart kettle, had a particular resonance. The iKettle allows users to remotely monitor the amount of water, set a variety of temperatures and create bespoke settings. Water can be boiled specifically for formula baby feeds, and the kettle can be set to turn on at a given time each morning for that all-important first cup of the day.

Smarter's mission is to make any kitchen smart by helping people more efficiently use their appliances. With the Smarter app, users can link different appliances together to create seamless kitchen operations from afar.

The FridgeCam is the company's latest product. Created to prevent waste by alerting users whenever food expiration dates are near, the connected camera also provides recipe suggestions based on the current contents of the fridge and it automatically compiles shopping lists.

Magnetically mounted, FridgeCam takes only moments to set up and can be used in any style of refrigerator. Users download the app and then, with personalized notifications, receive an alert just before they run out of a favourite item.

The FridgeCam works by taking a photo of the inside of the refrigerator every time the door closes. Via Wi-Fi, alerts are then sent to everyone in the household who has signed up to the same account. The alerts contain information on which products are nearing expiry, recipes for using those products and reminders to replace frequently used items when supplies are getting low.

The app also compiles shopping lists of recognized favourites, which can be linked to each person's most-used online grocery store. UK households throw away an average of £700 worth of food each year, which equates to 700 tonnes (772 t.) of waste, more than half of which could have been eaten or drunk. The FridgeCam has been designed specifically to help reduce such waste, as well as save individuals and families significant amounts of money.

In addition to the smart kettle and refrigerator camera, Smarter has designed a smart coffee machine. Smarter Coffee can be set to brew from anywhere in a building and produces cups of coffee exactly to each person's taste, from strong and dark to light and sweet. It also grinds the beans on demand and can be set to clean itself as per various chosen settings.

Smarter will shortly be introducing the third-generation iKettle and second-generation Smarter Coffee machine. Other products in development include Smarter Mats and the Smarter Detect.

Waste prevention is essential to sustainability, and the food industry is a well-known culprit in not making best use of what is available. A multitude of projects is trying to combat this excessive waste and pollution. Copia is a California-based app that connects homeless shelters with companies that have leftover food, and the Solidarity Fridge in Spain and Brazil's Street Dish campaign provide ways for people with valuable leftovers to reach directly those in need.

TAKEAWAYS

1 How else could frequently used devices be made more intelligent by allowing for on-demand use or production?
2 Are there ways you could connect your company's product to the customer's likely use or uses to help provide added efficiency in their day?
3 How could your product or service be made more sustainable?

INNOVATION DATA

Website: smarter.am
Contact: claire@smarter.am
Company name: Smarter
Innovation name: FridgeCam
Country: United Kingdom
Industries: Access exclusive / Design / Food / Food beverage / Home garden / Internet of Things

86

BRINGING ONLINE COOKIE FUNCTIONALITIES TO THE MALL

The Physical Cookie is a device that could bring targeted digital marketing capabilities to malls and shopping centres worldwide.

In the face of ever more advanced e-commerce algorithms, the smartest bricks-and-mortar outlets are borrowing from their online counterparts to create hybrid shopping experiences that incorporate the best of both worlds.

Finland-based real-estate investment company Sponda has developed the Physical Cookie, a device that can bring targeted digital marketing capabilities – the kind readily available to online retailers – to city malls and shopping centres. It brings online cookie functionalities to the real world, enabling businesses to collect and use data about a consumer's shopping habits. The company describes the innovation as a 'disruptive loyalty programme for a shopping mall', explaining that 'instead of identifying the loyal customer at the end of the shopping process (purchase), the system identifies loyal customers as they enter the shopping mall'.

The device is a simple RFID key fob — costing 0.17 cents to produce — that the customer places in their pocket or attaches to their clothes. It doesn't need to be registered or retain personal data, instead focusing solely on the customer's time spent in stores.

The Physical Cookie collects data about the customer as they shop, monitoring their behaviour by tracking which displays they are lingering by, and communicating its findings with participating stores via electronic readers.

The system learns from the usage data and creates personalized messages, which are displayed to the consumer on screens in store in real time. Instead of annoying push notifications, the shopping environment reacts to the shopper, offering more relevant messages and personalized offers.

Sponda, in collaboration with ad agency TBWA\Helskinki, undertook a successful large-scale trial of the Physical Cookie in one of Helsinki's busiest malls, where 14,000 shoppers carried the device and were rewarded with targeted deals over a four-month period. The Physical Cookies were handed out at random to everyone who entered the mall. Sponda reported that customers with Physical Cookies spent 21.7 per cent more time in stores than those without them, and they also claimed to be able to guide 14.5 per cent more customers from the busiest ground floor to the mall's second floor via targeted, personalized electronic messaging. Throughout the trial, retailers benefited from real-time analytics, enabling them to optimize floor space and understand which displays were proving the most popular in their store.

The system has many advantages over similar technologies, such as the **iBeacons** used in the Dharavi slum. First, it doesn't inconvenience the shopper by asking them to turn on their Bluetooth and drain their phone's battery. Once it's attached to their keys or placed in their pocket, the customer can forget all about it. It also avoids overloading the shopper with information. Rather than spamming multiple alerts to their phone as they walk through the mall, the Physical Cookie causes the physical retail environment to react around them, displaying dynamic ads in response to their activity. It's both less obtrusive and requires less action on the part of the shopper.

TAKEAWAYS

1 Outside retail, how else could RFID be used to offer more personalized experiences?

2 If the Physical Cookie required users to create an account, how could e-commerce stores then make use of the customer's data from activity in the real world?

3 Could there potentially be privacy concerns with the Physical Cookie? (If it were to be rolled out at scale, opt-in rates may be affected by shoppers not wanting their 'real-world browsing history' reflected on in-store advertisements that others could see.) How could this be overcome?

INNOVATION DATA

Website: www.physicalcookie.com
Contact: juha-matti.raunio@tbwa.fi
Company name: Sponda
Innovation name: Physical Cookie
Country: Finland
Industries: Marketing & advertising / Retail & e-commerce / Smart cities

87

DOWNLOADABLE DESIGNER FURNITURE THAT CAN BE MADE LOCALLY

Opendesk is a platform that enables customers to download furniture designs from around the world, and have them made at a local workshop.

Shipping furniture can be costly and result in long shipping times, but one London-based company is looking to disrupt the furniture market. Opendesk offers designer furniture that can be made locally around the world.

Inspired by the words of the economist John Maynard Keynes, who said, 'It is easier to ship recipes than cakes and biscuits', the company connects local workshops with online designs.

Rather than buying individual items of furniture and shipping them across the world, customers can pay for access to the design as a file, and have the furniture built for them in their own country by local makers. The designs work for flatpack products that can be easily assembled on site, using locally sourced materials.

This approach leads to substantial cost savings for the customer. One of the company's trademark four-person desks sells for around £1,400, which is around 50 per cent cheaper than a high-end equivalent and only two or three times more than an Ikea equivalent. Equally, the designers stand to make more. There is typically a 200 per cent mark-up on such goods sold at retail, and a designer would receive around half of what they could get if they sold their design through Opendesk. Usually, of an Opendesk sale, 10 per cent goes to the designer, 60 per cent to the maker and the remainder to Opendesk.

Small-scale creatives and designers also benefit from the new opportunities that open up when the onus of production and shipping is taken off the table (no pun intended). They are able to host their designs on the global platform without having to worry about organizing shipping themselves.

Designers also have control over how they license their product designs. They can choose to publish them without any licence restrictions (under something like Creative Commons Attribution), or they can specify that they are free for non-commercial use only. They can also charge for downloads as a way to earn income. Elaborating on this 'open making' model, the company explains: 'We embrace open source because we believe that it can produce attendant benefits and a more ethical model of production without the intellectual property incumbency typically associated with "business as usual". This means that we're able to host professional product designs which can be freely downloaded and made by people themselves, for example in makerspaces, Fablabs, techshops or other suitably equipped facilities.'

The company is also aiming to appeal to customers through Opendesk Express, which enables customers to buy on-demand desks that are shipped within 14 days. Customers of the service can check out instantly, rather than wait for a quote from a manufacturer. Opendesk is also working on new smart features for their office ware, continuing development on utilities for desks such as phone charging points and touch sensors.

The company, which is backed by Innovate UK and Telefonica's Wayra accelerator, has raised around £640,000 through a combination of crowdfunding and investment. With a global network of over 1,000 designers and makers, and with over 30,000 downloads, the company has also attracted interest from a number of big brands. The likes of Nike, Greenpeace, Google and John Lewis are all using Opendesk designs, and the company has forecast profit for 2017.

TAKEAWAYS

1 In what other industries could an open making model be applied?
2 Without any showrooms, how could Opendesk designers best advertise their work?
3 How could your company look to cut out the 'middleman' in your supply chain to the benefit of your company and your customers?

INNOVATION DATA

Website: www.opendesk.cc
Contact: sales@opendesk.cc
Innovation name: Opendesk
Country: United Kingdom
Industries: Design / Retail & e-commerce / Workspace

88

A SCANNER THAT HELPS SHOPPERS FIND WHAT THEY WANT

Germany's Findbox is a device that enables consumers to find what they're looking for in store quickly by scanning similar items.

Regular readers of Springwise may remember our coverage of Partpic, the visual search app that lets consumers scan components to work out what they are and where to buy them. Bringing this capability to high-street stores, Germany's Findbox is a device that enables shoppers quickly to find what they're looking for by scanning similar items.

For large stores and DIY outlets with a wide inventory of similar products, customers can often become confused while trying to find a particular item and end up leaving without buying anything. Findbox is a kiosk that aims to avoid this scenario by acting as a digital assistant that can locate the items they need. The device features a scanner that uses an advanced image-recognition algorithm to recognize 3D objects and match them to products in the store.

For example, if customers need a particular type of light bulb, ink cartridge or screw as a replacement, they can take an old one into the store, scan it and the device will tell them if it's in stock and which aisle and shelf it's on. The Findbox also offers up similar items: customers can scan any product to see what other related options are available to them. Otherwise, they can also search manually by keyword, using the device's touchscreen. Either way, the kiosk offers up rich information – brand, specifications and price – to help customers make a decision.

The system is ideally suited to large stores such a supermarkets or DIY warehouses, where finding the precise model or item required can be tricky, even if sections of the store are indicated with overhead signage.

Anyone who has had to visit a large DIY store and hunt for the correct screw type can testify to this. And while the shopper benefits from the time saved searching, vendors also learn about their customers. For example, Findbox could reveal that a certain item is highly sought after but out of stock, prompting the vendor to place a new order. As some shoppers are reticent about asking whether something is in stock or not, such insights can be hard to obtain otherwise. Findbox helps customers find what they're looking for more quickly, while businesses can reduce lost sales, free up staff and upsell related products.

The company also offers LightGuide wireless product tags, which can be used in conjunction with the scanning device. These tags replace the usual paper price labels on the shelves of smaller stores and, when customers search for an item using the kiosk, the tags can light up to show them exactly where they are.

Barcode scanners already exist which offer similar functionality to Findbox, but they are obviously unusable with any item that doesn't have its original packaging. Findbox is more versatile.

In three years the company has grown significantly and has installed devices in over 200 stores in Germany, France, the United Kingdom and the United States. Following this success, the company was purchased by SES-imagotag in November 2016.

TAKEAWAYS

1 Are there other ways for bricks-and-mortar stores to direct shoppers more efficiently to what they need?

2 What stores would be well suited to the Findbox solution? Could similar functionality be the cornerstone of modern retail environments, such as Amazon Go, in the future?

3 What other features could Findbox incorporate to emulate the speed and convenience of shopping online? Perhaps there could be an option to pay at a machine prior to picking up the item, for example?

INNOVATION DATA

Website: www.findbox.de
Contact: www.findbox.de/en/company/contact
Innovation name: Findbox
Country: Germany
Industry: Retail & e-commerce

89

A DELIVERY DRONE NETWORK CHARGED BY HOME SOLAR PANELS

Mobisol's Solar Air Distribution network is adding drone recharging stations to the roofs of homes in rural Africa, creating a delivery infrastructure for its customers.

German solar energy company Mobisol has an extensive customer network in eastern Africa and is focused on ridding the world of energy poverty. Providing solar panels throughout Kenya, Rwanda and Tanzania, Mobisol is currently developing a solar-powered delivery drone network.

The company's speciality is easy-to-install solar home systems that come with mobile pay-as-you-go instalment plans. Since its inception in 2010, Mobisol has installed more than 70,000 home solar units across the three countries. Within three years, almost all customers completely pay for the panels, thus saving money in the long run and significantly improving general standards of living.

Students who previously were forced to study via kerosene lamp, and business owners who were limited in the hours they could devote to their enterprise, are now free to study and work for as long as they like. Additionally, the use of solar energy in the home improves families' overall health, as air and noise pollution from lanterns and generators are greatly reduced.

Mobisol home solar systems are available in four different sizes, providing enough energy to power medium-sized homes through to running small businesses. Customers can also sell their excess energy to other local community members. The battery comes with a three-year warranty, and the panel itself with a 20-year guarantee. The Mobisol team also provides maintenance and repairs throughout the warranty period.

Now, having seen the success and continued growth in adoption of solar energy, Mobisol is expanding its work into delivery by drone. The company says that it wants to become the 'Amazon of the off-grid market' and plans to do so through its solar-powered drone delivery network. The beta project is being tested in Tanzania, and the team behind it believes it could leapfrog the continent's infrastructural deficits to become the main method of delivery.

Key challenges to worldwide acceptance and use of delivery copters are the lack of recharging capabilities and the distance needed to travel. In Tanzania, Mobisol is using its existing network of customers, none of whom is more than 5 kilometres (3 miles) apart, to test customer acceptance, technical constraints and the climatic conditions of the region. By installing recharging pads on existing customers' roofs, drones will be able to travel farther and provide a more reliable service.

Ideally, should the network prove a success, Mobisol customers who allow their solar panels to be used as part of the drone charging network will earn additional income, making the entire delivery system self-sufficient and self-perpetuating.

As well as bypassing many of the current infrastructural challenges facing many parts of the world, a carbon-neutral drone delivery network could go some way towards mitigating climate change and its effects.

Rural and remote communities are already some of those experiencing the most severe effects of climate change; eco-friendly improvements in connectivity therefore have great potential for supporting their long-term sustainable development.

TAKEAWAYS

1 What other types of energy infrastructure could also provide additional functionality?
2 Are there ways in which solar power could be incorporated into your business?
3 How could your product or service provide additional value to customers by layering on another purpose?

INNOVATION DATA

Website: www.plugintheworld.com/mobisol
Contact: communications@plugintheworld.com
Innovation name: Mobisol
Countries: Rwanda; Tanzania
Industries: Nature & sustainability / Retail & e-commerce / Smart cities / Transport & automotive

90

USING BEACONS IN MUMBAI TO HELP SMALL BUSINESSES ADVERTISE

This Google-backed project uses beacons to help small businesses in one of Asia's biggest slums to compete with online retailers by alerting smartphone users as they pass by.

Beacons are small, relatively cheap hardware that use Bluetooth connections to transmit messages or prompts to smartphones and tablets. Because they can detect very accurate location data, beacons are often used in innovations looking to deliver hyper-contextual content to users based on their location. Now, a project by Google, the Industrial Design Centre (IDC), the Indian Institute of Technology (IIT) and Swansea University is using the technology to improve an Indian slum market's visibility among smartphone users.

At 216 hectares (535 acres), Mumbai's Dharavi is one of Asia's largest slums. It has a manufacturing and retail sector worth around $1 billion and deals primarily in leather products, pottery, jewellery and textiles. Under the joint project, the use of beacons in the area enables local manufacturers and designers to send alerts to potential customers walking past, advertising new products, offers and other announcements.

Once mounted on a nearby wall, the beacons can broadcast an alert containing a website URL to anyone with a Bluetooth-enabled smartphone within 9 metres (30 ft). Nearby recipients can then open the link, which will take them to an online marketplace with information on what vendors in the locality are selling. Since many mobile users turn off Bluetooth to conserve battery life on devices, retailers have also been provided with posters that ask consumers to turn their Bluetooth back on so that they can receive the notifications.

The initiative is part of the Google IoT Research Award Pilot, and 100 beacons have been allocated for the project. The first 30 beacons have been designated to leather stores, while the remaining 70 are to be used in Kumbharwada – a century-old, 9-hectare (22-acre) establishment famed for its pottery, housing approximately 1,500 families of whom 700–800 are practising potters today. Researchers will be actively studying the performance of these beacons and the results for five weeks, but shopkeepers will be permitted to keep the devices after the project concludes. The beacons should continue to function for approximately three years in total.

According to Quartz India, the project had a slow uptake initially. During the first two weeks, only 11 beacons were adopted by local vendors, despite a good level of technical literacy in the area and a familiarity with other smartphone communication tools and apps. Chinmay Parab, a master's student at the IDC who worked on the project, commented, 'It is taking a bit more time than we expected to convince people, but we expected an inertia to [adopting] any new technology. Most people who might be passing by Dharavi's leather market might not even know that these markets have such good-quality crafty products. [This technology will give them] digital visibility.'

Some store owners explained that they were content with their existing, loyal customer base, but Parab and other early adopters feel there is a genuine need for the technology, particularly in response to increasing competition from e-commerce giants such as Snapdeal, Flipkart and Amazon.

But perhaps the project's greatest legacy will be how the slum is perceived in the future. As Parab explains: 'The economy that runs in parallel in Dharavi is always ignored under this "Asia's largest slum" image that we all have. We're attempting to give Dharavi, even though on a small scale, a new identity of being a digital hub.'

TAKEAWAYS

1 How could your company make use of beacons to link online and offline experiences?
2 How else could existing technologies be used to help developing economies amplify their local strengths and fight off competition from e-commerce giants?
3 How could beacons be used outside the retail environment?

INNOVATION DATA

Website: www.developers.google.com/beacons/
Contact: www.twitter.com/Google
Innovation name: Google beacons
Country: India
Industries: Retail & e-commerce / Telecoms & mobile

SUMMARY

Today, few areas of retail are not being seriously disrupted by new technologies and innovations. Twenty years ago, if you were to ask someone where they shopped, they would have perhaps named a shopping centre, a high street or marketplace. Today, they will tell you whether they prefer to shop online or in bricks-and-mortar stores. Tomorrow, they will be referring to virtual reality shopping locations, or waving a hand towards their smart-home interface, remembering how they used to laboriously order groceries online before their fridge took over.

From order to manufacture to delivery, innovation is rampant, offering consumers more choice, convenience and flexibility than ever before. Here are the key conclusions to draw from the ten innovations in this chapter to help you shape your own vision for the future of retail.

RETAIL TAKEAWAYS

1 **If something can be done online, do it offline, and vice versa.** Which advantages of the online experience can be recreated in the physical world? What does a real-world abandoned cart email look like, for example? How can we better show reviews in store for social validation? And what elements of physical stores would we like to see replicated online, through virtual reality or telepresence?

2 **Optimize the Internet of Things.** If IoT devices are to be endowed with the power to place orders on behalf of their human owners, retailers need to think seriously about how to best partner with, and optimize for, those devices. Catering to the algorithmic decision-making in these smart devices will be key for retailers in the near future.

3 **Incorporate sustainability.** Supply chains are a good place to start, and then think as widely as possible. Are the company's products or services used among sharing networks? Design your ideal scenario for such use, making sure to include some aspect of on-demand production or supply, and see what could be usable now. Finally, think creatively about future audiences, their use of new technologies and how your brand could use partnerships for improved provision.

4 **Deliver on delivery.** The technologies are still a long way from widespread adoption, but drones, 3D printing and local computer numerically controlled (CNC) machining hubs are all likely to seriously affect how we think about delivery networks in the near future. With 3D printing in particular, there is the bonus opportunity for customers to personalize their item before manufacturing. How could you reposition

delivery from being a number-crunching logistical challenge to a creative opportunity for an enhanced product experience?

5 **Don't forget the shop.** However much the actual retail transaction moves online, the store will always retain a critical role for retailers. This is the place. The place where customers can come to experience the essence of a brand – the products, the design and architecture, the people, the music, the smells, the energy. All these ingredients go to create an intangible impression in a customer's mind, which has been so important to merchants for centuries. And witness the raft of online 'pure-plays', including the mighty Amazon, now seeking out a physical, main-street presence. The shape, design, location and experience may change over time but the importance of a retail place will not diminish.

TRAVEL

Tourism and travel now contribute more than \$7 trillion to the global economy, and young people in particular are travelling more than ever before. Driven by disruptive technologies and new business models, the world has never been more open for tourists, and a new generation of travellers is taking full advantage.

The priorities have shifted, and the way we now plan and arrange our travel has fundamentally altered, as have the ways in which we experience our destinations. Many people now regard anything other than a highly personalized, bespoke experience as second rate. In this context, the Lonely Planet and Rough Guide books, two former staples of any well-planned holiday, have found their once 'invaluable' status diminished by online tips and review sites. Newer, digital offerings are now moving away from a one-size-fits-all approach in favour of guides that are truly tailored to each individual trip and the unique interests and priorities of the traveller.

Living like a local

As travellers seek out these ever more personal experiences, local, authentic knowledge has assumed a new premium. Only when equipped with local knowledge can travellers create truly bespoke and unique experiences, and while travel review sites are still a valuable resource, they struggle to provide the depth of knowledge that can come only from a true local in direct response to a traveller's questions. Western tourists are seeking new experiences that take them away from their everyday lives, gravitating towards new experiences and human connections.

This emphasis on local knowledge and personalized experiences lies behind innovations like **Kate's Goodness** – an Instagram-style feed of hotspots as photographed and described by locals – or Nectar & Pulse, which is an Austrian company enabling users to create personal city guides by zeroing in on the suggestions of locals with similar preferences. These innovations unlock local knowledge, enabling visitors to create unique and authentic experiences tailored to them.

The access economy

Airbnb has had a profound impact on the travel industry, and we have already touched on this company in the chapter on the sharing economy, but it is not the only access economy player in this space. While Airbnb casts its net wide, many of the start-ups we have seen on Springwise are taking that model and applying it to niche areas.

PandaBed, for example, is a peer-to-peer lodging service that enables homeowners to connect with guests who share their cultural or religious ideas. Located in Singapore and operating across Asia, the service lets homeowners open up their spare rooms to travellers and those seeking short-term accommodation. Meanwhile, over in Europe, Hotel Gelem uses the same model to overcome racial tensions, inviting visitors to stay in Romany communities. So-called 'embedded tourists' can apply via the website to stay in Romany homes in locations in France, Germany, Macedonia and Kosovo.

The objectives could not be more different. While PandaBed seeks to offer comfort by providing guests with a cultural framework that will be familiar, Hotel Gelem looks to break down barriers and encourage new ways of thinking. These contrasting outcomes are a testimony to how well suited the access economy is to disrupting hospitality as we know it, which will almost certainly see it survive inevitable regulatory challenges in the future. **Pearlshare** is just one of many innovations that feed directly off the Airbnb revolution.

Sustainable travel

With access and knowledge increasing, so too is an awareness of the damage tourism and travel can cause to the environment. Many travellers now make environmental concerns a pillar of their trip, doing what they can to offset or prevent pollution and expecting the companies they engage with to have a similar approach. Eco-tourism takes many forms, including staying off grid, volunteering abroad and staycationing.

Ticking the carbon offset box used to be enough for most travellers' consciences, but for the next generation it is just the start. Environmentally friendly behaviours from travel companies are no longer seen as 'nice-to-haves'. Rather, there is a now an expectation that, as they help travellers explore the planet, organizations should be behaving responsibly to help protect it.

GreenHotelWorld ranks hotels by their carbon footprint, helping travellers to find the most eco-conscious option. The company will even offer to help offset a traveller's CO_2 emissions from their stay for free. **Kind Traveler,** meanwhile, enables luxury holiday-makers to donate money to charity in exchange for exclusive deals with sustainable hotels.

With driverless cars and other mobility innovations just around the corner, the world is going to become even more connected over the coming years. In this context, the innovations featured in this chapter really only give a taste of what's to come, offering travellers more authentic, personal and sustainable adventures.

91

GUIDED TOURS WITH FORMER GANG MEMBERS IN PANAMA

The Fortaleza Tour in Panama City is a walking tour set up by rehabilitated graduates of the Esperanza Social Venture Club.

Travellers in search of an authentic experience can provide excellent business opportunities for local people in developing economies. Panama City's Fortaleza Tour is just such an example. Set up by rehabilitated graduates of the Esperanza Social Venture Club – an organization dedicated to demobilizing Panama's street gangs, integrating their members into society, and improving the area's economy – the Fortaleza walking tours have proven to be one of the club's most successful enterprises.

The Social Venture Club's mandate is simple and powerful: if their own communities cannot take on the gang members and young men on the periphery of gangs, who will?

Prison is counterproductive, despite the general public's preference for harsh punishments. The Esperanza Social Venture Club 'helps young men whose only contacts to formal society are through the police and the occasional politician ... to earn a stake in their society, learn its norms and see that their success is tied to its success'.

The club runs a ten-week intervention programme that works at the individual, group and community level:

- At the individual level, participants are helped to access public services and given training and support in either accessing employment or creating their own business.

- At the group level, the club measures success by demobilizing members of criminal-activity-focused, self-identified street gangs who form a team that continues to work together but now for different aims: broad social success.
- At the community level, the club helps to establish a zone of peace in the area that used to be controlled by the gang and encourages social events and the physical transformation of the neighbourhood.

After completing the club's intervention programme, graduates have a choice between finding a job or taking part in the Esperanza Social Venture Fund's three-week incubator circuit. The business development course culminates in entrepreneurial pitches by budding business owners to local leaders and funders.

Businesses that are approved for funding are then supported in making the ideas a reality. One of the club's most recent successes is the Fortaleza Tour. Conceived by former members of the Ciudad de Dios gang, the walking tour begins at the American Trade Hotel in Casco Viejo, an area that has been central to gang culture. The tour guides tell the history of the area and their personal stories, as they show the visitors their hangouts, their mothers' homes and gang graffiti. The tour ends at a street party, where guests can pay $10 for dinner and a mojito.

Tours last 80 minutes and cost $15 and have been an incredible draw as part of Casco Viejo's renewal. A large part of their appeal lies in the inspiring stories of growth and change, both in the lives of the tour leaders and the local community as a whole. In no way do the tours glorify violence or poverty.

Other ways tourists are being offered authentic local experiences are through Asia's BackStreet Academy and the United States' EatWith network. Backstreet Academy works with NGOs across Asia, enabling local hosts to offer tours and classes to visitors in search of authentic experiences. EatWith links travellers in need of a meal with residents looking to meet new people.

TAKEAWAYS

1 How could other cities use the model of rehabilitation to regenerate lives and neighbourhoods?
2 Does your business have unique local knowledge that travellers could use?
3 How could community experts contribute to your product or service?

INNOVATION DATA

Website: www.esperanzasvc.org/fortaleza-tours/
Contact: www.twitter.com/weareesperanza
Company name: Esperanza Social Venture Club
Innovation name: Fortaleza Tour
Country: Panama
Industries: Entertainment & culture / Non-profit & social cause / Tourism & travel

92

INTERACTIVE LOCAL GUIDES FROM HOLIDAY PROPERTY HOSTS

Pearlshare lets holiday rental hosts curate guides for the area around their property and set their listing apart from the competition.

Travellers are no longer satisfied with the mass tourism experience. They want to 'live like a local'. Locals always know an area best and are therefore the most valuable resource for inside knowledge and travel tips for visitors. Pearlshare is utilizing that resource and enabling vacation rental hosts to create guides for the area surrounding their property, and upgrade their listing profile so that it stands out from the competition.

Pearlshare is essentially a crowdsourced tour guide that collates recommendations from property hosts. To begin, contributors can view suggestions made by other users. They then add their own by selecting their favourite local spots – restaurants, parks and museums – and annotating them. Hosts can curate their selection into a personal area guide and insert it into their Airbnb profile, seamlessly providing potential guests with a view of the neighbourhood.

The guides built by hosts are fully interactive, complete with maps and personal comments. They can be shared via a link on the host's website or any messaging platform, so that anyone looking at a property can see the places of interest in the neighbourhood. They will then have all the details they need to find out whether a place is worth visiting and to book the property. Jim Breese, founder of Learnairbnb.com, says that 'Pearlshare is a powerful way to transform your guest's trip from an average vacation into a memorable, local experience.'

Guides can also be shared via an email link or by embedding it on a website using a simple embed code – meaning that visitors can start to explore recommended places even before they arrive. This aims to enhance a visitor's experience and lets the host get better reviews. The Pearlshare web and mobile apps allow hosts to update guides on the go and means that they are always at hand for the user. Pearlshare is designed to work on any mobile device and hosts can create as many guides as they wish, for free.

Visitors can use Pearlshare to save all the places they want to visit on their travels and add quick private annotations of their own. If they do not have time to plan ahead, they can use the service to find places of interest nearby while they are out and about exploring a destination. They can then share recommendations with friends, guests and fellow travellers if they choose.

Pearlshare suggests that any local expert – whether they are a travel writer, someone with a deep knowledge of a city or a specialist in a particular field who has an online presence – can use the service to build interactive guides. They can then share them with their followers and audience via a link. Every guide allows users to put in a link back to their own blog, website or social media channel, so it can be an effective way to build presence in the mobile space.

Examples of travel guides previous users have created include '7 London Food Trucks to Visit in 2017', 'Places to Go That Are Far Away from Your Awful Relatives' and '7 Unique Budget Places to Stay in Ireland'. Hosts can send the guides to guests in a welcome email and the platform is available via desktop or through a mobile app.

We have seen numerous tourism start-ups offer live smartphone tours, like Lopeca in Turkey, which enables users to 'see' the world via remote smartphone video tours from locals. The future of travel advice is surely in the hands of the locals.

TAKEAWAYS

1 Could businesses make use of this platform to offer special deals or discounts and entice new customers?
2 How else could crowdsourcing be used to raise the profile of a tourist location?
3 How could your business benefit from unique local insider knowledge?

INNOVATION DATA

Website: www.pearlshare.com
Contact: feedback@pearlshare.com
Innovation name: Pearlshare
Country: United Kingdom
Industries: Food & beverage / Home & garden / Marketing & advertising / Tourism & travel

93

A ROBOT SERVICE FOR LOST AIRPORT TRAVELLERS

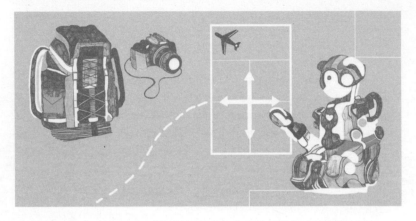

Electronics giant Hitachi is trialling a hospitality robot service at Haneda Airport, Tokyo.

The variety of tasks that robots now undertake is mind-boggling. One of the more visible ways in which they are being used is in customer service. In Japan, electronics giant Hitachi is trialling a new humanoid robot that will guide lost travellers around Tokyo's Haneda Airport. Hiroshi Sato, Hitachi's senior vice-president and executive officer, says, 'Japan has seen a recent increase in the number of foreign visitors, an increase which has raised the need for a variety of services to enable them to make the most of their visit.'

In development since 2005, the EMIEW3 humanoid robot uses a remote brain that combines built-in sensors and cameras to provide a realistic response and allow it to adapt to a changing environment. The version being used in Haneda Airport is the most advanced, and uses a cloud-based system that enables multiple EMIEW3s to communicate with one other.

The EMIEW3 currently speaks in English and Japanese and offers spoken guidance as well as more information via a large interactive display screen installed next to the counter that serves as the robot's base in the airport. The robot switches effortlessly between the two languages, pointing to potential use in translating crises for harried airport workers and late-running passengers. The robot travels smoothly around the airport at a steady 6 kilometres (3.7 miles) per hour and can even pick itself up without human assistance if it falls down – essential if sprinting passengers accidentally collide with the bot.

The introduction of the EMIEW3 to Tokyo's airport will follow three phases. At the start of the trial during phase one, the robot will be stationary. It will be seated at the counter that serves as its base, directing users with questions to the information available via the display system.

Following success at that stage, phase two will begin. In this phase, the robot will be able to move to the information displays of its own accord and answer questions in conversation with travellers. At this point, the robot will be working much more like a concierge.

The last phase of the trial will see the robot accompanying members of the public to their chosen location in the airport. Able to navigate a crowded space with ease, the robot will also be able to ask and answer questions visitors have on the journey.

The company plans to continue developing and introducing the EMIEW3 technology and will soon add Chinese and Korean to the languages spoken by the robot. Hitachi is also exploring the robot's use in other customer service-centric areas such as shopping malls, festivals and other public facilities.

Other interesting uses of robots include Spyce Kitchen's 1.6-square-metre (20-sq.-ft) automated kitchen that takes care of everything so that restaurants can spend more money on ingredients. Robots are also being used to help ease the burden on overworked health professionals. AiTreat's physiotherapy robot provides bespoke sports massage and acupoint therapy, while measuring patient progress over time.

TAKEAWAYS

1 What aspects of your company's customer service might adapt well to the addition of robotics?
2 Is there an unexpected area of the tourism industry that your product or service could contribute to?
3 How does your business cater to visitors? If it doesn't, is a robot something you might consider?

INNOVATION DATA

Website: www.hitachi.com/New/cnews/month/2016/09/
160902.html
Contact: www.hitachi.com/contact/index.html
Company name: Hitachi
Innovation name: EMIEW3
Country: Japan
Industry: Tourism & travel

94

A SUSTAINABLE TRAVEL PLATFORM
THAT IS REINVENTING TOURISM

Kind Traveler is a new site that lets travellers donate to
charity and receive exclusive discounts for luxury hotels.

Over 1 billion trips are taken globally each year. That represents
1 billion opportunities for travellers to make a difference in the
countries they visit. Kind Traveler enables luxury holidaymakers
to donate money to charity in exchange for exclusive deals with
sustainable hotels.

The enterprise works in partnership with a number of 'Kind
Hotels', whose sustainability initiatives are displayed on the Kind
Traveler site. Customers select a destination, make a booking and
choose from either human or environmentally based initiatives in
ten main areas that are aligned with the United Nation's sustainable
development goals. The platform then enables users to donate to any
of their charity partners from a selected list of local or global charities.
Under animal welfare, for example, holidaymakers can choose a local
charity such as the Pacific Marine Mammal Centre or a global one

such as Wildaid. In exchange for a donation, customers are offered exclusive rates: a donation of $10 can result in discounts as high as 20 per cent. Holiday destinations are from a growing list of locations, among them New York, Miami, Mexico and the Caribbean.

As well as charities focused on animal rights, other environmental causes include putting an end to trophy hunting and tackling deforestation. The human causes that collaborate with this project focus on feeding the hungry and providing clean water. Other causes that can be helped through this scheme include arts education and literacy, improving health care and improving overall equality.

Kind Traveler was co-founded by Sean Krejci and Jessica Blotter. Krejci grew up in Hawaii and served in the US Air Force before becoming an entrepreneur and launching three successful businesses by the time he was 25. As the eldest in a family of ten, with two blind parents, he has developed a unique and compassionate worldview. Blotter began her career as an earth sciences teacher at the UCSD's Preuss School. She then moved into working with a series of global publications, which focused on her main areas of interest: travel and hospitality trends, sustainability, welfare and social impact.

In 2012 the pair took a trip to the Mayan ruins of Belize. They couldn't help but notice the extreme poverty the local people were enduring, while wealthy tourists enjoyed their country. This inspired them to combine their entrepreneurial skills with their passion for travel, to create an opportunity to help both people and animals.

Luxury resorts can often stand in high contrast with a country's overall economic situation, and tourism often does not contribute to national economic growth. When tourists are aware of this contrast, it can make for an uneasy experience. Kind Traveler's 'give and get' model proposes to solve this problem. According to a recent study, one of the main barriers to the growth of sustainable travel is visibility. Through Kind Traveler, Krejci and Blotter aim to keep sustainable, socially responsible tourism at the forefront of travellers' and travel companies' minds from now on.

There is already a platform called OneSeed Expeditions that organizes trekking tours in South-East Asia, donating a percentage of their revenue to support female entrepreneurs. Now, sustainable travel is available to the less adventurous.

TAKEAWAYS

1 What other innovations could help raise the profile of sustainable tourism?
2 How else could the huge numbers of tourists visiting developing nations every year be used as a force for good?
3 Could your company introduce a similar scheme where discounts are offered in return for charitable donations?

INNOVATION DATA

Website: www.kindtraveler.com
Contact: hello@kindtraveler.com
Innovation name: Kind Traveler
Country: United States
Industries: Nature & sustainability / Non-profit & social cause / Tourism & travel

95

SHARING A BOUTIQUE HOTEL WITH YOUNG REFUGEES

Magdas is a boutique hotel and social enterprise in Vienna, providing employment for young refugees alongside open-minded guests.

Tourists are often shielded from the harsh realities of life that exist in some of the countries they visit, but not at Vienna's Magdas Hotel. Financed by 57,306 euros in crowdfunding and a 1.5 million-euro loan from the Catholic non-profit organization Caritas Vienna, this boutique guesthouse was launched in 2015 to help refugees arriving in Austria to find their feet.

Having noticed that many of the refugees they were working with were struggling to find employment, Caritas decided to take matters into its own hands.

Based in a former Caritas retirement home, the hotel acts as a way to provide employment and housing for refugees while simultaneously raising awareness of their plight. Of the 30 staff members who work at the hotel, 20 come from countries including Iran, Somalia, Chechnya and Syria, while the other ten are more experienced hoteliers from Austria as well as countries such as Poland and Nigeria. In total, the hotel employs staff from 16 different countries and more than 20 languages are spoken within its walls.

There are two suites at the hotel for asylum seekers under the age of 18 who are living in Austria with no family. They use the hotel lounge as their living room, and a social worker visits them and all the staff every week. The staff members are actively encouraged to interact with guests, who in turn appreciate the social impact of the initiative. CEO Gabriela Sonnleitner, in a 2017 interview with *Condé*

Nast Traveler, said, 'We realized they were the ideal people to work in tourism. They're well travelled, speak multiple languages, and many of them come from countries where being a host comes naturally.'

Dinis and Omid are just two of the hotel's success stories. Despite speaking French, Portuguese, Spanish, Italian, Swedish, German and English, Dinis the receptionist from Guinea-Bissau had struggled to find work during ten years in Austria before he joined the Magdas Hotel. Omid, from Afghanistan, can speak five languages and joined the hotel as a night porter before being promoted to deputy front-desk manager in 2016, and he has ambitions to continue moving further up. In conversation with *Condé Nast Traveler*, he explained, 'I've changed a lot, working here. Before, I was very nervous, but I'm more sure of myself now. Magdas is a really good project – it shows the world that there are many different types of people.'

Rooms are available from 62 euros a night, and the hotel is rated four out of five stars on TripAdvisor. Occupancy rates average at 70 per cent and the hotel, which is self-financing, is on track to break even. Staff pay is in line with industry standards, from around 20,000 euros a year for the most junior positions.

In 2015 the Magdas Hotel was awarded the Austrian State Prize for Design and numerous NGOs from other European cities have expressed interest in the self-sufficient project. The arrangement encourages guests to recognize refugees as individual human beings – who are making a contribution to society – rather than as faceless statistics.

TAKEAWAYS

1 Where else could such a model work?
2 What other marginalized groups could benefit from a similar set-up?
3 Which other industries could help refugees while simultaneously improving their service?

INNOVATION DATA

Website: www.magdas-hotel.at
Contact: info@magdas-hotel.at
Company name: Caritas
Innovation name: Magdas Hotel
Country: Austria
Industries: Non-profit & social cause / Tourism & travel

96

A SITE THAT LETS AMATEUR TRAVEL AGENTS EARN CASH

Amsterdam-based platform TRVL is the sharing-economy approach to travel booking.

The travel and tourism industry grew by 3.1 per cent globally in 2015, and is forecasted to accelerate over the next decade. A by-product of this expansion (unfortunate if you already feel inundated by news and updates) is the amount of information available online. There are now countless numbers of booking platforms, flight aggregators and travel blogs, which may contribute to the fact that 49 per cent of travellers will not book a hotel that lacks online reviews.

Helping to make sense of the jumble of online travel information is Jochem Wijnands. Wijnands founded Prss, a company that was eventually picked up by Apple and turned into Apple News Format. Wijnands's latest venture is the TRVL platform, a peer-to-peer community marketplace for travellers.

Anyone passionate about travel and/or their local area can sign up to become a TRVL agent. Prospective agents must create a profile, detailing their travel experience and any tips they usually like to share with friends. Then, through the platform, they can connect to a wide range of travel suppliers, and book a trip for friends and family at discounted rates.

The travel suppliers, hotel chains, airlines, car rental companies and other businesses pay a commission that TRVL splits with its agents. Commissions can be up to 10 per cent of the cost of the booking.

'Studies show that we spend hours researching our trips online just to cut through the noise, narrow down our choices and build up enough confidence to book,' says Wijnands. 'Recommendations go a long way, especially if they are coming from people you trust.'

As well as becoming a TRVL agent, people with extensive knowledge of a particular area can qualify as a Local Expert. Local Experts provide travellers with personalized recommendations and can receive queries from the platform via their mobile phone. When travellers use the TRVL site to search for holiday destinations, a pop-up chat window allows them to contact a relevant Local Expert. TRVL also provides its own recommendations in the form of 'truly wonderful hotels' and offers price comparisons between some of the largest travel booking sites like Booking.com and Hotels.com.

TRVL is completely free to use with no subscription, booking, sign-up or administration fees. The platform also provides an online magazine of inspirational trips, photo tips, videos and various categories of places that include wildlife, adventure and islands.

Other peer-to-peer travel recommendation networks include Yonderbound and Jetpac. Yonderbound pays travellers for posting their opinions and generating hotel sales. Users simply write reviews of the hotels, hostels and resorts they've visited, much as they would on any other site, adding their personal knowledge and insights. Every time a reader clicks through to place a hotel booking from the review, the writer gains Yondercredits in the form of 70 per cent of any profit the site makes. Jetpac uses algorithms to trawl public Instagram photos and glean information about the vibe of city bars and restaurants, before curating them into visual travel guides. Visitors using the app can browse through categories that include 'Happiest places in town' and 'Hipster hangouts'.

TAKEAWAYS

1 How else can the sharing economy be merged with travel?
2 How could a business's supply chain relationships be turned into travel opportunities?
3 What, if any, categories of travel-related information could use an accessibility makeover?

INNOVATION DATA

Website: www.trvl.com
Contact: hello@trvl.com
Innovation name: TRVL
Country: The Netherlands
Industry: Tourism & travel

97

OFFSETTING YOUR CARBON FOOTPRINT BY BOOKING AN ECO-FRIENDLY HOTEL

GreenHotelWorld enables travellers find the most eco-conscious hotels and have the CO_2 emissions from their stay offset for free.

The hotel industry creates 1 per cent of the world's carbon emissions, and non-profit initiative GreenHotelWorld believes that the travel industry itself is the best place to start transforming the world's economic system into a sustainable one. This is because the organization says that there is hardly anyone in the world who does not interact with the industry in some way, thus placing travel in a unique position of potential leadership.

GreenHotelWorld advocates for a greener hotel industry, and helps travellers find the perfect hotel with excellent environmental credentials. Since every overnight hotel stay produces more than 20 kilograms of carbon dioxide, the company also offsets, at no charge to the customer, the carbon dioxide emissions of every hotel stay booked through its site.

While many individual hotels are making concerted efforts to provide a greener service, the GreenHotelWorld platform is stepping in on behalf of those hotels that have yet to begin making an effort to improve their practices. The carbon offsetting is done under the aegis of myclimate, a world leader in providing voluntary carbon-offsetting measures.

Eco-conscious travellers wanting detailed information on how green a hotel's practices are can search for their dream hotel using the GreenHotelWorld website. The organization has partnered with some of the largest online booking agencies, including TripAdvisor, Expedia and Trivago, and lists more than 130,000 hotels in 107 countries.

By connecting to a booking platform via the GreenHotelWorld site, any bookings then made earn the non-profit a commission. The commission is used to pay for carbon-offsetting projects and for further advocacy.

As with any regular travel site, customers begin by entering their destination and dates of travel. The platform then uses a green rating algorithm to filter the options, showing which hotels have certified green practices and which do not. GreenHotelWorld has more than 5,200 eco-friendly hotels in its database. Travellers can even prioritize certain green practices such as environmental protection and social responsibility.

The carbon-offsetting projects that GreenHotelWorld contributes to via myclimate all include an aspect of poverty alleviation as well. The organization is currently contributing to projects in Nicaragua, Kenya and India. Biogas is being installed in India for cooking fuel to help reduce communities' reliance on firewood; energy-efficient cookstoves are being installed in rural Kenya; and reforestation is being supported in Nicaragua. More information about each project is available on the GreenHotelWorld website.

Some of the advocacy work being done by the organization includes the promotion of green tourism certification labels and providing a green hotel density calculation. Eco labels are an important way for consumers to know at a glance which sustainability practices a business upholds. GreenHotelWorld estimates that there are 50 active eco labels specifically for the hotel industry.

In its Global Green Hotel Density review, GreenHotelWorld found that the worldwide density of green hotels is 6.2 per cent. There is considerable variation between continents, with North America leading the way with more than a 10 per cent concentration of green hotels. Asia has the lowest rate, at less than 1 per cent.

Specific hotels that Springwise has featured for their environmental responsibility are the Cottage Lodge in the United Kingdom and the Tubohotel in Mexico. An eco-chic bed and breakfast, Cottage Lodge features a number of sustainable initiatives including pedal-powered TVs in the guest rooms. Tubohotel is built from discarded concrete pipes and is priced reasonably enough to attract a range of travellers, from budget-conscious backpackers to visitors looking for something different as well as eco-friendly.

TAKEAWAYS

1 How else could customers be supported in pursuing eco-responsible tourism?
2 What incentives might encourage hotels to more widely adapt sustainable practices?
3 Are there areas in your business that could use an eco-boost?

INNOVATION DATA

Website: www.greenhotelworld.com
Contact: www.greenhotelworld.com/contact-us
Innovation name: GreenHotelWorld
Country: Switzerland
Industries: Nature & sustainability / Tourism & travel

98

NAME-YOUR-PRICE HOTEL ROOMS

FindBed enables customers to book a hotel room
at a rate of their choice.

Hotels are often left with unfilled rooms, which is why websites offering to cancel and rebook rooms for customers (and make the most
of fluctuating room prices) have already proved so successful. Polish
start-up Findbed reverses the booking process by enabling customers
to name their ideal price, leaving hoteliers to decide whether or not
to accept their offer. Simple to use, and with hoteliers answering in
real time, travellers have an opportunity to negotiate a great price and
ultimately pick up a bargain.

> As Findbed says on its site, the most expensive room is an empty room. So
> this new approach to the hotel industry could prove extremely beneficial
> to both buyers and sellers. Registration is free for both hotels and travellers,
> and Findbed does not charge accommodation owners a commission.

Travellers wishing to use the service fill out a simple form consisting
of desired arrival and departure dates, numbers of adults and children, preferred locations (such as mountainous, seaside or anywhere
in Poland) and what type of catering he or she would like (none,
breakfast only, or breakfast and dinner). Lastly, a minimum and maximum price must be listed.

Travellers are required to include an email address in order to
receive responses from the hotels, and Findbed emphasizes the site's
privacy and security. Once a request for a room is submitted, the
traveller sits back and waits for a response or responses.

Every request for a room has a unique reference number and is
live on Findbed for 24 hours, giving a range of hoteliers time to
consider and reply. Once potential visitors receive replies to their
query, they have a further 24 hours to make a decision about where

to stay. Generally, travellers will receive responses only from hotels happy to provide a room at the offered price.

Findbed says that the entire process often takes only a few minutes; the 48-hour limit is there to protect both sides of the bargaining table from wasting time and effort. Once a user has decided which hotel's offer to accept, he or she must contact the relevant business's booking department and use the unique reference number generated by Findbed to confirm the reservation. The booking then follows the typical reservation process, with fees confirmed, payment made and the visitor receiving final confirmation by email.

If a hotel does not hear back from a potential visitor before the end of the 48-hour period, it is safe to assume that the traveller chose another destination. Although the platform does not currently charge a commission to hotels that receive bookings through the service, Findbed does offer premium, paid-for marketing and sales packages to help hotels improve promotion and sales conversions.

Other industries testing out the pay-what-you-like model of economics include a taxi service in Los Angeles and the US-based Aspiration Bank. Opoli is a smartphone, desktop and tablet transportation app, which enables customers to confirm a price during booking, eliminating the surge pricing and unpredictable metered fees of other taxi services. Aspiration wants to see a move away from the profit-driven fees that investment banks attach to user accounts, instead opting for a 'pay what Is fair' fee model.

TAKEAWAYS

1 If these payment models prove successful, what other industries might be tempted to test similar options?

2 Is there an aspect of your business that customers could contribute more to in terms of fees and service provision?

3 Could there be a future scenario where customers set up a one-stop payment mechanism that covers all the different services they use throughout the day?

INNOVATION DATA

Website: www.findbed.pl
Contact: rafal@findbed.pl
Innovation name: FindBed
Country: Poland
Industries: Retail & e-commerce / Tourism & travel

99

TRADING LOCAL TRAVEL TIPS IN A 'GOODNESS' MARKETPLACE

Kate's Goodness is an Instagram-style, curated stream of travel recommendations from in-the-know locals.

Looking for useful travel tips in an unknown city, both online and off, can often feel like searching for the proverbial needle in a haystack. The idea of travel, for some, has become an event with such high expectations, so thoroughly researched and well planned, that on one side, the joy of serendipity and of 'getting lost' has almost completely vanished with GPS technology. On the other hand, users are more able to get exactly what they want, satisfying their personal, unique consumer needs.

Helping travellers do just that is Kate's Goodness, an app that curates an evolving stream of 'goodness' – places recommended by locals who know and love them – and creating a marketplace where local information is currency.

With an Instagram-esque layout, the app is an evolving stream of each city's 'goodness' – up-to-date recommendations by locals, who counter the excess of Internet noise by presenting their favourites in the form of a single picture, a short, intimate description and a location map.

After a visit, travellers can vote 'goodness' or 'not quite' depending on their experience, and writers earn or lose points – known as Goodness gold – accordingly. A place can only be written about once – at which point it 'belongs' to that writer. The founders say, 'Our long-term goal is to build a global community of people who share and appreciate Goodness, enabling anyone and everyone with a mobile phone to have rewarding, quality experiences across the world and in their home town.'

Places move up and down the ranks depending on users' votes. Visitors also earn Goodness gold by writing posts, voting and sharing. This way, the app maintains a diplomatic and up-to-date catalogue of tips. By crowdsourcing the votes from visitors to each destination, the recommendations become more reliable as more users sign up to the app.

An interesting aspect of the app is the Goodness currency. The app's stock exchange element sees users acquiring and selling articles to enhance their portfolio and in-app status, trading Goodness gold between users (because one business or local spot can be 'acquired' only by one user).

The company has now officially launched in the App Store, doubled its user base within one month, and increased the library of posts by nearly 20 per cent. The community of contributors also expanded, adding hundreds of locals, and email subscribers grew threefold.

'There is no tool in the App Store today that helps people discover Goodness in an intuitive way, using short curated friend-like recommendations,' one of the co-founders says. '[For the team], when someone has a great travel/human experience, it makes it all worthwhile.'

The start-up is now planning to build a more streamlined connection between posts in the app and bloggers' content, and create a culture of Goodness gold, awarding contributors titles such as 'The most influential theatre expert in Berlin' or 'The leading global authority on coffee shops'.

Other ways travel locals are linking up with interested travellers include Austrian company Nectar & Pulse, a travel site that creates personal city guides by helping visitors zero in on the tips and suggestions of locals with similar personalities and preferences; and Scouted, which allows anyone to create a guide for their city, picking their favourite places to go or following a particular theme.

TAKEAWAYS

1 How could this type of knowledge sharing be made even more useful for residents and their local businesses?
2 How could your company contribute to or get involved in a peer-to-peer recommendation network?
3 How could rating or recommendation systems be adapted for internal use with staff and rewards, both individually and company-wide?

INNOVATION DATA

Website: www.katesgoodness.com
Contact: www.katesgoodness.com/contact
Innovation name: Kate's Goodness
Country: United States
Industries: Entertainment & culture / Tourism & travel

100

DESIGNING YOUR OWN LUXURY POP-UP HOTEL

Bespoke travel experts Black Tomato introduce their latest service, Blink, for accommodation, location, amenities and adventures unique to each trip.

For seasoned travellers looking for something unique, Black Tomato's award-winning Blink service provides self-designed luxury tent accommodation in some of the world's most remote locations. Already an expert in exclusive, luxury travel, Black Tomato has taken its service into the realm of complete customization.

No one will ever have the same Blink experience, and Black Tomato emphasizes the sustainability of the offer. 'Once you have experienced your Blink camp, it will be taken down and we'll ensure that nothing is left behind, and no one else will have that same Blink experience. Our aim is to leave no trace and to let the natural environment remain in its perfect state.'

The Black Tomato Blink team has done its research, finding some of the most remote and untouched locations around the world. The service caters for travel groups of a range of sizes, from a romantic twosome to an extended family get-together. As well as offering help to book flights, the Blink team will organize as many or as few excursions and events as desired during a group's stay.

Potential guests start the process by filling out a detailed questionnaire that includes letting the Blink team know whether the group already has a specific area in mind. To help narrow down the options, the questionnaire includes choosing specific environments, such as polar, desert or jungle and a steer on how remote the guests would like to be. They can choose from unmapped territory, no other inhabitants, no Wi-Fi or signal, or within reach of a local community.

Camp structure options include yurts and a variety of styles and shapes of tents with layouts that could include a spa tent, en-suite bathrooms and an outdoor relaxing area. Camp furnishings could include local artwork, lanterns, electric lighting, antiques and specific types of textile.

Food, drink and the general running of the camp are no less opulent, with options including what type of food the chef is expert in and the preferred size of the Blink team. Guests can choose to have a concierge, an astronomer, a yoga instructor, waiters and more. Additionally, guests can choose how they would like to arrive at the camp. Supercars, helicopter, trekking and camel are some of the options.

The Blink team estimates that planning a trip will take three to five months, depending on the size of the group travelling. Costs will vary depending on location and amenities desired, with estimates ranging from $65,000 for three nights in Morocco for a group of six to more than $175,000 for four nights for six people on the Bolivian salt flats. Blink plans to provide up to 100 trips per year.

For travellers with smaller budgets, there are many other recent travel innovations focusing on planning and transit, with apps helping to provide personalized trips. The Hawaii Tourism Authority is testing facial recognition technology in its Discover Your Aloha video to gauge visitors' interest in different activities. And the United Kingdom's Whitbread chain has announced the Hub, a compact hotel room that guests can customize via their smartphone, even before they've arrived. Facial recognition software is also being tested out as a way to help travellers plan their ideal activities, and smart robots are helping to provide concierge services.

TAKEAWAYS

1 What other aspects of tourism could be tweaked to provide lower-cost customizations?
2 How could you build, or improve upon, personalized features in your product or service?
3 Are there luxury options you could provide as another tier in your business offering?

INNOVATION DATA

Website: www.blacktomato.com
Contact: jos@blacktomato.com, twitter.com/Black_Tomato
Company name: Black Tomato
Innovation name: Blink
Country: United Kingdom
Industries: Luxury / Tourism & travel

SUMMARY

At home or abroad, tourism is greatly enriched by the generosity practised by communities that share knowledge and services in a way that has only recently become possible. New innovations are placing human connections and authentic experiences at the heart of trips away from home.

So much must now be taken into consideration when planning a trip – from a region's geopolitical stability to carbon footprint – that there's never been a more crucial time for travel innovations that can help us navigate this new terrain, improve our understanding of the world around us and, ultimately, increase our overall wellbeing.

TRAVEL TAKEAWAYS

1 **Make mobile devices the ultimate travel companion.** More than a fifth of all bookings are completed on a mobile device, with 65 per cent of same-day hotel reservations made from smartphones. Have someone with minimal knowledge of your service take a look at your online presence. What are their impressions? What was easy to find and do and what required more effort? This is your chance to show off. Have fun!

2 **Personalize to make every travel experience unique.** Consider your audience or audiences. Do you know enough about them to be able to offer custom options? If not, what steps can you take to get the necessary data? This is a fantastic opportunity to make maximum impact with minimum change. Is there something you could add to or make more prominent in your offerings that could attract a group you'd like to do more business with? Take this as an opportunity to tweak your services and become more responsive.

3 **Connect with residents.** Building strong working relationships with locals will reap rewards in a number of ways. Not only will you be able to offer curated, bespoke experiences through residents' knowledge and expertise, but they could also prove a loyal customer base as well as providing products and services unique to your venue. Make sure to recognize their contributions: consider putting on an event in the off season exclusively for those living nearby. Encourage travellers to connect with locals for a taste of real life at your destination.

4 **Support your local community.** Social innovation is a big part of our work at Springwise and we see many examples of this type of innovation in the travel

and tourism space. As a tourism business, the better your relationships with the local community the more you will be able to engage and create positive change. Think about how you could use your team's expertise to support local charities and social enterprises. Are you employing local people? Can you provide related or even unrelated services to these local communities?

5 **Don't forget Mother Nature.** Last, but definitely not least, is the need to do all that you do in the most sustainable way possible. This is a tall order, but it is essential. No one has all the solutions and making a start is better than doing nothing. Many travellers judge destinations on their environmental credentials. Might an eco package be a welcome addition to what you currently offer? How could you leverage your community network for a smaller carbon footprint? This may be one of the toughest tasks but it could prove to be the most rewarding in the long term.

CONCLUSION

Writing this book has been a labour of love for the Springwise team and we hope you have enjoyed reading it as much as we have enjoyed writing it. On our journey of discovery, in celebrating some of the cleverest and most entrepreneurial innovators on the planet, we have perhaps only scratched the surface of what is to come. What is certain, though, is that there is no shortage of ideas and energy to bring them to life.

What is most encouraging is that in our day-to-day lives it is becoming clear that businesses, governments and large organizations are increasingly looking to understand and partner with start-up and innovation communities to drive positive change among their customers, employees and leaders. Although many are motivated purely by financial rewards, it is refreshing to uncover many more who are equally motivated by driving social change.

As demonstrated throughout this book, we believe that very significant advances will come from these partnerships, whose creative and ingenious thinking is stirred as the firepower, and cash, of larger organizations combine with the agility and creativity of the minnows. These collaborations will come to represent progress in the modern world, and as the pace of change continues the new norm will be collaborations where the sum of the parts is genuinely greater than the whole – for all stakeholders.

As we have seen, this is not easy, and in particular will require great foresight from global political and business leaders, as well as NGOs, opinion formers and the media. Springwise aims to be your finger on the pulse in this fast-changing environment, to keep you ahead of whatever game you are playing and to continue to uncover the Zeitgeist, wherever it may be. In this book we have brought you a snapshot of our ever-transforming innovation landscape and we will continue to do so, with our daily coverage at Springwise.com

From smarter cities, new ways of travelling, revolution in the automobile industry, to the new retail paradigm and across the environmental and educational agendas, this book is a reflection of the innovation lighting up the planet. Each example in this book was chosen with the goal of broadening your horizons, igniting your interest and setting your creative juices flowing.

So where does all this leave us as we move forward together on our journey of disruption? The answer we think, is to continue to think differently, to stand on the shoulders of giants from all walks of life and from all over the world – individuals, businesses and communities who are inventing and innovating every day and in every way, to solve their own individual, idiosyncratic issues. This book is here to inform, inspire and, most importantly, to help you think differently, to motivate you to create the positive change in your organization and your life that will be an engine of progress for you.

We have asked you many questions along the way and endeavoured to draw the threads of theory and thinking that knit this complex world of innovation together. We urge you to take this as a starting point, and to root your thinking in a framework of sustainable and positive innovation, in all senses of the word.

Next time you are sitting with colleagues discussing your product or service, or brainstorming ideas for a new innovation, we hope you will consider using *Disrupt!* as a stimulus or source of inspiration. The innovations collected here are united by the open-minded and collaborative spirit in which they were invariably designed – so do take these established ideas as prompts and build on them with imagination and verve. Take this book with you and, when you are feeling creatively uninspired, use it as a sort of recipe book, a resource from which you can take, imitate, adapt or redesign from scratch.

The takeaways within each section and at the end of each chapter are open questions designed to encourage fresh thinking that is lateral as well as rigorous. Always ask yourself, 'What here might be useful for me?' The questions asked in this book are posed in the spirit of curiosity and intended not just as hypothetical queries but also as workshop questions, so feel free to pose these questions to your team and see what they come up with. Every innovation in this book has the potential to light a spark that could change your business for ever. Use it well.

Perhaps the most engaging part of your journey through these ideas, however, will be to sit back and marvel at the ingenuity, creativity and extraordinary capacity of the human mind – to invent, innovate and evolve more rapidly than ever before. At Springwise we have every reason to feel positive about a future filled with innovations of all kinds and from all places, and we leave you with this thought from Kevin Kelly, one of the founding fathers of innovation, from his 2016 book *The Inevitable: Understanding the 12 Technological Forces That Will Shape Our Future*.

'There has never been a better day in the whole history of the world to invent something. There has never been a better time with more opportunities, more openings, lower barriers, higher benefit/ risk ratios, better returns, greater upside than now. Right now, this minute. This is the moment that folks in the future will look back and say, "Oh, to have been alive and well back then."'

REFERENCES

The sharing economy

www.opendesk.cc/openmaking-dot-is/field-guide/who-will-own-the-next-industrial-revolution

Smart cities

www.who.int/gho/urban_health/situation_trends/urban_population_growth_text/en/

Sustainability

www.planetaid.org/blog/recycling-rates-around-the-world
earthobservatory.nasa.gov/Features/GlobalWarming/page3.php

The workplace

Yvon Chouinard, *Let My People Go Surfing* (Penguin, 2006)

Communication

www.lifewire.com/how-many-emails-are-sent-every-day-1171210
www.youtube.com/yt/press/statistics.html

www.natureworldnews.com/articles/467/20130107/ict-sector-account-2-percent-global-carbon.htm

REFERENCES

Education

www.itu.int/en/itu-d/statistics/documents/facts/ictfactsfigures 2016.pdf

www.gsmaintelligence.com/

www.census.gov/popclock/world

Max Roser and Esteban Ortiz-Ospina (2016), 'Literacy'. Retrieved from ourworldindata.org/literacy/

www.census.gov/newsroom/blogs/random-samplings/2015/10/women-now-at-the-head-of-the-class-lead-men-in-college-attainment.html

uis.unesco.org/en/news/stem-and-gender-advancement

Retail

www.emarketer.com/Article/Worldwide-Retail-Ecommerce-Sales-Will-Reach-1915-Trillion-This-Year/1014369
www.vendhq.com/university/retail-trends-and-predictions-2016

Travel

www.wysetc.org/research/publications/new-horizons/
www.statista.com/topics/962/global-tourism/
www.statisticbrain.com/internet-travel-hotel-booking-statistics
www.theguardian.com/technology/2016/nov/29/airbnb-denies-liability-after-guests-plunge-two-storeys-from-balcony

371

SPRING
_.WISE
THE GLOBAL SOURCE FOR INNOVATION
EST 2002

The original and most relevant digital source of innovations and ground-breaking ideas that matter, from across the globe.

Springwise has been discovering and promoting the world's best innovation ideas since 2002. Our ambition is to unlock innovations that matter by bringing these ideas to a global audience, and to help Springwise innovators play their part in making the world a better place.

Visit **www.springwise.com** to see thousands more innovations that matter, published in real time, every day.

Create the future. Today.

Re_Set is London's leading transformation and innovation consultancy, uniquely powered by Springwise. From strategy to delivery, Re_Set's proprietary innovation operating system is helping the world's most exciting organisations create the future, today.

To learn more, see **www.thisisreset.com**

'Almost too good to share'

Seth Godin
Entrepreneur, Author, Public Speaker

Certified
(B)
Corporation
PENDING